TIME TO DECLARE

My Life in Church Music

TIME TO DECLARE

My Life in Church Music

Martin Neary

PUBLICATIONS

RSCM Publications is the trading name of RSCM Enterprises Ltd,
a wholly owned subsidiary of
The Royal School of Church Music
19 The Close, Salisbury, SP1 2EB, England
Registered charity 312828

Tel: +44 (0)1722 424848
E-mail: press@rscm.com Website: www.rscmshop.com

TIME TO DECLARE
My life in church music
Martin Neary

First Published 2025

Copyright © 2025 Martin Neary

Martin Neary has asserted his moral rights
to be identified as the author of this work.

The views and opinions expressed in this publication are those of the
author and do not necessarily reflect the official policy or position of
The Royal School of Church Music, its subsidiaries or affiliates

All rights reserved. No part of this publication may be reproduced,
stored in a retrieval system, or transmitted, in any form or by any
means, without the prior permission in writing of the copyright holders,
or as expressly permitted by law.

Edited by James Wilkinson
With assistance from Eleni Thwaites

Typeset by Regent Typesetting Ltd
Jacket design by Anthony Marks
Printed by Short Run Press

ISBN: 978-0-85402-358-5
Order Number: 9780854023585

Contents

Foreword by Stephen Layton — vii

Introduction — 1

Chapter 1 – Background and Childhood — 3
Chapter 2 – Joining the Royal Household — 9
Chapter 3 – The 1953 Coronation — 20
Chapter 4 – City of London School — 29
Chapter 5 – Cambridge — 34
Chapter 6 – St Albans and Tanglewood — 42
Chapter 7 – Getting started in London, 1963–71 — 48
Chapter 8 – St Margaret's Westminster, 1965–71 — 60
Chapter 9 – Musical evenings at No. 10 — 65
Chapter 10 – Moving to Winchester, 1972–78 — 79
Chapter 11 – 900th Anniversary of Winchester Cathedral, 1979 — 99
Chapter 12 – Bicentennial Fellowship — 107
Chapter 13 – Winchester, 1981–87 — 113
Chapter 14 – Andrew Lloyd Webber *Requiem* — 124
Chapter 15 – Arrival at the Abbey — 130
Chapter 16 – Special services and events — 138
Chapter 17 – Funeral of Diana, Princess of Wales — 158
Chapter 18 – Foreign tours — 168
Chapter 19 – Some honorary positions — 180
Chapter 20 – Suspension and dismissal — 184
Chapter 21 – Cricket to the rescue — 190

Chapter 22 – More Performances — 197

Chapter 23 – 70th Birthday Concert, St John's, Smith Square, London, 28 March 2010 — 202

Chapter 24 – St Michael and All Angels, Barnes — 205

Epilogue — 208

Appendix 1 – Interview with Jonathan Harvey — 211
Appendix 2 – Cathedral Opera: Passion and Resurrection — 222
Appendix 3 – Boston Globe — 224
Appendix 4 – The Millennium Consort Singers — 225
Appendix 5 – Commissions, Premieres and other Significant Performances of Contemporary Music — 227
Appendix 6 – Recordings – a selection — 230
Appendix 7 – A year of good grace — 234
Appendix 8 – Press Statement by Dr Martin Neary — 237
Appendix 9 – Crossword — 239

Index of Names — 241

Foreword

As a small boy, uprooted from my home town of Derby and finding myself in the unfamiliar world of Martin's Winchester choristers, one overwhelming thing struck me forcibly. I know it struck my fellow choristers, too. We sensed that Martin loved the music that we sang. We sensed his awe and joy at the gift of singing, his reverence for it as a means of divine worship, his deep respect for a great tradition. Learning how to sing in this tradition was about human thriving – past, present and future – and its renewal was a sacred duty. Out of this was born Martin's luminous ethic of excellence. We loved it, and we loved him.

The extraordinary inspiration we felt when Martin stood in front of us and encouraged us to make music is something that we choristers have treasured all our lives. I remember the first chorister rehearsal for the preparation of Stravinsky's *Symphony of Psalms*. As we rehearsed that soft slow uplifting moment – *Alleluia* – Martin sang to us. He sang how he felt we should phrase it. I see his face now and hear that emotive voice. For me and for many others, it was a call to something outside of our world.

Music has the power to transcend time, bringing together past and present in a symphony of continuity and evolution. In *Time to Declare: My Life in Church Music*, Martin Neary offers us an extraordinary journey through his life in music – a journey rich in artistry and rich in personal and historical significance.

From his own early days as chorister at the Coronation of Queen Elizabeth II to his role directing the music in Westminster Abbey at the funeral of Princess Diana, Martin's career has unfolded alongside some of the most profound moments in modern British history. His story is not just one of personal achievement but of dedication to the traditions, innovations, and challenges of church music in the twentieth and twenty-first centuries.

What makes this book so compelling is its balance – between personal reflection and professional insight, between the weight of history and the vibrancy of the present. Martin's deep commitment to music ranging from Purcell and Bach, to Wesley, to Tavener and Harvey, reveals a musician who is both a guardian of tradition and a champion of contemporary composition. His work has not only preserved the past but shaped the future of sacred music, inspiring generations of musicians along the way.

Yet this autobiography reveals how Martin's life and work have been enriched by other passions, not least of which has been cricket. Martin writes with warmth about his time at the City of London School, where he played alongside Mike Brearley, later one of England's most influential cricket captains. The same qualities that make a great conductor – discipline, foresight and the ability to bring out the best in others – are also the hallmarks of any great leader on the field.

Readers turning these pages will discover more than an autobiography, more even than an inspiring account of a lifetime devoted to excellence. This book is a testament to the power of music to elevate and move, to unite and ennoble. It is a reminder that great traditions such as choral music do not look after themselves. For future generations to enjoy and enrich this tradition, each generation must labour after excellence, and that labour will require leaders of the stature of Martin Neary.

Stephen Layton

Martin Neary at St Sophia, LA

Martin Neary in 1972

INTRODUCTION

Re-reading *A Westminster Pilgrim*, the autobiography of Sir Frederick Bridge (Organist of Westminster Abbey, 1882–1918), has prompted me to write an account of my own more modest "pilgrimage".

I particularly liked Sir Frederick's opening titles:

> Being a
> RECORD OF SERVICE
> In
> CHURCH, CATHEDRAL AND ABBEY
> COLLEGE, UNIVERSITY AND CONCERT ROOM
> With a
> FEW NOTES ON SPORT

Sir Frederick and I share(d) a number of interests, in particular championing the music of Henry Purcell and Samuel Sebastian Wesley, and we were both much involved in the celebrations marking two of their special anniversaries, albeit in different centuries.

In 1895, for the 200th anniversary of Purcell's death, Bridge put together a fascinating programme (including restoring the *Te Deum* to what Purcell had written!) while 100 years later I had the tercentenary, when there was some "rescuing" of a different kind, and we benefited from the latest musicological research.

Back in 1910, Bridge masterminded the Westminster Abbey centenary Commemoration of Wesley's birth, while in 1976 at Winchester Cathedral, we honoured the 100th anniversary of his death by including his unknown Symphony and the orchestral accompaniments to two of his anthems.

A Westminster Pilgrim runs to over 350 pages, but this will be a shorter read! It does though cover a significant period in church music, in which I have been privileged to play a small part – from singing at the Coronation of Queen Elizabeth II in 1953 to the Funeral of Princess Diana in 1997, my departure from the Abbey, the challenges and unexpected pleasures of my life thereafter, and in particular the stimulating experience of working with two of the most significant composers of our time, Jonathan Harvey and Sir John Tavener.

I do occasionally stray from musical matters. Bridge's reference to "a few notes on sport", has given me an excuse periodically to refer to cricket, of which I was once kindly described by no less a critic than John Woodcock, the late cricket correspondent of *The Times*, "as a true lover of the game". My family, I think, might describe me as an addict!

Speaking of family, there has also been a personal reason for learning more about my illustrious predecessor. Following the death of his second wife, Sir Frederick invited one of his Royal College of Music organ pupils to marry him. Alice Ibbetson, the student (and the second woman fellow of the Royal College of Organists) who turned him down, was my wife's grandmother!

This book would not have been completed without the constant advice, patience and support of Penny, our daughters, Nicola and Alice, indeed all our family and so many friends, including my marvellous editor, James Wilkinson – my heartfelt thanks go to them all. Another title could have been "Music for a While", but I discuss that in the closing chapters.

As will become apparent, it is indeed "Time to Declare"!

CHAPTER 1

Background and Childhood

*"I don't want a French girl living in my house ......
(two hours later) When is she going to move in?"*

In September 1933, a 17-year-old French girl arrived in London to learn English. Her father, Gérard Thébault ran a successful garage business in Paris, and he and her mother, Renée, had decided that their daughter, Jeanne, should spend six months living with an English family. And so it was that she came to meet the Nearys in Southgate, North London. Apparently, my grandfather George James Neary (a retired post office clerk whom I never met), was adamant that he did not want a French girl living in his house. But he reluctantly agreed to meet her. The conversation flowed – they discovered a mutual interest in literature – and as she was about to leave, against all expectations, George asked when she was going to move in! Jeanne Thébault gratefully accepted, and ended up staying rather longer than either her parents or her English landlords had envisaged.

The contrast between the centre of Paris – the Thébaults lived in the sixième district on the Left Bank, quite close to Les Invalides – with a quiet north London suburb must have been pretty challenging; Jeanne was the only foreigner in the street. There was little sign of the buzz of Parisian life, and absolutely none at all of its cuisine! Nonetheless, Jeanne became an increasingly close friend of all the family, and in particular of their second son, Leonard, despite his being 12 years older and at least a foot taller.

My father's siblings were all musical: elder sister Nellie played the piano; brother Horace, who became a bank manager, was a violinist who played in the Barclays Bank orchestra, and the youngest, Rosebud (yes, that is how she was known!) played the piano by ear, and only in flat keys! It was Papa, however, who was the most musical. A pianist and cellist, he had a beautiful baritone voice, and fitted in a lot of singing, in particular at St Michael's, Cornhill, while working as an accountant for the Eagle Star Insurance Company.

In due time, Leonard persuaded the Roman Catholic Jeanne to attend the Anglican services at St Michael's, and ecumenical differences do not appear to have interfered with their burgeoning romance. The two families met in France in 1938, and soon preparations were made for the wedding at St Michael's on 25 February, 1939. The service included the premiere of a beautiful short Benediction anthem, *May the Grace of Christ Our Saviour*, "composed for Leonard Neary's wedding" by Dr Harold Darke, the legendary organist of St Michael's, under whom Leonard had first sung as a treble. The "Fashionable Wedding" of Mr Leonard W Neary and Mademoiselle Jeanne M Thébault in the 900-year-old Church was the headline in the Palmers Green and Southgate Gazette, whose report quoted from the address, describing the bridegroom as a "true son of the church" and that he had been a "tower of strength to rector, organist and choir".

Little did Jeanne realise that, when her family returned to France after the wedding, she would not see them for the next six years, the onset of World War II making non-military travel between England and France all but impossible. Leonard, aged thirty-five at the start of the War, was not called up, but continued to work at Eagle Star and did regular night shifts with the local Auxiliary Relief Patrol (ARP).

During an air raid, on 28 March, 1940, I was born at Hackney Hospital. I was named after St Martin of Tours, the Loire town, just north of the *Poids de vins* region, while my other two names, Gérard and James, were those of my two grandfathers. I was not christened at St Michael's until I was 17 months old, already walking, and too heavy for Rector Ellison to lift. My parents had waited in the hope that the war would end and enable my mother's brother, Christian, who they subsequently learnt had been taken prisoner at Sedan in June 1940, to be present. It would be more than a year before they received news that he was safe.

Soon after the birth of my sister Denise in October 1942, with the war escalating, my father installed a Morrison shelter in the living room; my earliest memory is of the whole family huddled together under it at night. By the summer of 1944, however, my father had become increasingly worried about the family's safety in London, and arranged for his mother, wife, and two children to be evacuated to North Wales. The train from Euston was so crowded on a hot August afternoon that we all were bundled into the Guard's van. After changing trains at Crewe we reached Mold, then, after a bus journey, arrived at the small town of Leeswood. There we met our formidable landlady, Miss Parry, who was letting out two of the ground floor rooms in her house but did not seem best pleased that one of her tenants was a rather active four-year-old boy. On the other hand, my sister, Denise, not yet two years old, could do no wrong.

Our Welsh 'digs' were dark and claustrophobic, and the plumbing basic, the outdoor lavatory we were allocated being close to where Miss Parry kept pigs. But at least we were safe. My mother organised a few outings: one was a bus trip to Rhyl, where Denise and I saw the sea for the first time. There were occasional visits from Papa, who was somewhat taken aback to hear his son talking with a Welsh accent. I started infant school in Wales, but little from this period survives in my memory until March 1945, when we broke free from the reins of Miss Parry, and moved to a nearby house which had space, and above all a view. Even now, eighty years later, I can feel the relief which this modest move brought, with the peaceful sight of cows grazing contentedly across the fields. But that was nothing compared with the joy of returning to London a few days after VE Day on May 8th. I was reunited with my (English) family, with my friend John Witt, who lived next door, and with one or two toys such as a double-decker bus which I particularly prized, and which had been too big to take to Wales. The Morrison shelter had gone, and we could hear Papa accompany himself on the Bechstein upright piano, now back in the living room. It was certainly the most beautifully toned piano I had ever heard, and I really wanted to play it.

Shortly after our return, at the age of five and a half, I was taken to a teacher in nearby Palmers Green, Miss Winifred Collier, to begin piano lessons. According to Maman, after four weeks Miss Collier made it plain

Aged 3 in the garden at Southgate, 1943.

that I was too young to teach, and that there was nothing she could do with me. However, this did not daunt Maman, who despite having had only a few piano lessons as a child, took it upon herself not only to teach me the musical alphabet but to introduce me to Chopin's little *Prelude in G major*. Within six months she was able to hand me over to another teacher, John Roberts, with whom I was to study for the next eight years.

Aside from the piano playing, Leonard was hoping that I would follow in the family tradition and have a reasonable voice, but until I was seven he despaired that I would ever be able to sing in tune. Then one day, in an almost 'road to Damascus' moment when Papa was at the piano and I was some distance away, I asked him why he played a particular note, telling him what it was; it was the first indication that I had perfect pitch. That certainly meant that there could be no more excuses for singing out of tune. Papa started teaching me a few simple songs, and quite soon I was 'performing' at family gatherings, which often included some music.

Following my sixth birthday, Papa would often take me along with him to St Michael's, Cornhill, on Sunday mornings, and have me sit through a choir practice followed by a solemn (low church) Matins, attended by a congregation barely reaching double figures. The special musical events there, however, frequently drew full houses. The St Michael's organist, Dr Harold Darke, had a considerable following, and he conducted his St Michael's Singers in some notable premieres, including several by Ralph Vaughan Williams. RVW was quite a regular at the St Michael's concerts, and after hearing his *Mass in G minor*, recommended the soloists (including my father, who was singing bass) to Sir Malcolm Sargent for a performance Sir Malcolm was conducting in Cork. Similarly, after attending the annual performance in Holy Week of the *St John Passion* at St Michael's, he invited my father to sing the part of Jesus in the Leith Hill Festival *St John*, which Vaughan Williams conducted in 1947. I still have the vocal score RVW gave to him, marked with the cuts (although there were none in his part), and a handwritten letter, apologising for the cold conditions in the Dorking Halls – it was the bitter winter of 1946–47 – but promising a hot meal between the rehearsal and the performance. A few weeks later, I was allowed to go to St Michael's to hear Papa sing the part. I cannot pretend to remember much, but the music and the drama did make an impression, as will be revealed later.

However, my father's time at St Michael's was drawing to a close; the church no longer had a regular Evensong on Sundays, so Papa accepted an invitation to join the Evensong choir at Holy Trinity Brompton (the church at the back of Brompton Oratory, whose parish included most of Knightsbridge). The services, led by the dynamic preacher Bryan Green, had a terrific atmosphere, often with congregations of a thousand. The choral resources were more interesting than at St Michael's, and relatively soon Papa decided to resign from St Michael's and to sing at Brompton on Sunday mornings as well.

I too 'transferred' to Holy Trinity, and it was not long before the gifted organist and choirmaster, Frank Woodhouse, suggested that I should put on a cassock and surplice and sing in the choir. Most of the other choristers were members of the London Choir School, a kind of 'chorister factory' based in Bexley, which supplied boy singers to various fashionable London churches with few children among their parishioners. The choir was good enough to be invited to sing an Evensong at St Paul's Cathedral, but my own contribution was distinctly limited. A few weeks before the service, Papa had noticed that I was having difficulty reading the notice boards at the tube stations, and decided to have my eyes tested. There was a problem, however, as the drops administered daily before the eye test left me with blurred vision, and I could hardly read the music.

A few months later, at the age of eight, I found myself being prepared for an audition to another choir, which sang at St James's Palace.

Thanks to a singing colleague, the alto Robin Lock, my father was given an introduction to Dr Stanley Roper, Organist, Choirmaster and Composer to His Majesty's Chapels Royal. At the audition there were just three candidates, for what transpired would be three vacancies at the beginning of the Autumn Term. I sang last, and Dr Roper, perhaps taken aback by how young I looked, said to my father, "you take him through", which he duly did. I sang a few scales, and a short setting of Psalm 15, composed by my father. The whole process lasted barely ten minutes, and I had no idea whether I had passed or not. However, a week later, a letter from the Comptroller to the Lord Chamberlain arrived at 73 Oakfield Road, inviting me to become one of the Children Royal, provided I was accepted at the City of London School (CLS), like the other 'Children'. This was some proviso, because the entrance exams for the next academic year had already taken place, and in any case I was considered too young for CLS. An option would have been for me to wait a year, and not join the choir (or the school) until I was nine, but my father had other ideas. Discovering that the main concern of the Lord Chamberlain's Office was that I should attend the chorister practices at St James's Palace on

Stanley Roper, Organist, Composer and Master of the Children of the Chapel Royal, who awarded MN his place there, 1948.

weekday afternoons, he asked the Headmistress of Hazelwood Lane School, if I could be granted special permission to leave an hour and a half early at 2.30 pm on Tuesdays, Thursdays and Fridays, to attend the Chapel Royal choir practices. Miss Belfontaine referred the request to the Middlesex County Council and, rather to her astonishment, permission was granted.

The next challenge was how to transport me four times a week from North London to St James's Palace.

CHAPTER 2

Joining the Royal Household

"Don't try to play all the notes"

For centuries the Kings and Queens of England have had their own choir, not only to sing services in the Royal Chapels, but also to accompany them on the battlefield – as at Agincourt in 1415, when France was brought to her knees during the Hundred Years War.

In its golden age, until approximately 1800, the Chapel Royal had attracted, and even conscripted, the best young boy singers from all over the country to its ranks. It also recruited many of England's greatest composers as either Gentlemen or Organists. But the situation after the Second World War was very different. There were just ten Children and six Gentlemen and, compared with today, the repertoire was very limited. On Sundays we sang at the morning services in St James's Palace Chapel – Sung Communion on the first Sunday of the month and Prayer Book Matins on the other Sundays, when the *Te Deum* and *Jubilate* were often sung to chants, and anthems were few and far between.

When I joined, aged eight, I was barely able to see above the choir desks in the Chapel. I was by far the smallest and rather chubby with large glasses; some of my friends used to call me 'The Owl'. What use I was vocally during my first two years at the Chapel I cannot imagine, as my voice was very small. But I had been making some progress on the piano; and I remember an occasion early on when Dr Roper was late arriving and the Head Boy told me, the youngest boy, to play the piano, so that the rehearsal could begin. We practised a simple hymn and were working our way through a Psalm when Dr Roper walked in. He was very kind, but somewhat disarming: "Don't try to play all the notes". Of course, *he* knew which ones could be left out.

While I have comparatively little memory of my first services, I do remember having to learn to walk in step, and the time it took us to robe.

MN as one of the Children of the Chapel Royal, 1953.

The Children's uniform (dating from the Restoration) included, as it still does today, black patent shoes with buckles, black stockings, red breeches, red frock coat (with black velvet stripes, and yards of gold braid) and a white ruff.

There were some unforgettable occasions during my seven years as one of 'The Children'. The first was the 1948 Service of Remembrance at the

Cenotaph. As we processed out from the Home Office, the army band played solemn arrangements of Chopin's *Funeral March* and Purcell's *Lament* from *Dido and Aeneas*. As soon as the Royal party were in their places, everyone was silent as Big Ben sounded 11 o'clock. The two-minute silence, followed by the *Last Post* and *Reveille*, remains one of my most moving experiences. The crowds were enormous, stretching to both ends of Whitehall, and among the vast throng was my French uncle Christian Thébault, who had been a prisoner of war for five years and had come to London especially for the Remembrance Observance. Even at the age of eight, I could sense the national mood of sorrow and thankfulness.

Our next outside engagement was to sing at Buckingham Palace for the Christening of Prince Charles. To our excitement, the choir rode in three of the Sovereign's horse-drawn carriages from St James' Palace to Buckingham Palace. The Christening, and indeed all the services at Buckingham Palace during my time as a chorister, took place in the Music Room, as the Chapel had been bombed on Friday 13 September 1940 and the King and Queen had insisted that any repair and renovation should wait.

There were four generations of royalty present: Queen Mary, the King and Queen, Princess Elizabeth and Prince Philip, and Prince Charles. I tried not to look at them as it had been firmly instilled in us that on no account were we to stare at any member of the Royal Family. This provided a convenient excuse for my being unable to describe to my mother, later that evening, what either the Queen or Princess Elizabeth was wearing! I could remember, however, that the young prince had not uttered a sound. According to Dr Geoffrey Fisher, the Archbishop of Canterbury, who officiated, the Prince was "as quiet as a mouse" while being baptised with water specially brought from the river Jordan. I also remembered the delicious chocolate *éclairs* which were served to us after the service.

(In 2023, shortly before the Coronation of King Charles III, when I was fortunate enough to speak to the King at a Royal Victorian Order reception at Windsor, I mentioned that we must be the only two people present who had been at his Christening. He asked: "When was it? Was it in January?" I replied saying that it had been on 15 December. He then kindly asked if I was still playing the organ.)

Less than two weeks later we were unexpectedly back at Buckingham Palace for a short carol service, the Royal Family having been forced to stay in London over Christmas because of the King's ill health. On Christmas

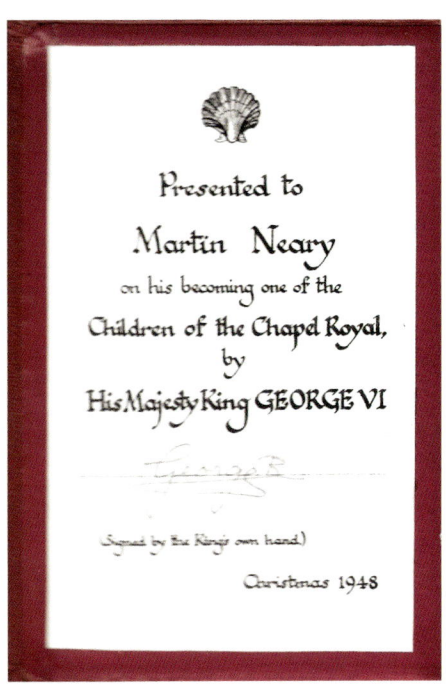

Day, my fellow new boys and I were presented with Bibles, signed by King George VI. Years later I said to Queen Elizabeth how much this gift had been appreciated, and she asked me if I still had mine, I replied that I had! Probably the most colourful ritual of the year was at Epiphany, 6 January, when Beefeaters with their halberds lined St James's Palace Chapel as His Majesty's representatives offered gifts of gold, frankincense and myrrh at the altar.

In May 1949 I passed the Entrance exam for the City of London School. By remaining at my local state primary school for my first year as one of the Children, I had in fact saved the Royal Household the cost of one year's school fees (which I believe were £30 per term), and I gathered later that my parents received a quarterly allowance (£5) as a retaining fee for the services of their son in the Chapel Royal Choir. I still have the letter, dated 30 September 1949, from Buckingham Palace explaining: "Now that he has commenced at the City of London School this allowance will no longer be paid".

The City of London School (CLS) dates back to 1442 and the death of John Carpenter, town clerk of London, whose will included a bequest to care for and educate four poor children from the City. Over the years the numbers greatly expanded. By the time I joined, the school had grown to take around 850 pupils in a huge building on the Victoria Embankment close to Blackfriars Bridge. On my first day I got lost, much to the annoyance of the school porters, who went on a search to find me when my mother arrived to collect me. Since the 1920s the Chapel Royal Children had been educated there, as had the Temple Church choristers. As well as the choristers, whose fees were paid by the Royal Household, there were John Carpenter scholars and a few 11–plus scholarship holders, whose fees were paid by their local authorities. (After I stopped singing at the Chapel Royal, Middlesex County Council covered my school fees.)

My closest friend, with whom I have remained in touch, was Peter Lough, eldest son of Ernest, the famous Temple chorister who had been the brilliant treble soloist in the ground-breaking recording of Mendelssohn's *Hear my prayer – O for the wings of a dove*. Peter joined the Chapel Royal Choir because the Temple did not resume services until the war-damaged church had been restored in 1954.

From its early days, the CLS included pupils from non-conformist and Jewish families. During my time something like 20 per cent of the intake were Jewish, who, after the notices had been given out at the daily assemblies, would leave the school hall for their own short

With MN's friend Peter Lough, son of Ernest Lough (who famously recorded Mendelssohn's *O for the wings of a dove*), 1954.

service. Historically, the Headmaster had been a classicist but in 1950 the City Corporation appointed Dr Arthur Willoughby Barton, a highly distinguished scientist who had been a research student at the Cavendish Laboratory, working with Lord Rutherford on the atom.

Dr Barton's arrival led to a number of important changes. Arguably, the most significant was forming a school orchestra, apparently against the advice of the Director of Music, Leslie (known by the choristers as 'Tubby') Taylor, who resigned as a result. His successor was Dr John Wray, who persuaded several members of the school staff to play in the school orchestra with the boys. The excellent leader was Dennis Moore, who taught classics. One of the physics teachers, Arthur Campbell, was not only a fine horn player, but seemed to be able to play whatever instrument was needed. He also helped me with playing the drums and learning to count rests.

Dr Barton, who grew up in Nottingham, had retained his Northern accent, somewhat to the amusement of the boys and even the staff. The final words of the Head's end of term addresses became somewhat predictable, invariably giving us an exhortation to "read some good books, see some good plays, and listen to some good music" which we duly imitated with an exaggerated Northern brogue. I remain extremely grateful however to Dr Barton for kindly allowing me in my O level year to have five individual music lessons per week with 'Doc Wray' when the rest of the form was studying science. (I was the only boy in my form who was taking the O level music exam.)

Believe it or not, the best voice in my time at the Chapel belonged to a treble I had 'recommended' to Dr Roper. When I started at the City of London School in 1949, I found myself in the same form as a boy who, in our weekly class music lessons, showed he had an exceptional voice. So having told Dr Roper about him, I took Michael Wilkinson to one of our weekday practices at the Chapel, at the end of which he duly passed his audition. But there were no chorister vacancies and no provision for probationers. Undaunted, Dr Roper arranged for Michael to sing as an unpaid volunteer until a choristership became available.

I had no idea at the time that Michael had already had a somewhat colourful career as a chorister, having been first at the London Choir School in Bexley (which used to supply choristers to several London churches, such as Holy Trinity, Brompton), and then for a while at St Paul's Cathedral. It transpired that because of some difficulties with the authorities at St Paul's, Michael was removed from the school when he was only ten years old, and his father, Lambton, a fine alto who had sung in the St Paul's Choir as a Vicar Choral, got him into the City of London School instead. Michael soon came to the attention of Leslie Taylor, the CLS Director of Music, who wasted no time in finding opportunities for him to sing on Sunday evenings at the Church of the Annunciation, as well as at some quite glamorous solo engagements, such as singing the part of the boy Nicolas, alongside the great tenor, Peter Pears, in the first broadcast of Benjamin Britten's *St Nicolas*.

Another annual outside engagement was at Westminster Abbey, on the Thursday before Easter, for the Royal Maundy Service at which Maundy money is distributed to deserving recipients by the Sovereign. This commemorates Jesus washing the feet of the Disciples at the Last Supper. After the rather limited rations of the Sunday musical menu at St James's Palace, it was thrilling to sing some much more exciting music, as we combined with the Abbey Choir. By far the most popular work was *Zadok the Priest*, one of the four anthems composed by Handel for the Coronation of George II in 1727.

At these services, the organ was always played by Dr Osborne Peasgood, Sub-Organist of Westminster Abbey, who was a phenomenal accompanist. We loved the way he produced a slow but eventually rousing *crescendo* during the 22-bar introduction, before the Choirs came in *fortissimo*. Frankly, the standard of the Abbey choristers was far superior to what we could offer from the Chapel; and I remember admiring the confidence with which each year an Abbey boy would sing the opening solo in Wesley's anthem *Wash me throughly*. I also loved the beautiful chant by Walter Alcock to Psalm 91, "Whoso dwelleth under the defence of the most high", which has remained a favourite of mine ever since. On returning to St James's, each of the Children was given a set of Maundy money, four coins totalling ten pence; 1, 2, 3 & 4, in respect of our services.

Towards the end of the summer term, the Sub-Dean would announce during the Notices that there was to be a summer outing for the "Children", and, somewhat to our embarrassment, invited donations from the congregation. I learnt later that most of those attending the Sunday services were members of the Royal Household, who unlike their bosses stayed in London at the week-end. We hardly ever met any of the congregation, as we went in and out of the Palace through the back door in Colour Court, but there were two women who regularly sat together, who attracted our attention. One was always dressed as a man. I would quiz my family about this when they came, but I was never given any kind of explanation.

We never knew what the Summer Outing collections amounted to, but we always had a good day at the sea, on the South Coast. The Sub-Dean, Canon Foxell would come with us on the train, and then, having set us up on the beach, would wander off for several hours, to go and sketch, which he did rather beautifully. None of us came to any harm during his absence, apart from one year, all ending up horribly sunburnt. For the last Sunday of term, Dr Roper invariably put down the first part of Stanford's anthem *Awake my soul*, after which we had ten weeks off, when the Court disbanded for the summer.

Our next visit to Buckingham Palace was in 1950, this time for the Christening of Princess Anne. We were all amused when two year-old Prince Charles, after behaving impeccably during the short service, decided that he wanted to take the service sheet away with him. Someone told him not to, I think it was Queen Mary, but when their back was turned, he quickly retraced his steps, picked up the copy and hid it behind his back!

It is difficult today to describe the air of excitement in 1951 which was created by the Festival of Britain, and the opening of the Royal Festival Hall (RFH) on Thursday 3 May. In 1951 the rubble on the ground, both from war damage and the building preparations, was still to be seen as I and my fellow Chapel Royal Choristers made our way from Waterloo station to the Artists' Entrance at the RFH to rehearse. We were but part of a huge number of singers, drawn from the Choirs of Westminster Abbey, St Paul's Cathedral and seven London choral societies, but had a central position (where three years later the organ console would be placed). In front of us were the instrumentalists (selected from five London orchestras) and the State Trumpeters of the Royal Horse Guards.

The two conductors were Sir Adrian Boult and Sir Malcolm Sargent, whose biographical notes in the Souvenir Programme make for interesting reading: "Only the incontrovertible evidence that he was born in 1895 can ensure acceptance of the fact that Sir Malcolm is 56", and continued: "For Sargent, all life is such fun". Well, Sir Malcolm's self-evident enjoyment certainly communicated with his young choristers, as did Sir Adrian's deep love and talent for music, which had been "discerned from an early age at school, and had grown in wisdom and stature in pace with his physical and mental growth".

The hall itself was quite unlike anything I had ever seen. With a seating capacity of over 2,500, it felt ultra-modern, and acoustically amazing, as absolutely no trace of sound could be heard from the trains going in and out of Charing Cross Station across the Thames barely twenty yards away. It was also very intimate, as I was to find out years later when seated at the organ console.

The programme of entirely English music was ideally suited to our taste.

Handel: *Zadok the Priest* (the first time we had sung it with orchestral accompaniment)
Parry: *Ode at a solemn music*
Arne: *Rule Britannia* (in what became Sir Malcolm's famous arrangement at the last night of the Proms)
Vaughan Williams: *Serenade to Music*
Elgar: *Pomp and Circumstance No.1* (with *Land of Hope and Glory* almost bringing the house down)
Purcell: *Soul of the world*
Handel: *Hallelujah Chorus* and *Amen* chorus from *Messiah*.

There was quite a debate among the choristers about the respective merits of the two conductors, some preferring the restraint and subtle control of Sir Adrian, while others liked "Flash Harry". When we rehearsed *Rule Britannia* Sir Malcolm told us: "Sing the first three verses as loud as you possibly can, and in the fourth verse ... you sing still louder".

Both men were able brilliantly to communicate what a piece of music was all about, and both had us eating out of their hands. It remains a fantastic memory, and I was amused to find myself, many years later, the size of a small dot, in a wide-angle photograph of the opening concert, hanging in the (then) Artists' Bar.

Another occasion with interesting repertoire was the service in honour of St Cecilia, a Roman virgin martyr who became the Patron Saint of music and musicians. In due course, festivals in her honour were held to mark her Saint's Day (22 November), and there were a series of beautiful Odes to her composed by Henry Purcell and his contemporaries in the 1680s and 1690s. From 1905 these festivals included annual services, sponsored by the Musicians Benevolent Fund and held at St Sepulchre's, Holborn. We joined singers from Canterbury Cathedral, St Paul's and Westminster Abbey for a festival service which traditionally had a new commission each year. Not all these new works have gone into the regular Cathedral repertoire, but in 1951 Gerald Finzi's *God is gone up* absolutely hit the spot. Another vivid memory from a St Cecilia Festival Service was hearing Alfred Deller (of St Paul's) and John Whitworth (of the Abbey) singing the solos in Maurice Greene's anthem *God is our hope and strength*. They had a ringing tone so different from our more elderly altos at the Chapel, who, incidentally, sang at all four Coronation services during the twentieth century, first as boy trebles and then as adults.

It was at the St Cecilia Day Service in 1952 that we first met Mr Harry Gabb (Sub-Organist at St Paul's Cathedral) who directed the choirs that year, and who in 1953 was to become Composer and Organist at the Chapel, succeeding Dr Stanley Roper, who had retired after a long illness. Both of them were quite shy men, but I have to thank Dr Roper for placing his trust in me at my audition, when I was barely eight and making such a small sound. I also remember the way he played a phrase on the piano so that it always had elegance and charm. On the other hand, I wish he had been more adventurous with his choice of music and more challenging to his charges. Whether in summer or winter, he always wore a white scarf, and seemed to be continually ill, but that did not stop him conveying to us his love of beautiful sounds, even if I have to admit that neither he nor his successor gave the Children one lesson in voice production – nothing even about breathing – throughout my entire time as a chorister. When I first joined, the expectation was that you would sing like the older boy next to you, who sang like the boy next to him; and the result was often pretty dull and hoot-like. There were some exceptions, but I was not one of them.

Professor Taylor was a highly successful operator, who combined teaching at CLS with work at the Guildhall School of Music, as well his church job, and acting as a deputy from time to time for Dr Roper at the Chapel. At one point 'Tubby' Taylor ran three cars – claiming that in this way, even when one was being serviced, he would have one in reserve. He also directed a very good choir at the Church of the Annunciation (behind Marble Arch), with several treble voices much better than could be found at the Chapel. From the age of eleven I would sing there for Evensong, and at last I had a chance of singing some of the rich Evensong repertoire, denied to us at the Chapel. Tubby also invited some of his trebles to act as part of a guinea-pig choir for conducting candidates' exams at the Guildhall School of Music; and I fear that several of us took delight in obeying instructions to sing the occasional wrong note or ask tricky questions. And once again there was financial inducement. Leslie Taylor also did most generous work for several London hospitals, and each year we would sing carols outside many of the wards at St Mary's, the Middlesex, St Batholomew's and Guy's.

Thanks to Leslie, I also sang at a concert in the Royal Albert Hall in the *Lift thine eyes* trio from *Elijah*. Placed in the highest gallery, we could barely see the distinguished Austrian conductor Josef Krips, but we could hear his disapproval of our intonation. One of the older singers, David White, has since told me that by the time the orchestral sound reached us it sounded flat, just as by the time our sound reached the platform it also sounded flat! Not surprisingly, this did not go down well with a conductor, described in the New Grove Dictionary of Music, as "a benevolent despot in performance", and, to try to improve the situation a violinist from the London Symphony Orchestra was dispatched to join us in the gallery, with instructions to play our cue a semitone higher!

From time to time there were also extra services such as weddings and funerals at the Chapel, for which we Children were extremely well compensated. Our fee was seven shillings and six pence, which, in the late

1940s and early 1950s, was considerably more than my weekly pocket-money, and at today's rates would probably be at least £40!

Although the Royal Family had again stayed in London over the Christmas period in 1951 and we had once again sung at Buckingham Palace, I still remember the shock of *The Evening News* headline on 6 February 1952, "The King is dead". The whole country was plunged into mourning and, as members of the Court, we wore black armbands on our coats for six months. Our first duty was to sing with the Westminster Abbey Choir in Westminster Hall at the opening of the King's Lying-in-State, a ceremony that was as simple as it was poignant. We were also allowed off school to watch (from a gallery in Marlborough House) as the gun carriage passed by on its route to St George's Chapel, Windsor, for the State Funeral. By then it had already dawned on me that, as one of the Children of the Chapel Royal, I would be involved in one of the most momentous services of my life.

CHAPTER 3

The 1953 Coronation

"The Crown of the year"

Today we tend to associate Coronation music with what is played and sung inside Westminster Abbey, but from the Middle Ages until 1821 the Great Procession from Westminster Hall also had musical accompaniment. In 1189, Richard I was led to the church, "with an ordered procession and triumphal chanting", while for George II in 1727 there was a host of drummers. This all made for a great spectacle, which later seems to have got somewhat out of hand, causing Horace Walpole in 1761 to describe George III's Coronation as a "puppet show"!

This 'concert' element went largely unchecked until 1902, when, thanks principally to the Dean of Westminster, Armitage Robinson, the liturgical and theatrical elements were brought closer together. A striking example is Sir Hubert Parry's setting of Psalm 122, the opening words of which – "I was glad" – had been sung at the entrance of the Sovereign since 1661. Henry Purcell's setting was almost certainly used from 1685 until 1821 when, on the orders of George IV, it was replaced by the *Hallelujah Chorus* and Thomas Attwood's *I was glad*. For Edward VII's Coronation, Parry had the inspired idea of incorporating the words normally shouted by Westminster School's King's Scholars, "*Vivat Rex*" (Long live the king!) into his anthem. This arrangement worked so well both musically and liturgically that, like Handel's *Zadok the Priest*, it has been performed at every Coronation since (with appropriate words "*Vivat Regina*" substituted for a Queen.)

The *Vivats* go back at least to 1685, when Sandford recorded that the 40 King's Scholars of Westminster School, who were placed in a Gallery "adjoyning to the Great organ loft, entertained His Majesty with this short prayer of salutation."

Fairly soon after the death of King George VI, preparations were underway for the Coronation of Queen Elizabeth II, and long before we saw any of the music, we were measured for new robes. Quite a lot of guesswork must have been involved in estimating how much boys aged between 9 and 14 would grow in nine months. In February 1953, the 183-page Service books arrived. There were 22 separate musical items, most of which were unknown to us and, from then on, almost every practice included some of the Coronation music.

In May intensive preparations began. There were eight preliminary rehearsals, all of which were compulsory, and we were each issued with a card, which had to be stamped to show we were present at every one. My copy of the Service book still bears the markings made at these rehearsals, in particular the counting of rests. The thought of coming in one beat early or putting in one 'Alleluia' too many was terrifying. For the Homage, several anthems had been printed in the service books. As no-one knew how long it would take for the various representatives of the nobility to pledge their allegiance, we had to pencil in a number for each of the anthems. A white card would be held up to tell us which anthem was next so that one or more of the anthems could be dropped as the Homage approached its end.

The choir rehearsals were held at St Margaret's Westminster, close by the Abbey; the first four were for boys only, and the rest with the adult singers. As well as altos, tenors and basses, there were also twenty sopranos and contraltos from the 'Dominions', to the consternation, I later learned, of several eminent English women singers, none of whom had been invited to sing and who made their feelings plain. After the Coronation, Sir William McKie, who was the Director of Music for the Coronation, and the Archbishop of Canterbury met to discuss how to avoid this problem at the next Coronation, and recommended that in future there should be no women singers at all.

The final three rehearsals were in the Abbey, which had been closed for six months, with train tracks laid down so that the heavy loads of scaffolding and the extra staging could be more easily transported. Rehearsals began at 9.15am and lasted until lunchtime, as if to train us for the endurance test of Coronation Day itself. We could hardly believe our eyes when we saw the huge galleries on either side of the nave and quire that would somehow accommodate 386 singers. We ten Children were very fortunate to be placed in the second row, behind the Abbey choristers, enabling most of us to see not only the two sub-conductors, John Dykes-Bower (St Paul's Cathedral) and William Harris (St George's Chapel, Windsor) on either side of the quire, but also some of the amazing ceremonial. The sub-conductors were needed for those in the choir who could not see the main conductor (William McKie) because they were behind pillars or the organ cases. Unfortunately, some of the singers complained that they could not follow Harris's beat. It was therefore decided that he should have a sub-sub conductor, whereupon Dykes-Bower insisted that he should also have one, so as to avoid any undue comparison.

The last practice was a complete dress rehearsal, with no interruptions and almost everyone present wearing full Coronation robes: the Duchess of Norfolk stood in for the Queen. Many years later, Hugh Marchant (William McKie's administrative assistant) told me that by the end of this rehearsal Dr McKie (he had yet to be knighted) had become extremely stressed, and was on the brink of calling for a doctor and telling the Archbishop of Canterbury that he would have to pull out. However, after lunching with Hugh at the Athenaeum Club, McKie relented, and the music at the service was widely acclaimed. He was a meticulous choir trainer, but at times he had a short fuse.

The weekend before the Coronation, the Royal Family stayed in London and the Queen and Prince Philip attended the Sunday Service at Marlborough House Chapel, when special prayers were read, in common with every church in the UK. The following night, 1 June, during the Earl Marshall's final inspection of the Abbey, there was apparently some amusement when a black cat, who turned out to be a well-known resident of the Abbey precincts, belonging to one of the minor canons, was found asleep in the Coronation Chair!

It had been decided that the ten Children should stay in London overnight, so as to guarantee our presence at Westminster Abbey by 7.30am next day. Earlier, on that warm, sunlit, and strangely peaceful evening, Papa had delivered me to St James's Palace where the Chapel had been turned into a temporary dormitory, with ten mattresses and sleeping bags laid out on the stone floor between the choir stalls. It was very hard to sleep. Quite apart from the excitement, none of us was used to boarding, and my neighbour had hay fever. But despite our awesome surroundings, not least the Holbein painted ceiling, we young choristers were not deterred from enjoying ourselves, and I expect that this was the first and last time that the chapel was the scene of pillow-fights. It was not exactly the ideal preparation for the rigours of the day ahead, given the length of the service and the amount of music we would be singing. However, we had been getting to know the music for nearly four months, and this preparation seemed to overcome the effects of any lost sleep.

The 1953 Coronation

On a dull Coronation Day, Her Majesty the Queen on her way to the Abbey in the Gold State Coach, 1953 *(Photo: Getty Images)*.

Coronation Day dawned, and we were up well before 6.00am. After a cooked breakfast, served in the Chapel, we left by coach for the Abbey, where individual tickets, issued on the orders of the Earl Marshall, told us to report by 7.30am. (By 1953, sadly the practice of "chauffeuring" us around in horse-drawn carriages, which we had all so much enjoyed, had been dropped.) We were led into Dean's Yard and, just before we went into the Song School, the first excitement was hearing that Edmund Hillary and Sherpa Tensing Norgay had climbed to the summit of Everest; the world's highest mountain had been conquered and a new Elizabethan age was beginning. The other exciting news was that William McKie was to be knighted.

We had an extra rehearsal with the Abbey Choristers that morning, practising part of the semi-chorus in the *Coronation Te Deum* and the opening of *O taste and see*. By 10.00am sharp we were duly in place to sing the Litany in procession from one end of the Abbey to the other. Following the choir in this procession were members of the clergy carrying the Regalia, from where they had been kept overnight in a private room in the Deanery, to the west end of the Abbey, where a large annexe had been built. It was here that the Regalia were laid on an altar-like table, ready for the great Coronation procession in which they would be returned into the Abbey – this time carried by members of the nobility, followed by The Queen herself.

How can I describe the scene as we processed through the Abbey? First there was the colour – the rich crimson robes and glittering coronets of the Peers, the copes of the Bishops, the uniform of the State Trumpeters and the glowing banners. Between the transepts and in front of the High Altar was a square dais, known as the 'Coronation Theatre', where the Queen was to be presented to the congregation by the Archbishop for the formal Recognition. We could also see The Coronation Chair, where the Queen would sit for the Anointing with holy oil and the Crowning itself. We passed the Peers, the Prime Minister, Sir Winston Churchill and members of the Cabinet; then the senior Ministers of the Commonwealth countries and Heads of State, who were sitting in the quire. We later realised how fortunate we were to have this advance view of everything, for when we finally reached our places in the choir gallery, several of the Abbey choristers and Chapel Royal Children found their vision restricted by pillars, even when they were sitting in the front rows. I was one of the lucky ones.

Everything then went ahead as planned, notwithstanding a brief moment of confusion when the doors opened and the whole congregation stood up for the arrival of the Queen, only to see four cleaners with carpet sweepers enter the Abbey to do a final tidy-up, resulting in ripples of laughter.

Unlike some of the peers and members of the royal party, who seemed to have turned the Lady Chapel of Henry VII into a temporary refectory, we choristers were given little sustenance to keep us going throughout the four hours we were on parade in the Abbey, apart from a plentiful supply of glucose tablets (though the Westminster Abbey choristers had been given a packed picnic lunch in their cassock pockets consisting of ham sandwiches, an apple and barley sugars). There were also specially installed lavatories at ground level in the choir aisles beneath our galleried seating.

At last, after all the months of preparation, the Service was actually happening! I think we were all conscious of taking part in a unique moment of English history and thrilled by the music we were singing. First of all, Hubert Parry's incomparable setting of *I was Glad*, as the Queen processed through the Quire towards the Altar, with the *Vivats – Vivat Regina Elizabetha*! (Long live Queen Elizabeth!) – sung quite raucously by the 40 Queen's Scholars of

Westminster School, placed high up in the Triforium above the organ screen. Even at that age I could appreciate the beauty of Herbert Howells's Introit, *Behold, O God, Our Defender*, with the wonderful soaring phrase "For one day in thy courts is better than a thousand". On to the Anointing and Handel's *Zadok the Priest*, specially re-orchestrated for the occasion, and (to quote the Service Book) a chance to let forth all our "pent up feelings of rejoicing" as the Central Rite of the Service was reached. As well as the musical highlights, we loved the numerous opportunities to shout, "God save the Queen".

For me, some of the most memorable pieces came towards the end of the service; Stanford's *Coronation Gloria* and William Walton's specially commissioned and very challenging *Coronation Te Deum*, in which the composer used all the forces at his disposal – the State Trumpeters from Kneller Hall, two semi-choruses, full orchestra and the organ (which was given a brilliant antiphonal solo part), not to mention nearly 400 voices.

Among all the pomp and majesty, there was also Ralph Vaughan Williams's exquisite miniature, *O Taste and See*, sung quietly as the Queen and Prince Philip received Communion. I later learnt that Vaughan Williams had declined to compose a new *Te Deum* for the service, but his music was still the most prominent feature. More than 70 years later, whenever I hear the opening of the *Sanctus* from the *Mass in G minor* with its timeless triads, I think back to the Coronation Service, even though it was sung to English words in place of the Latin text and was originally composed for Westminster Cathedral.

Strangely enough, there was some controversy over the inclusion of Vaughan Williams's setting of the *Old Hundredth, All people that on earth do dwell*, with its awe-inspiring trumpet fanfares, the lyrical trumpet solo over the choir's quiet unaccompanied verse 3, and the last verse "with all available trumpets". The Archbishop remained unconvinced about the hymn arrangement, possibly because the unfamiliarity of the introduction left some members of the congregation uncertain when to come in – indeed, congregations to this day are tempted to join in during the organ play over, as happened at the service marking the 60th anniversary of the Coronation in 2013. Some of the miscreants should have known better.

An hour after the service was over, we were driven back to St James's Palace. It was still raining, but our coach stopped where Horse Guards Road meets The Mall, giving us splendid views of the Royal processions and the State Coach on their way back to Buckingham Palace. At St James's we were given our Coronation medals, and soon I was on my way to join my family and to watch some of the ceremony on a tele-recording (as it was then called). But there were no pictures of the choirs, not even of the Litany which the Westminster Abbey and Chapel Royal choirs had sung in procession.

Over the years, the music at Coronations has been a barometer of the tastes, and sometimes the prejudices, of each period. Several of the commissioned works have not really stood the test of time; certain texts inspired composers more than others. But is there another country in the world that could boast such variety and inspiration for these great occasions – be they exquisite miniatures such as Vaughan Williams's *O Taste and See*, the rousing marches of Elgar and Walton, Britten's *Gloriana*, Stanford's inspired *Coronation Gloria* or Handel's *Zadok the Priest* – all composed to mark Royal celebrations? That being said, it would appear that the impeccable ceremonial of 1953 was not always achieved in the past. Queen Victoria's account, written at the close of her Coronation Day in 1838, gives a delightful insight into her emotions, as well as a hilarious account of various (non-musical) mishaps, and she completely agreed with the Dean of Westminster that "there really should have been a rehearsal". This moment in history did not fall victim to such mishaps. Horace Walpole's celebrated comment of 1761, after the Coronation of George III: "What is the finest sight in the world? A Coronation. What do people most talk about? A Coronation", also rang true in 1953.

A week later, the Chapel Royal Choir was involved at St Paul's Cathedral, where there was a Coronation Thanksgiving Service by the peoples of the Commonwealth. Although the service was simpler and much shorter than the Coronation itself, there were some individual moments just as powerful in their way, for example Sir Winston Churchill reading the lesson from Ephesians VI: "Finally, my brethren, be strong in the Lord, and in the power of his might". Other highlights included another Coronation anthem by Handel: *The Queen* (changed from *King*) *Shall Rejoice* and Vaughan Williams's *Te Deum in G*.

Later that summer, people also talked about 'The Ashes', as Test matches between England and Australia are known. In 1953 England had managed to go into the final match at the Oval all square, thanks in part to some questionable negative tactics by the English all-rounder, Trevor Bailey, in the penultimate game at Headingley. The game at the Oval was very tense. The Surrey spinners, Tony Lock and Jim Laker, however had come into their own, and on the final afternoon Bill Edrich and my idol, Denis Compton, saw

England home, with Denis hitting the winning runs. We were on holiday at Frinton, and my family somewhat grudgingly waited to go out until the end of the match, which I followed ball by ball on my small portable radio. In the post-match discussions the Australian commentator and former opening batsman, Jack Fingleton, generously described England's victory as the "Crown of the Year".

It is a tribute to Harry Gabb, to say that there was no sense of anti-climax for the rest of my time as a chorister, even though it was very much back to the usual routine. Then in July 1954 my closest chorister friend, Peter Lough, and I represented the Chapel Royal celebrating the move of the Royal School of Church Music to Addington Palace.

Representatives from a number of choirs sang at the opening of the RSCM at Addington Palace, 1954.

The service included an anthem, specially commissioned from Sir William Harris, *Behold, the Tabernacle of God*, and I was delighted when I arrived at Winchester Cathedral nearly thirty years later to find it in the repertoire there.

My last visit to Buckingham Palace as one of the Children was at Christmas 1954, when we took part in a short carol service. Despite my modest voice, Harry Gabb allocated me the solo in *I Saw Three Ships*, and very nervous I was too! One of our practices was recorded for the seven o'clock news on the

BBC Light Programme, and when I heard the broadcast, I was not inspired by the sound of my own voice. The most interesting setting that afternoon at the Palace was Stanford's *The Monkey Carol*, a delightful choice of Harry Gabb's, which amused both us and our audience. At the end of the service, Her Majesty presented a signed copy of the Bible to the newest recruit, John Murray – the only time this presentation was made in person while I was one of the Children.

Sunday, 25 July 1955, was a day of desolation. I had had an exceedingly long run as a chorister, lasting for seven years from the age of eight until past my fifteenth birthday, and had been appointed Head Chorister in April 1954. By then I had come to feel so much a part of the Chapel and could hardly imagine life without the weekly routine of practices and the Sunday service. Around Easter, Harry Gabb had gently mentioned *en passant* that "of course I would be leaving in July", and quite right too, as my voice was beginning to break and I was having to do warm-up exercises as I walked from Green Park Station to St James's Palace. Harry Gabb kindly came to my rescue, however, by offering to give me organ lessons, often at St James's Palace, as soon as I left the choir. He was unassuming and, on the few occasions when he conducted, very undemonstrative. However, to have had a choirmaster who cared about his choristers in this way is something for which I shall be forever grateful, and it certainly contributed to my eventual decision to take up a career in church music.

CHAPTER 4

City of London School

"The quality of mercy is not strained"

I was a committed Anglican, veering towards Anglo-Catholicism, and was confirmed in the Crypt Chapel of St Paul's Cathedral after catechism classes with the Sub-Dean. Regular church-going was very much part of our family agenda and before leaving the Chapel Royal Choir, I became a server at Christ Church, Southgate on Saturday mornings. With the church overlooking the Walker cricket ground, I have to confess that there was an added incentive to arrive early for Sunday Evensong – to watch some cricket. The first game I remember was in 1949, between a Middlesex eleven and the Southgate Cricket Club – a benefit match for Denis Compton, who duly made a century, and I became a fan for the rest of his life. Within two years I became an avid follower of the England Test Team, and during the 1950–51 tour of Australia used to tune in on my radio each morning of a Test Match to find out the overnight score.

I enjoyed a number of sports at the City of London School, particularly cricket. The school sports ground was at Grove Park in south-east London and a 20-minute train journey from Charing Cross. I was selected as wicketkeeper in the junior house matches, but sometimes there were clashes with Chapel Royal Choir practices, and on several occasions I was promoted to open the batting before having to leave early to catch the train.

I managed to represent the school at Fives, when one of my partners was Michael Brearley (son of the maths teacher, Horace). I never was good enough a cricketer to play in the first eleven with Mike, who in due course became one of England's most successful captains. I did however open the batting for the CLS second eleven with another Michael (Apted), later a notable film director. And yes, I had the privilege of being caught on the boundary in a house match by Mike Brearley, who politely asked on my way back to the pavilion why I had not kept the ball on the ground!

My most formative influence at school was the English master, Geoffrey Clark, who produced the annual school play. Indeed, I cannot overstress how important Geoffrey was to my life – as I later acknowledged in an article for The Times Educational Supplement's series, *My most important teacher*.

I think I first came to be noticed by Geoffrey when he was the adjudicator for the Beaufoy Shakespeare Recitation prize, and he awarded me the prize for my rendering of the St Crispin's Day speech from *Henry V*. It was however because of my singing voice that I first appeared in a school play. In my last year as a treble, I was given a minor part in Sheridan's *The Critic*. This involved singing some rather ridiculous, albeit entertaining, lines (concocted by another master, Mr Carruthers) and cleverly adapted by the School's Director of Music, Dr John Wray, to familiar melodies by Mozart and Beethoven.

MN, in the centre, taking part in the City of London School's production of Sheridan's *The Critic*, 1955.

We were very fortunate that our annual school plays were performed in the theatre of the Guildhall School of Music and Drama, then on the opposite side of John Carpenter Street. The following year the school play was *The Merchant of Venice*, chosen, I suspect, by Geoffrey because there was an outstanding candidate to play Shylock: his name was Brian Lapping, the future eminent English journalist and television producer, who became renowned for his historical documentaries, such as *Obama's White House* (2016); *Putin, Russia and the West* (2011) and several others. To my surprise I found myself entrusted with the role of the leading lady, Portia. This involved learning over 400 lines and delivering such well-known speeches as 'The quality of mercy is not strained'. I also had to play a male judge after endeavouring to act as a woman. Another Shakespearean part was Titania in *A Midsummer Night's Dream*, when we performed an extract at the Recitation prize-giving, in front of the Lord Mayor.

MN as Portia in *The Merchant of Venice* at the City of London School, 1956.

Physically I was a late developer, with no signs of a hairy chest until I was nearly 17, which I suspect was one of the reasons why Geoffrey always gave me girls' parts. His choice of plays was unusual to say the least. My other roles included the genteel Lavinia in George Bernard Shaw's *Androcles and the Lion*, which retells the ancient tale of Androcles, a Christian slave who is saved by the requiting mercy of a lion in the Roman Colosseum. Then in my last year, I played the more complicated but rewarding part of Sheila in J B Priestley's *An Inspector calls*, which revolves around the apparent suicide of a young woman called Eva Smith.

I learnt so much from Geoffrey, about timing, the value of silence, and how to convey the meaning of the text. He was really a *manqué* actor, and each Lent term he became completely absorbed in the school play. He was extremely demanding, but my goodness, this paid off.

This all went down very well with my father, who was always insistent on clear diction; when we were very young, my sister Denise and I had extra elocution lessons. I am sure this must have helped when I competed at the age of 13 in a French competition recitation prize at the *Institut Français*, and was awarded first place after reciting La Fontaine's poem *Le rat de ville et le rat des champs*. I wish though I had shown more aptitude with French, and regret that, despite having a reasonable accent, my vocabulary has remained *très limité*. It was hard for my French grandparents that communication with their English grandson was so restricted, whereas Denise presented no such problems. In my defence, I can plead that our mother, out of courtesy to her English mother-in-law (who did not speak a word of French and lived with us until I was seven), in my early years deliberately avoided speaking to me in French. Language limitations however did not prevent me from enjoying some marvellous French holidays, when we stayed with our cousins and greatly enjoyed the French *cuisine*.

As well as all these varied activities, there was academic work to be done. My A level subjects were History, English and Latin and I particularly enjoyed history for which the special subject was Napoleon. By the time I was 17, however, I had begun to think of ordination and, in December 1957, I was awarded a place at New College, Oxford to read theology.

I was also making some progress on the organ, and in January 1958, at the age of 17, I was invited to become organist of St Mary's Hornsey Rise, in north London. This enabled me to 'cut my teeth', learning how to play hymns and accompany the psalms (to Anglican chant) as well as to take choir practices. For this I had received some training when, in my final year at the City of London, 'Doc' Wray had appointed me conductor of the school's small chamber choir.

All this was an enormous help as, at the suggestion of the school, I prepared for the Organ scholarship exam for Gonville and Caius College, Cambridge, in April 1958. The examiners were Patrick Hadley, the Professor of Music and Precentor at Caius, and Raymond Leppard, the eminent conductor and Fellow of Trinity College. After the first round, the candidates were told that six of us had been selected for the final and would be called out in alphabetical order. When five names had been announced by the time they reached 'M' I was worried, but my anxieties were soon relieved; "Neary", mercifully, was the last name called. The final round consisted of some aural tests and improvising, for which Ray Leppard gave me the slightly mischievous theme of *Twinkle, twinkle, little star*. I decided to play a series of variations, the first of which started slowly in the minor key, before the variations became increasingly lively, not to say, jazzy. By the time I had finished, everyone was laughing, and the following day I received a telephone call from the Senior Tutor, Ian

McFarlane, offering me the Organ Scholarship, in the course of which he told me that, "we like to save a man from Oxford, if we can".

Here is how my record at the City of London School was described in the 1958 Chapel Royal magazine (which Peter Lough and I, much aided by his father, Ernest, started in 1954):

> "Martin Neary, (Chapel Royal 1948–55) was elected to an Organ Scholarship at Gonville and Caius College Cambridge. He used to play the organ at School prayers and was also well-known not only for his energetic performances on percussion instruments in the school orchestra, but also for his accomplished portrayals of female characters in the school plays."

There was no reference to the occasion when I played an extra verse in the hymn, unaware that it had finished, and ground to an embarrassing halt. Nor was there any mention of cricket.

CHAPTER 5

Cambridge

"I'm out. Over to you"

Greek was not the only language challenge I would face at Cambridge, for the Part 1 Theology course also required a knowledge of Hebrew. So, in company with some future distinguished clerics, including Bishop Richard Harries (Oxford) and Bishop Stephen Sykes (Ely), I attended Hebrew classes three times a week, taught by Henry St John Hart, the redoubtable Dean of Queens' College. And I rather enjoyed it. I have often wondered whether learning to read from right to left helped me when playing pieces like the Bach trio sonatas, with a separate part for each hand and the bass line played on the pedals.

I was also quite absorbed by my Old Testament studies with the distinguished scholar, Peter Ackroyd, and at the end of my first term I spent a weekend being vetted at Cuddesdon Theological College, following which I was offered a place to train as an Ordinand after completing my degree at Cambridge.

The set-up in Caius Chapel was colourful, to say the least. The Dean, Hugh Montefiore, just about managed to tolerate the Precentor, Patrick Hadley, and vice-versa. Paddy (as he was universally known) never forgot that in the College hierarchy he was senior to Hugh.

The choral evensongs were sandwiched between the two sittings in Hall for dinner, between 6.55 pm and 7.15 pm, and followed a weekly pattern:

Monday: Plainsong, sung by the 12 Choral Scholars (tenors, baritones and basses).
Tuesday: Choral Scholars and volunteers, whom Paddy called the "Foothills".
Wednesday: Choral Scholars, with more demanding repertoire; at that service the Dean allowed the director to conduct, while on all other occasions, the direction was undertaken by two Choral Scholars, called "nodders" – effectively conducting with their heads (and rather weird it looked!)

Thursday: Choral Scholars and the "Foothills".
Friday: 5.30 pm Practice, normally taken by the Precentor, who was always keen on the clarity of the words "JAS" (Just Accentuation of Syllables was a constant concern).

When I arrived at Caius, I had no idea that I would be coming into contact with such a remarkable person as Patrick Hadley, nor what an influence he would have upon me. As Vaughan Williams had written to Paddy on his appointment as Professor of Music in 1947: "You have the heart of music in you, and you will make it live for all those young people whose musical conscience is in your keeping". He certainly did, having a magical way with 'the chaps', as he always referred to the Caius chapel choir (which then consisted only of tenors and basses).

Although by then composing very little, Paddy put his heart and soul into the music of the college and in particular the chapel choir. He continued to make male voice arrangements of such works as Verdi's *Stabat Mater* and *Te Deum*, thereby enabling us to perform repertoire beyond our normal reach, with the Organ Scholars expected to provide accompaniments on the modest chapel organ. *En passant*, I should say that the chapel's very dry acoustic meant that every error was heard.

Paddy's philosophy: "way beyond us, therefore we do it" made a huge impact, and I am sure inspired me to perform some of the wilder Tavener pieces when I became Organist of Winchester Cathedral.

At Caius, the incoming Organ Scholar generally had a one-year overlap with his predecessor organ scholar, and in my first year the main organ scholar duties were undertaken by the senior organ scholar, John Edwards. He was already a fine organist, but quite shy when taking choir practices, and on several occasions when Paddy was 'hors de combat' John generously gave me the chance to direct the rehearsals, for which he would play the accompaniments at which he excelled.

Paddy was very keen that the Caius undergraduates should have a chance to conduct at the College concerts, and in my second year I was given a chance to direct a performance of Corelli's *Christmas Concerto*. I have to confess that I felt out of my depth conducting a small orchestra, with hardly any supervision. So, the following summer I spent an invaluable week at a conductors' course, led by Sir Adrian Boult, and at the 1960 Caius Christmas concert I was entrusted with a more complicated work, Jacques Ibert's

Divertissement, when several people were kind enough to say how much I had improved since the previous year.

Paddy was devoted to, and expected a lot from, his Organ Scholars. I was not the only one whom he asked to help him take off his wooden leg – his right leg having been amputated below the knee towards the end of World War 1. This disability inevitably left a lasting impact on him, although it did not prevent him from riding his bicycle nor from undertaking quite long walks in his beloved Ireland. He certainly had his unpredictable, not to say exasperating, moments, often not unconnected with alcohol. One I will not forget was receiving a telegram, sent from his rooms in college, a day before we were due to perform his arrangement for men's voices of part of Berlioz's *L'Enfance du Christ*. The telegram had two sentences: "I'm out. Over to you". So I found myself conducting the concert with just a day's notice.

He was never short of a colourful phrase such as when he greeted me on Election Day, October 1959, at the "You have never had it so good" victory of Harold Macmillan: "Hello Martin! I have made the sign of the Cross". Paddy had a sharp wit, which at times could be quite biting, such as when he would greet a latecomer to a rehearsal by stopping the practice and saying pointedly: "Thank you SO much for coming".

Paddy was very generous and whenever we found ourselves travelling on the same train to London, he would insist on paying for me to travel first class with him. "I'll sport you." Despite the 40 years' difference in our age, we became close friends, and I spent many evenings with him in his rooms, when, as well as playing on the piano selections from his favourite operas (Puccini's) he would open up about his life. More than once he spoke to me melancholically of his disappointment over his career and how he had become disillusioned with the musical establishment. In the summer of 1958, his most recent work *Connemara* had been rejected by Oxford University Press. His compositional style, which had been warmly appreciated in the 1930s, had by then become unfashionable, and previously acknowledged masterpieces such as *The Hills* and *The Trees so high* were hardly ever being performed. "I wanted to be a great composer or conductor, and I am neither". He died in 1973, aged 74.

Why then is his music not better known? As Simon Heffer wrote in the Daily Telegraph (April 2023), Patrick Hadley "left behind an underappreciated canon of music of the highest quality; and those who grow to love it will always ask what else might have been, had fate not dealt with him in so brutal a fashion ... It is not surprising that much of his music has a darkness, as well as a profound beauty. After Cambridge, he studied with Ralph Vaughan Williams at the Royal College of Music. One of the most remarkable features of Hadley's music is that the influence of RVW is apparent everywhere, but there is no pastiche. He often goes off in exotic directions that Vaughan Williams might have followed had he been as fond of alcohol. Hadley loved lyricism and was adept at displaying it with a lack of inhibition his teachers did not share."

One of the privileges/duties of the Caius Choral and Organ Scholars was to sing grace at the annual nine course Feast celebrating Stephen Perse, one of the College's principal benefactors. In the afternoon we would rehearse the grace with Paddy, but without the (notoriously tone-deaf) Dean, Hugh Montefiore. To prepare the singers Paddy mischievously would imitate the Dean by growling his part deliberately off-key – how the singers managed not to collapse laughing when Hugh 'sang' on the night, I do not know.

Hugh Montefiore, later Bishop of Birmingham, became an outspoken figure in the Anglican Church, who was often controversial for speaking out on such issues as the environment and women in the priesthood. Born to Jewish parents, Hugh had shocked his family by converting to Christianity while a student at Rugby School. He attributed this conversion to having seen Jesus in a vision. Forty years later, Hugh was extremely supportive when my wife and I faced difficulties at Westminster Abbey.

Unusually, there was no-one reading music in my year at Caius, and by my second year I found myself taking an increasingly prominent role in the College's music, even though I was not studying for the Music Tripos. There were however some highly talented musicians, from whom I learnt a great deal. In the year above was the prize-winning composer David Blake, whose opera *Toussaint* was later performed at the Coliseum.

One of my closest friends was David Gaine, whose day would generally begin by his listening to a recording of Bach cantatas. He was extremely fond of BWV78 *Jesu, der du meine Seele*, and in particular the aria for soprano and alto duet *Wir eilen mit schwachen*, and in due course this was the first Bach Cantata I conducted in the College Chapel.

My knowledge of opera was embarrassingly limited, but another Caius contemporary opened my ears to the operas of Richard Wagner. Richard Weeks was a brilliant classicist, who in his first year was awarded the prestigious Porson Prize for Greek poetry. He had developed a love of Wagner when a pupil at Clifton, where the Director of Music was a remarkable musician, Douglas Fox, who had lost his right arm in the First World War. Douglas had retired to Cambridge, where he became the Organist of Great St Mary's (the University Church) where he was able to play brilliantly using one hand and two feet. Thanks to Richard's introduction, Douglas not only took me on as an organ pupil, but also invited me to the Royal Opera House to hear a number of Wagner operas. Little did I think that 20 years later I would have the opportunity to direct extracts from *Parsifal* and *Tristan* with the Bournemouth Symphony Orchestra in Winchester Cathedral.

Douglas Fox was an inspirational teacher, from whom I benefited enormously. He also had some scatter-brain moments, such as losing his music. I was told on good authority that, when he was at Clifton, he was convinced that someone had stolen his score of the Wagner work he was about to conduct. He became so agitated that he called in the police and persuaded them to launch an inquiry. Happily, this yielded a quick result after one of the officers asked Dr Fox if he would mind getting up from the piano stool, whereupon the 'stolen' score was discovered.

In my first term, the Cambridge University Musical Society performed Paddy's cantata *Fen and Flood*, which had been orchestrated by Vaughan Williams for four-part choir and full orchestra (the original having been for the Caius 'chaps' and piano duet), and I was able to experience at first hand Paddy's wonderful gift for melody, which we Caians thought deserved to be better known.

With this in mind, I was persuaded in my second year by some of Paddy's staunchest Cambridge supporters, including the horn players Tim Reynish (later the renowned wind band director) and Guy Woolfenden (later to become Director of Music at the Royal Shakespeare Company), to ask the Caius College Music Society to promote a concert of music entirely by Paddy at the Recital Room at the Festival Hall. They agreed and we hired the Recital Room on 11 March 1960 for £25. The principal work for the chorus was *Connemara* which to this day still remains unpublished. Despite a rocky start to *Connemara*, there was a sympathetic review in *The Times*, written, I later learnt, by Frank Howes. Paddy was very self-effacing, and at the end of the concert it was quite difficult to get him to come to the front and acknowledge the applause.

There was a full house, and we were invited to repeat the programme at the Arts Theatre in Cambridge, where Paddy was a member of the Board.

Despite his reluctance, we went ahead, and once again drew a good audience. Paddy was already thinking about retiring and took a Sabbatical in 1960–61. Several members of his family had died around the age of 60, and he thought he might well follow suit. For his Sabbatical, Paddy persuaded Caius to appoint as Precentor, Peter Tranchell, a Lecturer in the Music Faculty. He was another huge influence, above all encouraging me to believe in myself as a musician. A brilliant pianist with an astonishing mind, he had already made his mark with his colourful personality, his musical *Zuleika* and the opera *The Mayor of Casterbridge*. On hearing that Peter would be deputising for Paddy, I asked him if he would have time to compose something for the Caius May Week concert. The result was the very entertaining *Aye, aye, Lucian* with its racy choruses such as *"What shall we do on the earth without women?"* Two years later came *The Mating Season* – a perfect marriage of the humour of P G Wodehouse with Tranchell's musical wit and compositional flair.

Peter was not attached to any college, having been controversially rejected for a fellowship at King's on the advice of Benjamin Britten. However, towards the end of my third year, I became indirectly involved in Peter's election as a Fellow of Caius. My opinion had been sought by the two opposing factions, one led by the Regius Professor of Classics, Charles Brink (chairman of the Caius College Music Society), who was in favour, and the Dean, Hugh Montefiore, who was against. In the event, to my delight, Peter was duly elected.

Towards the end of my second year, the thrill of making music had really got into my system, and I began to question whether ordination was going to be right for me. More than 60 years later, as I try to recall what caused this change of mind, I believe I felt increasingly that music provided me a means of expression, with a power beyond that of words. As I explained at my 21st Birthday party at our home in Southgate, I regarded becoming an Organist rather than a Priest as another way of serving the church. I had come to realise, however, that, if I were going to develop as a musician, I would need to read for a degree in music. So I decided to explore the possibility of changing from the Theology to the Music Tripos. Thanks to the unflagging support of Paddy, Peter and Ian McFarlane, the University authorities passed a motion enabling me to change subjects at the end of my second year.

During my time, there were some exceptional musicians at Cambridge, of which the outstanding Organ Scholars were Simon Preston at King's, Brian Runnett (who tragically died young in a car accident) at St John's and the opera conductor, Richard Armstrong (Corpus Christi). Other brilliant contemporaries included the pianist and conductor, Philip Ledger, the violinist Simon Standage, the conductors, John Eliot Gardiner and Christopher Seaman, the composers, David Blake, Derek Bourgeois, Sebastian Forbes and Jonathan Harvey, not to mention highly regarded academics such as Philip Brett, Alan Brown and Geoffrey Chew, my first successor as Organ Scholar. There were also some superb instrumentalists at Caius, such as the violinist, David Beck, and viola player, Richard Bruce-Wilson, with whom I performed Mozart's *Sinfonia Concertante* in our last year.

Without exception, all the members of the Music Faculty had something special to offer, even if Paddy did not always agree with them. Among them were notable scholars, Thurston Dart and Peter Le Huray, music historians such as Philip Radcliffe, and two brilliant choral conductors, David Willcocks and George Guest, whose choirs at King's and St John's were second to none. Indeed, hearing their Evensongs on days when we were not on duty at Caius was inspirational. I particularly remember one Ash Wednesday, when I unexpectedly found myself involved in a broadcast Evensong from King's. As I entered the chapel for the service David Willcocks spotted me and asked if I would mind listening to the service from the organ loft, as his Organ Scholar, Simon Preston, was away giving a recital in Birmingham. The service was unaccompanied, but David wanted to have someone at the organ ready to play a G minor chord before the Allegri *Miserere*, should he feel it necessary. I gladly accepted, whereupon David gave me detailed instructions about how to play the chord (with a small *crescendo* and *diminuendo*), and that it should only be played if he looked up towards the organ loft at the end of the Third Collect. He did, and I duly obeyed his instructions.

A number of the King's and John's choral scholars became friends, and I was very pleased when some of them asked if I would like to conduct a programme with them. I took up the offer enthusiastically, and we duly formed the Ionian Consort. Our first concert, in Jesus College Chapel, was well reviewed in *Varsity* and gave me more of a taste for conducting.

One unexpected activity at Caius was the Gilbert and Sullivan Society, which had been founded by Paddy. The G and S Society rehearsed on Sunday mornings, and by the time I joined, Paddy had handed over the conducting to students. In my time we gave concert versions of *HMS Pinafore, Iolanthe, Pirates of Penzance* and *Ruddigore*, the last two of which I conducted.

At Caius there were some extremely talented choral exhibitioners, Alec

Broers, the brilliant Australian scientist, who became Master of Churchill College and Vice-Chancellor, Richard Frewer, who, as well as being an exceptional architect had a beautiful baritone voice and Stephen Walsh, who wrote his first reviews for *The Times* while still an undergraduate, is a world authority on Stravinsky, Mussorgsky and Debussy, and who has written several books, his most recent being on the Romantics – *The Beloved Vision*.

Thanks to my changing subjects, I spent five years at Cambridge, which gave me extra time to develop as an organist. To my astonishment in March 1962, shortly before my 22nd birthday, I was shortlisted for the post of Sub-Organist of Westminster Abbey. But I was not in the least surprised that I was not selected, as one candidate, Simon Preston, was in a different league entirely, and he was appointed.

However, in due course it transpired that I had been noticed by one of the Canons, Michael Stancliffe, who was also Rector of St Margaret's Westminster. I learnt several years later that, when he arrived home after the interviews, Canon Stancliffe had told his family that he had just seen the man he would like to be his next Organist at St Margaret's. Within a year I found myself auditioning for the post of Assistant Organist there, with the expectation that within two years I would take over from the then Organist, Herbert Dawson.

CHAPTER 6

St Albans and Tanglewood

"Everyone has been looking for you ..."

I owe a great deal to all my organ teachers but, as I look back over 60 years, I have no doubt that the most influential was the Welshman, Geraint Jones, whose performances of Baroque music anticipated the "authentic" style long before it became fashionable. In the late 1940s and early 1950s Geraint had been the first British organist to record the organ works of J S Bach on the renowned instrument at Steinkirchen, which dates from the time of Bach himself.

Before my last year at Cambridge, one of Geraint's former star pupils, Peter Le Huray, strongly recommended me to study with him. My first lesson (at St Gabriel's, Cricklewood, in Northwest London) was very revealing. After listening to me play through the Bach *Toccata (Dorian) in D minor*, Geraint commented on my technique, or rather lack of it. He asked simply but pointedly if I wanted to take my organ playing seriously. I replied positively, whereupon he said this would mean "going back to basics". I would need at the very least to double my practice time each day and work daily on keyboard exercises such as Hanon prescribed in his *Virtuoso Pianist* or the extremely demanding Brahms *Fifty-one Exercises*, including training the brain and fingers to play four-time against three.

Geraint was unique in many ways. A brilliant organist, he was also a ground-breaking conductor, whose performances of Purcell's *Dido and Aeneas* with soprano Kirsten Flagstad and baritone Thomas Hemsley in the opening season of Bernard Miles's Mermaid Theatre in 1951 were highly acclaimed. He was also an exceptional sight-reader. It was infuriating when, after I had played a piece which he had not seen before, he would instantly know how to play it. As far as I am aware, he was the only major British organist of his day not to hold an important church position. Instead, he apparently enjoyed profitable dealings in the antiques business. He had a love of smart cars, and one of the pleasures, after a challenging lesson at St Gabriel's, was being driven to West Hampstead tube station in his Rolls Royce.

In April 1963, together with other Oxford and Cambridge Organ Scholars, I received a letter about a new Organ Festival to be held at St Albans, inviting applications for the Interpretation and Improvisation competitions. I had no idea what the likely standard would be, or whether I had any chance of being accepted. During my next lesson, I discussed the letter with Geraint, who thought that there would be nothing lost in applying. The one specific organ qualification I had was the Fellowship of the Royal College of Organists, which I had received the previous January. I can only assume it was on the strength of this that my application was successful, as, without having had to play a note or send in a tape, I was invited to enter the Interpretation competition and to have a Master Class in Improvisation. Today's candidates will be astonished to hear how little in terms of repertoire was demanded of us in the 1960s, as they would be by the limited amount of practice time we were given on the Abbey organ and the "generosity" (if that's the word) of being allowed one, and only one, general piston – the divisional pistons were unalterable. There was one compulsory piece, Buxtehude's *Prelude and Fugue in F# minor* and an open choice for a second work lasting not more than 12 minutes. I chose Liszt's virtuoso *Prelude and Fugue on BACH*. In both pieces Geraint Jones was in his element; indeed, his Liszt, as I now look back, was revelatory. So, a few weeks before the competition, I arrived at St Albans to spend an hour registering the two works. The first shock was the layout of the newly refurbished organ, with the Positive at an angle to the player's right, providing an incisive sound such as I had never heard before. Ideal, I felt for Buxtehude, and so I duly made a registration scheme, after which I went back to Cambridge for my last 'May Week'.

A few days before the competition I had another lesson with Geraint but, when I showed him my registration proposals for the Buxtehude, he dismissed them with a brisk: "Well, this is how I would play it". Such was my confidence in him that, even though I was not going to have any more practice time in the Abbey, I completely revised my plans, which I am sure was a vital factor in my being chosen for the final.

However (and it seems strange to have to admit this, nigh on 60 years later), I was unaware of my progress in the competition. Because I had previously promised to play at the wedding of the Caius Chaplain on what turned out to be the day of the competition's final, I was not present for the announcement of the finalists. Nonetheless, once the wedding was over, I thought I had better get back to St Albans, catching a train to Welwyn Garden City and completing the journey by bus. On arriving in the Abbey just before 7.00pm, I casually asked one of the stewards if he could tell me who was in the final. He said: "Are you Martin Neary?" I was. "Well, you are in the final. We've been trying to contact you all day, everyone has been looking for you, and if you don't report by 7.00pm you are going to be eliminated. And you are first on at 7.30." At least there was no time for nerves, and as the repertoire for the final was the same as for the first round, I do not remember being unduly worried. I heard the other finalists play and was incredibly impressed with the electrifying performance of Messiaen's *Dieu Parmi Nous* by Susan Landale, who duly won. Despite the commotion less than half an hour before I played, my Liszt apparently persuaded the Jury to award me second prize.

The following morning, I was back at St Albans for the Master Class in Improvisation with Marie-Claire Alain. I was the only candidate, as no-one else had applied. Marie-Claire was charming and so constructive. Starting with a plainchant melody, she asked me to play it first in two and then in three parts. Inevitably I was soon struggling, but it was a great experience to spend even a short while at Marie-Claire's feet – speaking of which, I still remember her pretty silver organ shoes! In the afternoon there was the Prize-winner's recital, when Susan, Guy Bovet, the brilliant Swiss winner of the Improvisation Competition, and I all played.

The frequent use of the word 'prize' may today seem somewhat inappropriate in terms of monetary reward, as I believe the first prize was £30 and I received £10. But much more important was the feeling that our playing had communicated and had won the approval of such an eminent jury. This was a wonderful confidence boost. Both Susan and I were immediately invited to record recitals for the BBC Third Programme, which in the 1960s regularly included 30 minutes of organ music at 2.30 pm on Sunday afternoons. This was arranged by one of the Jury, Harry Croft-Jackson, then in charge of organ programmes for the BBC. When I made my recording two days later, little did I realise how distinguished my page-turner would become; his name was Andrew Davis.

At the time, I don't think any of us realised just what Peter Hurford's vision would mean for the organ world, and indeed for the organists fortunate enough to play in that and subsequent International Organ Festival competitions. Peter's timing was right; the 'organ reform' movement was just beginning to catch on, and above all he made the musical world at large realise that organists were no longer playing in ivory towers on instruments when clarity of texture was not necessarily the most important thing on their minds. Through his own experience on the Continent, where he had had numerous successes both as a player and improviser, Peter almost single-handedly broke the insularity of the English organ world. In this, he followed and developed the path so bravely trodden by Ralph Downes, with the design of the Royal Festival Hall organ in 1954. Ralph was a member of the five-strong Jury in 1963, with Piet Kee from Holland and François Roboulot, the blind Parisian organist at St Germain des Près. For me, the chance of hearing the jury members play, as well as fellow competitors, was inspirational.

The day after I recorded my BBC recital I flew to America to take up a conducting scholarship, awarded by the Berkshire Music Center at Tanglewood, the summer home of the Boston Symphony Orchestra. Ten weeks earlier, after sending in an application to the Music Center, I had received a telegram asking if I would meet the Chairman of the Faculty, the eminent American composer, Aaron Copland, on Good Friday for tea at the (very grand) Connaught Hotel in Mayfair. He was extremely charming, asking why I wanted to go to Tanglewood and how I thought I would benefit from the experience. I explained that I felt the need for some concentrated tuition in conducting and was drawn to Tanglewood after reading about the Festival in a British Sunday newspaper. Little did I realise what was going to be in store, for Tanglewood that year had a truly remarkable range of talent on the faculty and among the students.

Apart from Stewart Kershaw (who later conducted the Seattle Ballet Company), I think I was the only British conducting student to apply that year, which may have been one reason why Dr Copland told me at the end of the interview that he was going to recommend that I be invited. My scholarship would pay for tuition and accommodation, and I was left to find the cost of travel to the States, which Caius generously covered. When I discussed this possibility with my supervisor, Thurston Dart, he told me with typical forthrightness: "My dear Neary, if you want to go, you will go".

This was to be a very illuminating period, as I learnt for the first time what it was to really know a score, as well as how to communicate. It was stimulating, if sometimes alarming, to be studying alongside fellow conductors who were streets ahead of me, and to come under the eagle eye of Erich Leinsdorf, who had succeeded Charles Munch as Music Director of the Boston Symphony Orchestra. I remember trying to conduct the opening movement of Beethoven's 8th Symphony and being asked by the Maestro if

I thought I knew the score. I had worked so hard at trying to be clear in my movements and about the numerous tempo changes, but I clearly needed to do more work.

It was also stimulating getting to know some of my Tanglewood contemporaries, among them David Del Tredici the composer, who became a Pulitzer Prize winner and achieved fame with *The Works of Alice*. He had also created works celebrating "gayness", acknowledging that many great composers had been gay and that "it's something to be celebrated". Another British student was the outlandish Welsh composer, John Cale, some of whose compositions, according to his website, were considered too violent and dangerous to be performed in public. One of his pieces involved smashing a table (or was it a piano?) with an axe.

There was also a charming Greek student, Alexander Symeonides, with whom I went sailing several times in a small boat on the local lake. This may sound idyllic, but there was one occasion I shall never forget when there was a sudden change in the weather and a storm blew up, forcing us to take down the sails. The only way we could reach the nearest shore (on the other side of the lake), was by taking off the rudder and using it to row. By amazing good fortune, we were spotted by some people on the bank, who insisted we come back to their lakeside house to recover. In due course we discovered that our hosts had a Canadian organist staying with them whose name was John Weatherseed, Music Director at the Metropolitan United Church in Toronto. When John heard that I too was an organist and was going to stay with some cousins in Toronto, he said he would arrange for me to practise at his church, which turned out to be a most welcome bonus.

Talking of Greeks, there was another extraordinary musician on the Faculty, the 40-year-old Giannis Xenakis, the Romanian-born Greek-French *avant garde* composer, music theorist, architect, performance director and engineer, who applied the kinetic theory of gases to some of his musical compositions. I also became a friend of the world-renowned organist of the Boston Symphony Orchestra, Berj Zamkochian, known by his many friends for his generosity, keen intellect and sense of humour. As well as introducing me to the delights of eating lobster, he kindly arranged for me to practise on the electronic organ in the Music Shed, as the Tanglewood concert hall was known. This was invaluable, as I found myself playing the organ part in Respighi's *Pines of Rome* with the Berkshire Music Center Orchestra under Eugene Ormandy. In fact, the organ part is undemanding, the biggest challenge was counting the huge number of bars rest and coming in at the right place.

Other notable musicians and composers that year included Gunther Schuller, whose music seemed to bridge the gap between classical and jazz, and Lukas Foss, who was also a fine pianist. Today it is hard to believe that at one of the Boston Symphony Orchestra concerts, conducted by Charles Munch, the solo keyboard part in the 5th Brandenburg concertos was brilliantly played on the piano rather than the harpsichord by Lukas Foss. Somewhat to my surprise, a few months later when I described this to the eminent harpsichordist, George Malcolm, his reaction was "how sensible – at least the piano could be heard without amplification". I also remember, towards the end of a rehearsal of another Brandenburg concerto, Munch saying to the orchestra, who had obviously played the work many times with him before: "Last four bars". And that was all they rehearsed!

To be honest, I was less enamoured with some of the chorus masters of the Berkshire Music Festival Chorus. The student conductors were encouraged to sing, and it is fair to say that our patience was tested at one rehearsal, when we sang through Mozart's *Ave verum* more than a dozen times, and to my mind, it got progressively worse. On the other hand, it was thrilling to take part in Stravinsky's *Symphony of Psalms*, directed by Erich Leinsdorf and, likewise, the American premiere of Britten's *War Requiem*.

I needed to keep up my organ practice, as the Director of the St Albans Festival, Peter Hurford, had kindly written to a number of organists in the USA and Canada, encouraging them to invite me to give a recital in their churches, and several invited me to play. So, after the Tanglewood Festival was over, I spent a further month in the USA and Canada, principally to give organ recitals. One of these was at St Matthew's Church, Ottawa, whose organist, Gerald Wheeler, I had known from the days when he took the occasional choir practice at the Chapel Royal. Small world!

The reviews of my recitals were not always entirely complimentary – one Ottawa paper noted that it took me "a little while to get the measure of the auditorium", and another that my rendition of César Franck's *Cantabile* "seemed altogether too tame". I can now see that, rather than communicating the essential character of a piece, I was often too concerned with playing accurately.

My next challenge was to develop my organ playing and to find work in London.

CHAPTER 7

Getting started in London, 1963–71

"He's a good organist"

Before going to America, I had been introduced by a friend of my parents to Herbert Dawson, Organist of St Margaret's Westminster, who it transpired was looking for an assistant. After a brief audition, 'Bertie' recommended me to the Rector, Canon Michael Stancliffe, who remembered me from the interview for Sub-Organist at Westminster Abbey the previous year, and I was duly appointed. On the recommendation of Harry Gabb, I was given some organ pupils at Trinity College of Music, so that when I returned to London from America, I had two modest jobs to begin.

I was determined to improve my organ playing, continuing to have lessons with Geraint Jones. Then, during the course of a visit to United Music Publishers in Montague Street, I had a fortuitous meeting with the Armenian music critic and organ enthusiast, Felix Aprahamian, which led to a life-long friendship. Felix was a small, dapper man with a neat grey beard. As his friend, John Amis, wrote in his obituary in *The Guardian*, "Felix was a

Alice (cello) accompanied by Felix Aprahamian, 1992.

mixture of characters from Proust to P. G. Wodchouse". He was also a very able pianist and score reader, and many years later he played through part of the Elgar *Cello Concerto* with our daughter, Alice. When Felix heard that I had come second behind Susan Landale at St Albans, he was absolutely adamant that I should go and study with Susan's teacher, the blind French organist, André Marchal – which is exactly what I did.

The *Maître* was wonderfully warm-hearted; when teaching, he claimed to know only two words of English, "Good" and "Not good". Short, with quite long hair and a smiling face, he became a great friend of my parents, often staying with us on his visits to London and, despite his blindness, managing to repair our grandfather clock. He was one of the initiators of the twentieth-century organ revival in France. Seemingly undaunted by his disability, his own playing was always beautifully articulated, and I learnt a great deal about the release of a note. It was also uncanny how he seemed to know how I was pedalling, saying on one occasion: "Why are you not using your left foot?"

Marchal had been Chief Organist at St Eustache from 1945 to 1963, eventually resigning over a dispute concerning who should be responsible for rebuilding the organ. I had most of my lessons in France on the practice organs in one of his two houses, in Paris near the *Institut des Jeunes Aveugles*, where he had been a student and a teacher, or at his holiday home at *Hendaye sur Plage*, on the Atlantic coast close to the Spanish border. He swam intrepidly in the sea, despite being blind, and enjoyed being buffeted by the powerful Atlantic waves. Susan Landale arranged for me to be a guest in the organ lofts at St Sulpice and St Clothilde on Sunday mornings, to see their respective organists, Marcel Dupré and Jean Langlais, improvise. I was intrigued to see Dupré stand on the pedals while continuing to play, in order to see when the celebrant was ready to continue. They both had a *coterie* of female fans!

Felix encouraged me to explore a wider repertoire, such as Max Reger's *Toccata and (double) Fugue in D minor*, Op 135b, as well as some of Vierne's organ symphonies. He was instrumental in my playing at St Margaret's, Lothbury, in the City of London Festival in July 1964, although my programme was limited by the modest organ. However, I did play the premiere of *Sonatina for Organ* by Peter Tranchell; he was present at the recital, but I think we both felt that it was not one of his more interesting works. This was one of several engagements that came my way, chiefly because of the St Albans competition. Word seemed to have got around that I was available, and I was soon being invited to accompany a number of choirs at their rehearsals and in due course at their concerts. These could be quite challenging undertakings, such as attempting to realise, on the organ, the orchestral accompaniments for Bach's *St John Passion* and Mendelssohn's *Elijah*.

Another important contact was the brilliant harpsichordist, George Malcolm, who had been a boy prodigy, and whose father had been a colleague of my father's at the Eagle Star Insurance Company. Sometimes Papa went to the Malcolms' house in Clapham, where George would accompany him on whatever he had brought to sing. He was a reticent man, who was much admired by Benjamin Britten. It was George who recommended me to the conductor, Harry Blech, when he needed an organ continuo player for a London Mozart Players concert at the Festival Hall. Playing continuo in Bach's Cantata 82, *Ich habe genug*, with a professional orchestra was pretty daunting, not least because they played so far behind the beat, and at the concert I was too nervous to play the first chord. Luckily, Harry Blech was very tolerant and I became one of his regular continuo players, including playing in one of the opening concerts at the Queen Elizabeth Hall.

An even more significant guest organist invitation, however, came my way in 1966 when I accompanied the Saltarello Choir, whose singers had mostly just finished at University or Music College. The choir, who were giving a concert in Godalming in Surrey, were keen to give a performance in London as well. I suspect they thought that if they engaged me, I might arrange a concert for them at St Margaret's Westminster, where I was by now the Organist and Choirmaster, which I did! As well as watching the conductor, Nicholas Braithwaite, I also had a good view of the sopranos, one of whom, as well as being to my mind the most attractive, I discovered was the choir's treasurer, Penny Warren. We got talking, and when she asked where I was living, I explained that I lived in Winchmore Hill, North London but was hoping to find somewhere near to St Margaret's. To my complete surprise, Penny replied that there might be room on the top floor of her mother's house in Chester Square. The following Sunday, she arranged for me to meet her mother and to see the accommodation on offer. It was beyond my wildest dreams, and I had no hesitation in accepting "the deal" of £6 per week, Penny having told her mother that I was an impecunious organist.

Quite soon, Penny and I started going to concerts together. Then on Ascension Day, when I returned to Chester Square after a flying visit to Paris for a lesson with the *Maître*, Penny kindly asked if I needed a page-turner for a recital that I was giving on behalf of the Royal College of Organists two days later in Bournemouth. And the rest, as will be revealed, is history.

Both Penny's parents, who had divorced in 1961, were eminent doctors. Her mother Josephine Barnes (later Dame Josephine) was the first woman consultant in gynaecology at Charing Cross Hospital and the first woman President of the British Medical Association, while her father, Sir Brian Warren, had a fashionable London practice as a GP, with patients including several Tory MPs, such as Edward Heath. Ted was godfather to Penny's half-brother, Marcus, and attended the Christening at St Margaret's Westminster at which I played, and apparently told Brian that I was a good organist.

Penny and I became engaged in July, and in August we had a holiday in France, when I was able to introduce her to some of my French relations. She enchanted them all, and they did their best to make her feel at home, one example being when "Tonton" Charles, with whom we stayed in Pontaillac on the coast north of Bordeaux, proudly brought home some English Cheddar cheese from the local market, erroneously thinking that she would prefer this to their "fromage du pays". Most, diplomatically, she took some cheddar whenever it appeared on the table.

On returning to London, I was involved in a unique event at the Royal Albert Hall, devised and master-minded by Peter Hurford (then organist at St Albans Abbey) to mark the centenary of the Royal College of Organists – "ORGAN IN SANITY AND MADNESS. An investigation into the monarchical Rights and Wrongs of the King of Instruments". An unexpected scene was the "Arrival of the Queen of … shhhhh!" from Handel's *Solomon*, when 'the Queen', Peter Hurford, was carried by King's Choral Scholars from the back of the hall on a 'palanquin' (actually a stretcher kindly loaned by Charing Cross Hospital). Francis Jackson (Organist of York Minster) and I performed Antonio Soler's *Concerto in C for two organs;* I was also the soloist in a Handel organ concerto and took part in a spoof arrangement by Peter Hurford of the opening of Bach's *Prelude in D*.

Penny's next "engagement" was to turn the pages at my debut recital at the Royal Festival Hall. This had a varied reception, being described in the *Musical Times* as a "brilliant success", but also by my being loudly booed after I had played *Chants d'oiseaux* from Messiaen's *Livre d'Orgue* (I hope because of the music, not my playing). I had become increasingly attracted to Messiaen's music and felt that the Festival Hall organ offered the chance of playing a work

Royal Albert Hall programme cover for the organ extravaganza, 1966.

such as *Chants d'oiseaux* with the precise registration Messiaen intended. The movement is constructed around two contrasting ideas: a highly organised refrain, with its haunting Hindu rhythm and, alternating with this, some seemingly improvised birdsong sections, imitating the blackbird, robin, thrush and nightingale.

I had been fortunate during my visits to Paris for organ lessons with Marchal to attend some of Messiaen's analysis classes. These were fascinating, although I had been surprised at his not entirely favourable comments concerning the *Sanctus* in the Bach *Mass in B minor* – "Bach n'était pas Catholique". Messiaen's music featured prominently at our wedding at St Margaret's on 22 April 1967, when Susan Landale kindly flew over from Paris to play *Dieu parmi nous* from the suite *La Nativité du Seigneur* as Penny and I processed joyfully down the aisle. Susan, who had become one of Marchal's star pupils, had married a Frenchman and lived in Paris, where she continued her glittering career of playing and teaching.

St Margaret's, Westminster, 1967.

Other music in the service included Parry's *I Was Glad*, sung as Penny and her father walked up the aisle, and the beautiful Mozart *Missa brevis*, K192, accompanied by our friends, violinists Miranda Bulmer-Thomas and Nicky Ferry and cellist Gordon Leadbetter, with Richard Armstrong at the organ. The service was conducted by the Rector, Canon Michael Stancliffe.

For nearly 60 years Penny has been my greatest supporter and most perceptive critic. She had played the oboe and cor anglais in the Oxford University Orchestra and came from a musical family; her maternal grandmother, Alice Ibbotson, having been only the second woman to become a Fellow of the Royal College of Organists, receiving her diploma on the same day as Harold Darke, the Organist of St Michael's, Cornhill. When they met up again at our wedding reception at Apothecaries' Hall, around 60 years later, they did a splendid job probably pretending they recognised each other.

In 1968 I returned to the Queen Elizabeth Hall to make a recording on the recently installed Flentrop organ of Bach, Sweelinck and Mozart – his *Fantasia* K 608, which was originally composed for a mechanical instrument. There have been several attempts at making this remarkable work playable by two hands and two feet. The arrangement I used, and still like because of its late eighteenth-century style, is based on the edition by Walter Emery, who in his introduction wrote that he had "removed the impossibilities, but by no means all of the difficulties, many of which seem fully justified by the satisfaction to be derived from overcoming them". He concluded: "As this is an arrangement, no one need hesitate to alter passages that he finds unreasonably difficult or cannot make effective on his organ". During one of the recording sessions, I followed Walter's advice unashamedly, getting Penny to play one note which was causing me repeated problems. Many of the reviews began by questioning the decision to play the *Fantasia* on such a small instrument, but all agreed that it worked surprisingly well.

I had really enjoyed playing the Flentrop organ, and I decided to take the risk of giving a self-promoted recital at the Queen Elizabeth Hall on New Year's Day, 1969. To begin with, however, box office sales went slowly, prompting my father not only to buy 50 tickets, which he managed to sell to members of the congregation at Christ Church Southgate (where he had become a church warden), but also to hire a London Transport double-decker bus to transport the Christ Church party to and from the hall. To my relief, we ended up with an audience of over 800.

As well as a Bach *Trio Sonata* and the Mozart *Fantasia*, the programme included the premiere of *Sonata* by our friend Sebastian Forbes. This called for many changes of registration, most of which were fixed by Penny who had to move "ballet-like", as a friend wrote, from one side of the organ to the other. The recital drew favourable reviews, and the upshot was that the following year I was invited to play two more recitals in the 'Wednesdays at 5.55' series at the Festival Hall.

Back in July 1969 Penny had even more duties when acting as my registrant in Oxford, in the extraordinary solo organ movement in Peter Maxwell Davies' *O magnum mysterium*, which Lina Lalandi had included in her Oxford Bach Festival. The Oxford Town Hall organ had very few registration aids and my copy still has the markings with the registration instructions for

Penny, as well as a complimentary note signed by the composer. I was rather surprised, however, when he said he preferred the less squeaky sounds we produced to those of previous performances. I did not tell him that this was partly due to the Town Hall organ not having the highest notes, forcing me to make "adjustments" to the score.

Reverting to the Festival Hall; between 1966 and 1983, I gave eight recitals in the Wednesdays at 5.55 series, including 30 works by Bach. I increasingly enjoyed playing at the RFH, although I can still remember the shock of changing to the choir manual (a debatable move I now admit) in Bach's *Prelude in C minor*, BWV 546, and hearing nothing. Penny thinks she may have touched a button when turning a page. I quickly moved back to the Great, and picked up playing where I would have reached. Another testing moment was in 1983, when I took over a programme originally chosen by Susan Landale, who had had to withdraw. This started with the notoriously dangerous *Prelude and Fugue in D*, BWV 532, which opens with a sequence of ascending scales on the pedals. In the 15 minutes before the recital, I was a nervous wreck. In the event, mercifully all was well, but it took me some time to feel at ease.

The last chord – cartoon by Michael Hickey of MN and PN at the Royal Festival Hall organ, 1983.

My experience of playing recitals in North America in 1963 made me keen to make an organ recital tour there. Thanks to recommendations by friends (and before I had an agent) I was able to arrange a seven-week-long coast-to-coast tour in the "Fall" of 1968. A number of American and Canadian organists who had attended my recitals at St Margaret's Westminster were kind enough to invite me to play in their churches; in particular, Thomas E Wilson arranged a series of engagements in Southern California, including the dedication recital on the new Reuter organ at Riviera Methodist Church, Redondo Beach. I also played the outdoor Spreckles organ at Balboa Park, where there was competition from noisy aircraft flying into San Diego airport.

I gave a total of 21 recitals on a variety of organs, but I have to say that my favourite instrument was the Flentrop tracker-action organ, installed in 1958 in the Busch-Reisinger Museum at Harvard University; I did not give a recital, but, thanks to the pre-eminent organist, E Power Biggs, I was able to play it. The Baroque style voicing and the mechanical action made it ideal for playing Bach, and not least the trio sonatas. Back on the East Coast, Penny and I spent Thanksgiving with her distant American cousin, John Spencer and his family. They lived close to the Biggses, who kindly invited us to tea, after which he played some Schubert for four hands on his pedal piano. We then moved to New York, staying with another cousin, Ed Spencer, for my final recital of the tour at the Church of the Ascension.

Penny had been a marvellous help not only with registrations, but also in introducing the programmes – "chic in mini-dress", as described in the *Los Angeles Times*, while the Washington *Evening Star* praised her "valuable contribution, not without humor, by her reluctance to dwell on the obviousities". Each concert had a contemporary work, including the North American premières of Kenneth Leighton's *Et Resurrexit* and Simon Preston's *Vox dicentis*. Three years later, in 1971, I made two more tours to America, before being taken on by the Lilian Murtagh Concert Agency.

Thanks to support from the British Council, I also played quite frequently in Europe, ranging from a church in Koszalin in northwest Poland (where our interpreter was a constant presence – could she have been a spy?), West and East Germany, Holland, France, Switzerland and Italy. Until the birth of Nicola, Penny would generally be my registrant, although when we were in Modena, this was not permitted, because the only access to the organ loft was via a monastery where women were not permitted.

·

Another piece, for which my registration skills at the Queen Elizabeth Hall were tested, was Bernstein's *Chichester Psalms*. This was conducted by Louis Halsey, from whom I learnt so much, not least in the organising of rehearsal time, and later when he worked with period instrumentalists. Louis was just one of several conductors whom I was lucky enough to play for, and who fuelled my desire to direct concerts as well as to play in them.

One of my more unusual experiences was playing organ continuo for John Tobin in his annual performances of *Messiah* with the London Choral Society at the Festival Hall. John thought that in his quest for authenticity, the soloists should insert some dazzling cadenzas at the end of the arias, but the general verdict was that these excessive cadenzas were at times somewhat embarrassing. Thanks to my friendship with the flautist and ex-Caius choral scholar, Chris Yates, who had become the orchestral manager of the Philharmonia, I also played at the Festival Hall the organ continuo in the Bach *Magnificat*, conducted by Daniel Barenboim, and the virtuoso organ solo in Leoš Janáček's *Glagolitic Mass*, with its very exposed pedal *obligato*, conducted by Edward Downes.

I accompanied the BBC Chorus (as the BBC Singers were then known) often directed by Peter Gellhorn, previously chorus master at Glyndebourne, in a wide ranging repertoire including all six Bach motets. So far, nearly all my engagements had been to play the organ until, in September 1966, I was recommended by one of my father's singing colleagues, Sheila McShee to the Twickenham Musical Society (TMS), who were looking for a conductor. For my audition we worked on some choruses from Mendelssohn's *Elijah*, which I had never previously conducted. So, it was a delightful surprise to receive a telephone call from the indefatigable choir secretary, Barbara Muir, offering me the job.

The first challenge was to choose a programme for my opening concert in December. Rather than play safe, I opted for a varied menu, ranging from a Bach cantata to Benjamin Britten's *Rejoice in the Lamb*, which for most of the choir was unfamiliar. Everyone responded very positively despite some initial rhythmic problems, the irregular bar lengths causing quite a lot of consternation to the choir and conductor, who was rather flummoxed by one of the tenors relying on *tonic sol fa*. But our first performance at All Hallows Church was well received, not least thanks to our organ accompanist, Richard (now Sir Richard) Armstrong, and some excellent soloists, one of whom was a 12-year-old chorister from St Margaret's Westminster, Gunther Wassertheurer.

Most of our concerts were at All Hallows Church, though we did give a programme at St Mary's Twickenham, including the Kodaly *Missa Brevis* which, with its stratospherically high soprano part, was somewhat stressful. Perhaps the most adventurous choice during my time, however, was Handel's rarely heard oratorio, *Joshua*. Thomas Morell's libretto had some curious lines such as "And grateful marbles raise to thee", when it was hard to keep a straight face, but it was good to break new ground.

My Twickenham concerts were absolutely invaluable in helping me develop as a conductor, and benefit from working with gifted (and extremely tolerant) instrumentalists, whom I had come to know through playing continuo; for example the woodwind section in the Mozart *Requiem* included Thea King, playing the basset horn in a programme that included Schubert's *Eighth Symphony*.

My final concert with TMS was in March 1972, when we performed the *St Matthew Passion* (albeit with a few cuts) with the Bournemouth Sinfonietta – the first time I had conducted Bach's masterpiece. By then Penny (who sang regularly with TMS) and I had moved to Winchester *(see Chapter 10)*, and I therefore sadly had to step down as conductor. But what a way to finish! I was sorry to leave Twickenham, where we had made many friends, but by then I was already finding my duties at Winchester both fulfilling and time-consuming. I also felt I should not be directing another choral society when I was about to take over as conductor of Winchester's Waynflete Singers. Since then, it has been inspiring to see the way the TMS has continued to thrive, and I would like congratulate Christopher Herrick not only on his staying power, but also for all he has done to develop the choir; the outstanding performance of Herbert Howells's *Hymnus Paradisi* that I heard in 2022 was in a different league from what we were achieving 50 years ago. *Laus Deo!*

On 11 August 1969, our first child was born at the old Charing Cross Hospital (close to Charing Cross Station), a girl whom we named Nicola Marguerite and who brought us great joy. On that very day her grandmother, Josephine, told us that on her 30th birthday there would be a total eclipse of the sun. I don't know if this fact has had any influence on her life, but I think it fair to say that Nico has not often been eclipsed. Apart from her own outstanding academic record and her work as a Consultant at St George's Hospital, Tooting, where her care and concern for her patients are greatly appreciated, she has always given so much to her family and friends. Nicola took time out of her training in endocrinology and general internal medicine to do a PhD on gut hormones, relating to current treatments for obesity such as Wegovy. Later when she and her family moved to Washington DC for her husband James's work at the British Embassy, she was awarded a fellowship at the National Institutes of Health doing clinical and research work in endocrinology. In her current consultant role at St George's, Nicola leads the Type 1 Diabetes service and is relishing the development in technology with insulin pumps and sensors becoming more accessible. She also has a senior management role in acute medicine and above all values looking after and treating patients as a physician in the context of their overall wellbeing.

Nico is generous with her expertise and supports the rest of the family and close friends with their concerns about their health. It is wonderful for Penny and me that Nico and Alice and their families have always been so marvellously supportive of our autistic son Tom, for example taking holidays close enough to where he lives so that he can join them each day. (See Chapter 10)

In addition, Nico has somehow found time to sing, as a Choral Scholar at Trinity College, Cambridge (where she read maths and became a Senior Wrangler), and subsequently with some excellent choirs, as well as joining me in fund-raising recitals on both sides of the Atlantic.

CHAPTER 8

St Margaret's Westminster, 1965–71

"Je n'aime pas les 'woods'"

In August 1965, after nearly two years as his assistant, I succeeded Herbert Dawson as Organist and Choirmaster at St Margaret's Westminster. "Bertie" had had a remarkable career, dating back to 1900 when he became a Westminster Abbey Chorister. As well as being a highly regarded accompanist, from 1929 to 1965 he was Organist at St Margaret's. I only heard him play at the end of his career, but was staggered by the way he performed, quite masterfully, all six trio sonatas of Bach at six organ recitals only a year before retiring at the age of 75.

Bertie, who succeeded Stanley Roper (my first choirmaster at the Chapel Royal), also directed a good choir, although when I took over the number of trebles had dwindled to just seven boys. Among them, however, was an absolute star, Gunther Wassertheürer, whose parents worked at the Austrian Embassy and who had a vocal quality worthy of the Vienna Boys Choir. Like the other boys, Gunther was a pupil at Westminster City School. It was not long before Harry Mudd, of Abbey Records, heard about Gunther and offered to make a 45rpm record of Mendelssohn's *Hear my prayer* with our star soloist, accompanied by my first Assistant Organist, Richard (now Sir Richard) Armstrong, then a student at the London Opera School, who was to become a renowned opera conductor.

According to a review in the *Musical Times*: "Mendelssohn's hard-worked old warhorse comes up as fresh as a daisy, thanks mainly to an outstanding treble soloist. Gunther Wassertheürer, an Austrian living in England, has a voice of decidedly continental rather than English tone quality; but what is so impressive is the poise and security of his singing. The breath control is superb … Quite simply this is one of the best pieces of treble singing I have heard for a long time. The choir and organ backing is all that is needed, and the recording gives us a very nice balance between the forces employed. An issue that is a great credit to all concerned."

That September we had a good intake of new choristers, but one had to be realistic. Expecting the boys to turn up twice every Sunday was no longer a viable option, and so for Evensong on alternate Sundays the Rector agreed that the boys should be let off and be replaced by a small group of young women sopranos. This turned out to have other benefits, because it meant we acquired a pool of sopranos for any extra services in the week, rather than having just altos, tenors and basses, and it also enabled us to be more adventurous with the repertoire.

By this time the men's voices had been augmented by the presence of several ex-Oxbridge choral scholars (including a number from Caius College). I was becoming acutely conscious however that I had little idea about training boys' voices. I do not remember any voice-training as such when I was a treble – and I was most indebted to an ex-King's Choral Scholar, Bruce Pullan, for coming to oversee the boys' singing. This made a huge difference and, from then on, I resolved to find the means for the choristers to have regular vocal training.

This bore fruit, and in 1967 we were invited by the BBC to take part in the radio series 'Choirs and Places where they sing'. There was, however, some controversy – not over the music, but about some new windows along the South side of St Margaret's, designed by John Piper to replace those destroyed during the Second World War. Piper chose to use predominantly shades of silvery grey, with splashes of greens, yellows and blues in abstract designs, so as not to detract from the church's beautiful east window, dating from 1504, of which he was a great admirer. The plan had been for each of the 11 programmes in the series to be introduced by the Poet Laureate, Sir John Betjeman. However, it transpired that Sir John so disliked the new windows that he declined to take part in the broadcast from St Margaret's, his place being taken by the Rector, Canon Michael Stancliffe. The St Margaret's musicians did not share Betjeman's views, and they helped to raise funds for the windows.

In five successive years we gave a fund-raising concert at the Banqueting House in Whitehall (from where Charles I had walked to his execution), joined by a distinguished soloist each time – Leon Goossens *oboe*, George Malcom *harpsichord*, Gervase de Peyer *clarinet*, Julian Bream *guitar* and Alan Civil *horn*. One must admit that the over-resonant acoustic was not always ideal, but we managed to draw large and appreciative audiences. The choir for these concerts was newly founded St Margaret's Singers, the church choir expanded with other singing friends.

In the summer of 1966, we revived a series of Saturday afternoon organ recitals. The organ, built in 1897 by J W Walker and overseen by the star organist of the day, Edwin Lemare (Organist at St Margaret's, 1897–1902), still sounded very fine, although the action was in need of a major overhaul. These recitals were promoted by the Organ Music Society, led by Felix Aprahamian. At the beginning of the twentieth century, organ recitals at St Margaret's had attracted huge crowds, with queues stretching all the way round Parliament Square, drawn no doubt by Lemare's reputation and his repertoire, which included many of his remarkable transcriptions of movements from Wagner's operas – at that time the most likely way of hearing any Wagner in London. Later I was interested to learn that the Lemare family was thought to be (like my French family) of Huguenot extraction.

We also invited my teacher, André Marchal, who gave a beautiful all-Franck programme, despite his reservations about the specification – *"Je n'aime pas les woods"* – and we persuaded Walkers to remove these stops from the stop combinations. Although nothing like as popular as those given by Lemare, our recitals normally drew respectable attendances. But on 30 July 1966 there was an embarrassing exception due to a rival attraction – the triumphant Football World Cup Final at Wembley between England and Germany. The match had been due to finish before 5 pm, but, as the scores were equal, extra time was played. Parliament Square was completely deserted, and the distinguished organist, Ralph Downes, played a mostly unfamiliar Bach and Schumann programme to a miniscule audience.

In my own recitals, I would sometimes move from the Walker organ to the Lincoln Chamber organ, which worked very well for early English voluntaries; and on one occasion, when Grant, Degens and Bradbeer had temporarily installed one of their mechanical action instruments in the north aisle, I played all three instruments. There has always been a tradition of fine preaching at St Margaret's, from the time of Samuel Pepys, who would bring his hourglass to check the length of the sermons. The church was also renowned for its weddings, including those of Pepys and Winston Churchill.

Among the numerous special services, there are three (apart from our wedding) that for different reasons I particularly remember:

The Memorial service for Lady Megan Lloyd George (daughter of the former Prime Minister, David Lloyd George, and the first female Member of

Parliament for a Welsh constituency). Her family was very keen to have at least one hymn sung in Welsh. So, after listening several times to a vinyl recording, I made a version using phonetics to help the choir with the pronunciation, only for our efforts to be drowned out by the authentic and incredibly fervent voices of 50 members of the London Welsh Male Voice Choir.

In 1969 the wedding of Viscount Hereford, a Patron of the Royal Philharmonic Orchestra, who had the idea of inviting the orchestra to play. There was barely room to accommodate the instrumentalists in the south aisle, but somehow, they fitted in. I made orchestral arrangements of the hymns and found myself conducting the RPO in Mascagni's *Easter Hymn* from *Cavalleria Rusticana*.

The annual carol service of a Charitable Trust, set up to 'help the lame dog over the stile' called the Guild of Nineteen Lubricators, whose charity extended to giving cases of wine to the Rector, the Organist and Preacher. This was normally the Bishop of Guildford, George Reindorp, who never lost an opportunity of telling me that we were gradually approaching the standard of Barry Rose's choir at Guildford Cathedral!

The re-opening of the restored St John's Church in nearby Smith Square provided a better venue for the St Margaret's Singers concerts, and in 1970 we performed Bach's *St John Passion* there, when my new assistant organist, Alastair Ross, persuaded me to make the recitative continuo accompaniment more stylish – generally by playing short chords when the bass line moved, and not holding on to the chords throughout – one of my earliest moves towards a degree of authenticity.

The concert gained a complimentary review in the *Daily Telegraph* which began:

"Singing from the heart, and natural musicality of a high order, sustained with exceptional consistency by all the participants, resulted in a moving performance of Bach's *St John Passion* at St John's Smith Square last night – and also made an invincible case for chamber music treatment of it. The small group of St Margaret's Westminster Singers, under the admirable direction of Martin Neary, sang the sequence of dramatic exchanges with Pilate with ample tone. Only in the opening chorus was the need for a more massive sound felt."

At my final concert at St John's with the St Margaret's Singers in December 1971, I shared the conducting with my immensely talented successor, Richard

Hickox, who was a great catch for St Margaret's. In Part 1, Richard conducted Haydn's *Nelson Mass* and his *Organ Concerto No.1 in C* (for which I was the soloist), and in Part 2, I directed the Bach motet, *Singet dem Herrn*, and two of Handel's Coronation Anthems, *My heart is inditing* and *Zadok the Priest*.

On Christmas Day 1971, it was necessary to collect the choristers from their homes, because London Transport no longer operated on 25 December. My duties at St Margaret's, however, continued after Christmas Day and up to 11.59 and 30 seconds on 31 December. The BBC still broadcast a televised watch-night service on New Year's Eve, which that year was from St Margaret's. The service was to lead directly into the chimes of Big Ben, ushering in the New Year. Timing was therefore crucial. The challenge was all the greater because we did not know precisely when the previous BBC programme, starring the comedian Frankie Howerd at the Café Royal, would finish. So, the Rector, David Edwards (who was giving a short address), and I had to be prepared for last-minute cuts and we had six different versions to hand. In the event, Frankie went on much longer than anticipated, and we had to drop several verses of the psalm and of the hymn *O God, our help in ages past* (for which I had written my first descant). Thanks to the hand signals of Willie Cave, the BBC producer, we finished two seconds before Big Ben struck. And, after saying the closing prayer in the vestry, the Rector introduced the "new Organist of Winchester Cathedral".

CHAPTER 9

Musical evenings at No. 10

*"Martin Neary regards an electronic organ
as you and I do a made-up bow tie."*

Before moving on to Winchester, I must describe some more events in Westminster.

One of the duties of the Organist of St Margaret's, which for many years was the Parish Church of the House of Commons, is to play for ceremonies in the Chapel of St Mary Undercroft in the crypt of the Houses of Parliament. The chapel comes under the control of the Speaker of the House of Commons, and the majority of the services are conducted by the Speaker's Chaplain, who has generally been Rector of St Margaret's Church. Because of the Chapel's special situation outside the jurisdiction of the Diocese of London, it was possible to hold different denominational services there (mainly weddings and memorial services, including Roman Catholic ones) long before the ecumenical movement had begun to make its mark.

In 1966, soon after the general election, I played for a private Dedication of Government service in the Crypt Chapel, which was initiated by the victorious Prime Minister, Harold Wilson. The two clergymen taking part were both ardent socialists: Donald (later Lord) Soper, and the Bishop of Southwark, Dr Mervyn Stockwood, whose address began: "I am a socialist and *therefore* a Christian". He then went on to encourage the government ministers to ensure that "your light be seen before men, and that you *show forth* your good works".

At that time the chapel had a very moderate harmonium (American organ), although few people complained about the sounds emanating from it or about the inevitably limited repertoire because there were no pedals. I found this instrument increasingly frustrating to play, and eventually created such a fuss that Canon Stancliffe, the Speaker's Chaplain, persuaded the Speaker that something had to be done. Knowing of Edward Heath's background as an organist (he was a former Organ Scholar of Balliol College, Oxford), the

Speaker sought Mr Heath's advice, and the then Leader of the Opposition in turn sought mine.

The situation was complicated because no-one seemed prepared to allow into the Chapel an instrument which would hide any of the Pugin decoration. The simplest solution was to install an electronic organ, but I really could not countenance that – what signal would it send out to the organ world? Nonetheless, off I dutifully went to Harrods musical instruments department to try out several electronic organs, but I was not swayed by the sounds I heard and confess that I tried all the political wiles I could to prevent an electronic instrument being installed. For some time I felt I was getting nowhere until Canon Stancliffe, very much in sympathy with my pipe organ preferences, had the brainwave of telling the Speaker's Secretary, Brigadier Noel Reid, that "Martin Neary regards an electronic organ as you and I do a made-up bow tie". Only at that point did the tide turn. In due course a small pipe organ, to be built by Grant, Degens and Bradbeer, was approved, although I had to accept that the position of the console, far away from the pipes, was not ideal. And I was delighted when, 25 years later, *my* organ was replaced by a much finer instrument designed by William Blake, who had been given a considerably freer hand.

I had first met Mr Heath in January 1966, when he and three other eminent organists (Ralph Downes, Douglas Guest and Lady Susi Jeans) were made honorary fellows at a diploma prize-giving of the Royal College of Organists (grandly housed in those days in Kensington Gore, opposite the Albert Hall). After the presidential address it was (and still is) traditional that one of the younger Fellows plays a selection of the examination pieces, before as critical an audience as could be imagined – the successful examinees and their examiners. Perhaps, because of my association with the House of Commons, on this occasion the 'honour' had fallen to me.

It was to be the last official occasion when the College organ was played before a complete overhaul and rebuild. The organ certainly did need some attention, and it was difficult to find any bright sounds, there being no high-ranking mixture stops. To overcome this, I began my recital by playing Bach's Chorale prelude on *Komm, heiliger Geist* up an octave, with a sixteen-foot stop sounding as the fundamental. This obviously had its risks, but I seemed to be getting away with it until I decided, somewhat unstylishly by today's standards, to increase the pedal sound by pulling out the great to pedal coupler. I must have made a grab for it because, instead of moving out an inch, the stop came away in my left hand! Everyone who saw this was quite amused, and in a funny kind of way the incident removed the tension that I (and perhaps the audience) was feeling.

Despite a crushing defeat for the Conservative party at the recent Hull by-election, Edward Heath was on sparkling form, noting in his speech of thanks how one of the reasons he enjoyed playing the organ was that "it gave you a sense of power, which it was not always easy to find in the world of politics". Later in his book *Music, A Joy for Life*, he was to qualify this remark by writing "but not of power over people; it is the power of contributing sound to the general uplift of those making music together".

My next, albeit indirect, contact with a political leader came in 1967 through my Caius contemporary, the extraordinary TV presenter, David Frost, who had already made his name compering the hugely popular but short-lived satirical BBC TV programme, *That was the week that was*. David, who by then had transferred to ITV, invited the St Margaret's Choir to sing on his late-night show, *The Frost Programme*, and he asked me to produce an arrangement of a carol with words by Mary Wilson, wife of the Prime Minister, which had originally been set to music by Malcolm Arnold.

Not for some time did Edward Heath's political fortunes and 'power over people' improve, but on 9 June 1970 the Conservative party won a surprise victory in the General Election. Barely 48 hours before polling day, when he pounced on some bad trade figures previously denied by the Labour government, did Edward Heath's message finally register; and so "Sailor Ted", as the *Evening Standard* headline proclaimed, "sails in". Not only did Britain now have a prizewinning yachtsman as Prime Minister – he had captained the winning crew on his yacht, *Morning Cloud*, to win the Sydney to Hobart race in 1969 – he was also the first resident of No 10 Downing Street to have been an Oxford University Organ scholar.

Soon after taking office, Ted Heath began to hold musical *soirées* at Chequers, the country home of Prime Ministers, in Buckinghamshire, establishing a unique musical focus for his time in office. On 9 September Penny and I attended the first of these, a Beethoven programme performed by Isaac Stern, Leonard Rose and Eugene Istomin; but to everyone's regret our host had to stay behind at No 10. The concert that evening came at the height of the crisis in the Middle East over a hijacked aircraft, with more than 100 passengers being held hostage in the Jordanian desert. This drama also involved Leila Khaled, who had been taken off an Israeli aircraft in London and was being held by the immigration authorities, "and it became obvious", wrote the PM, "that I could not leave No 10 to go down to Chequers for the concert". Nevertheless, the recital went ahead. Isaac Stern spoke movingly, and later told Ted that as he was playing the *Spring Sonata* he realized that Beethoven's music was even stronger than the anxieties and horror of the political situation.

The next communication I received from 10 Downing Street was a letter from the Prime Minister's Principal Private Secretary, Robert Armstrong, asking if I could bring a small choir to sing Grace before dinner at 10 Downing Street on the two occasions when the PM had invited the House of Bishops. Robert, himself a fine musician (and son of a former Principal of the Royal Academy of Music, Sir Thomas Armstrong), admitted he was not quite sure which grace it was that the PM would like although, as far as he could tell from his rendering, it resembled the opening of *O quanta qualia* and the hymn-tune we associate with *O what their joy*. A little research confirmed that the grace they had in mind was *For these and all thy mercies given* (from the *Laude Spiritual'*, 1545), and that Robert's interpretation of the PM's singing had been absolutely right. I have to say I never heard Ted sing, although there were numerous services when I saw him definitely *not* singing!

With the Prime Minister Edward Heath, who regularly invited Martin and his singers to entertain guests at No 10.

Before the first dinner, I was invited to No 10 to meet the Appointments Secretary, Sir John Hewitt, to discuss the arrangements. In those days, there seemed to be very little security, and I walked into 10 Downing Street without requiring any proof of identification, although I was very impressed that the front door always opened just as I was arriving. We discussed where the choir should be placed, and indeed where (and what) the singers should eat and drink, as by then the Prime Minister had decided that he would like a grace after dinner as well, for which William Byrd's canon on *Non nobis Domine* (Not unto us, O Lord), was chosen. We would perform in a small anteroom at the entrance to the elegant State Dining Room (designed by Sir John Soane), where the 60 guests would be seated around a long horseshoe-shaped table.

I was then asked if the choir would sing some madrigals as well. In view of the ecclesiastical connection, it seemed fitting to start with Thomas Weelkes's *Hark, all ye lovely saints above*. The appropriateness of the text (especially with the Northern Province of York) went down well, as did the Prime Minister's short speech, after the toast to the Queen, that he would not "pontificate" any more than his Episcopal guests would "politicate". Mr Heath was also generous enough in a letter of thanks to say that he did "not think the performance of the Purcell Catch could have been improved upon" and, as Rosamund Essex reported in *The Church Times*: "Purcell's *The London Constable*, with its reference to Jesuits and Tories, brought loud acclaim while the innocent harmonies of Weelkes, Orlando Gibbons and Thomas Morley made a gentle scene even lovelier".

In the general euphoria at the end of the evening, the Prime Minister's Press Secretary, Donald Maitland, arranged for me to record an interview for the BBC Radio 4's *Today* programme. When I arrived at Broadcasting House at midnight, I discovered that my interviewer, Bob Friend, and his producer had been expecting to see and hear some of the singers, but all they got was me. Totally inexperienced to this kind of exposure, I fumbled my way through various questions. Although as far as was known this was the first time that there had been so much musical entertainment at a No 10 dinner, Bob Friend seemed less interested in what we had sung and rather more so about what was on the menu. During the interview I unwittingly disclosed that we had had a delicious soup (*Tortue Claire au Xérès*), which led to protests from the 'Save the Turtles' brigade. I did however manage to avoid discussing the wines; on our first night at No 10 there was a *Chateau Mouton Rothschild* 1943, so I have to say that the musicians were thoroughly spoilt.

Despite my gaffe, we received more invitations, and following the success of the musical menu at the dinners for the Bishops, I tried to select pieces with texts which would be appreciated by the guests, or at least by our host. At a dinner for the Treasury ministers on 9 February 1971, which coincided with the dramatic crash of Rolls Royce, I chose an early seventeenth-century three-part madrigal by Thomas Weelkes. The words of the opening verse seemed to take on a particular relevance:

> 'Late is my rash accounting,
> My fortune is amounting,
> *Fa la la la la.*
> And now all is undone,
> All courses backwards run.
> *Fa la la la la.*

Peterborough's report in the *Daily Telegraph* the following morning ended: "Mr Neary, perhaps wisely, leaves for an American concert tour today". The Prime Minister, however, was clearly amused and, after we had finished, insisted on my staying to hear him announce that I had been appointed Organist and Master of the Music at Winchester Cathedral – a warm human touch, typical of Ted's loyalty and friendship, which were sadly not sufficiently recognised, nor was his sense of humour.

The musical choice was always checked with Robert Armstrong, who himself often made delightful proposals, two of his most interesting (and mischievous) being the madrigals for five voices by Orlando Gibbons: *I see not friendship where I hate* and *I see ambition never pleased*, which we sang in late October at the Eve of Session dinner, when the cabinet and other senior ministers were entertained. These gatherings of Parliamentarians also gave us an excuse to include a charming catch *Mr Speaker* by an English contemporary of Handel, the composer and singer, John Baildon:

> Mister Speaker tho' 'tis late
> I must lengthen the debate.
> Question, hear him, hear.
> Sir I shall name you if you stir.
> Order, hear him, hear.
> Pray support the chair.

However, the Prime Minister missed one of these political dinners altogether, for while his guests were dining well upstairs, he was eating sandwiches with Trade Union officials, as they tried to reach agreement on a wages policy.

The visits of the Federal Chancellor of Austria, the Prime Ministers of Italy and Belgium, the President of the Commission of European Communities and of the French Ambassador gave us perfect excuses for including music from their countries. And although by 1972 our family was living in Winchester, the Prime Minister was keen that I should continue to direct the singers, so from then the choir was called the Martin Neary Singers.

On 29 March 1972 the Prime Minister gave a dinner in honour of Sir William Walton's 70th birthday, when the musical content was on an altogether different plane. Ted Heath had devised a most imaginative programme, abetted as always by Robert Armstrong, who had written a special text for a new grace, *Bless this house:*

> Bless O Lord, this house, we pray;
> Bless the food we eat today;
> God Save the Queen, preserve our host,
> And hearken to our birthday toast:
> May William Walton happy be
> In health and wealth and harmony.
> *Benedictus benedicat, per Jesum Christum Dominum nostrum.* Amen.

Many years earlier, when as a schoolboy he had been taking part in a local music competition, Ted Heath had made an impression on the distinguished adjudicator, Herbert Howells, who encouraged him to continue with his musical studies. The two had kept in touch, and now Howells, the doyen of English church music composers, was invited by his former *protégé* to set Robert Armstrong's text to music. Written for unaccompanied choir, the Grace has all the hallmarks of Howells at his finest – fluent word-setting, rich idiomatic harmonies and bold climaxes within a deeply felt and impassioned solemnity. In due course, Robert adapted the words for more general use, and we sang it at subsequent dinners at No 10.

Some time after the Walton dinner, I received an appreciative letter from Herbert Howells apologising for his delay in writing and adding: "To have written sooner would have been mechanical". Novello, Howell's publishers, wanted to make the Grace generally available, but it was not until the Howells centenary in 1992 that Ted Heath agreed to its publication. It was clearly something very personal to him and to his period in office at No 10, and he felt possessive about it. As far as I know, the Grace has only been sung there once since 1974 when in 1986, and in the presence of the Queen and the Duke of Edinburgh, the Prime Minister John Major hosted a dinner in honour of Sir Edward's 80th birthday. John Major decided, much to Ted's pleasure, to model the evening on how he had entertained his guests more than 20 years earlier. And so once again I was asked to bring some singers to perform 'Ted's graces' and a selection of his favourite madrigals and part-songs after dinner. It was inevitably a nostalgic evening, made even more memorable for me when, after leaving the dining room, Her Majesty found I was the only other person in the drawing room and kindly insisted on getting me a drink.

After the toasts to the Queen and Sir William Walton, there was a veritable musical feast, the first part choral, beginning with Arthur Bliss's *Ode for Sir William Walton on the occasion of his seventieth birthday*. Using amusing words by one of Walton's past collaborators, Paul Dehn, Bliss cleverly inserted numerous choral adaptations from Walton's most famous scores, such as *Henry V* and *Belshazzar's Feast*, as well as some clever pastiches. This delightful Dehn-Bliss frolic and tribute was followed by one of Walton's own most beautiful miniatures, the wedding anthem *Set me as a seal upon thine heart*. The singers then made way for members of the London Sinfonietta, conducted by David Atherton, to perform movements from *Façade* with narrations by Alvar Liddell. The Prime Minister later described the sparkling performance of "this precocious music to words by Edith Sitwell which had first made Walton famous", as bringing back "all the glitter, the fun and at the same time the hardness of the twenties".

So far, the musical items had been performed at the end of the dining room, with the guests remaining seated at the long horseshoe table. But there was more to come. The PM had remembered that Walton, when asked in an interview on his 60th birthday whether there was any piece of music he would have liked to have composed himself, had replied without pausing for a moment: "Yes, Schubert's *B flat Trio*". So now, with a galaxy of Britain's finest actors and musicians, including Benjamin Britten (whose presence, given past *frissons* with Walton, prompted Laurence Olivier to comment: "I see the enemy is here") seated in the drawing room, John Georgiadis, Douglas Cummings and John Lill played the Schubert piano trio in its entirety. Well past midnight no one had left until finally the Queen Mother made a move to go. On her way out she made a point of speaking to all the performers and kindly congratulated me on the 'exquisite singing'. The evening had above all been a musical triumph for the Prime Minister; he had overseen every aspect of the tribute to such an extent that I was told by his office it had been extremely difficult to get him to think of anything else throughout the day.

On 2 July 1973, the Prime Minister gave another 70th birthday dinner, this time honouring Sir Alec Douglas-Home (his Foreign Secretary and also his predecessor as Leader of the Tory party). At the end of a lengthy evening, Sir Alec's distinguished predecessor, Harold Macmillan, was heard on the telephone complaining to his manservant: "Stephenson, I am going to miss the train; it's all because of the madrigals they have here now". That evening our repertoire included Vaughan Williams's arrangement of the old Scottish song, *Loch Lomond*, with the baritone solo beautifully sung by Brian Kay, one of the King's Singers. I concocted a special arrangement of *Happy Birthday* but probably missed a trick by not including the Eton Boating Song. However, ten days later, when Ted entertained King of Hussein of Jordan, we sang a selection of Harrow School Songs.

I remember Denis Healey, at the time Shadow Foreign Secretary (and like Ted a Balliol man), lamented missing some of the Brahms *Liebeslieder Wältzer* because he had had to go back to the House of Commons to vote; on his return he told us: "I may not agree with Ted's politics, but I do like his choice of music". For the Brahms, Dr John West (my successor as Organ Scholar at Caius and colleague at St Margaret's) and I together played the small, rosewood Steinway grand piano which Edward Heath had bought in 1963, after being awarded the Charlemagne Prize in recognition of his unrelenting (but at that time unfulfilled) work of bringing the United Kingdom into Europe. It was a lovely instrument, and one of the press photographs when Ted Heath became Prime Minister showed the Steinway being moved into No 10 (there were more when he moved out). Ted had chosen very carefully after taking advice from his concert pianist friend, Moura Lympany, and whenever possible he would spend a few minutes after lunch playing a Bach prelude and fugue. But he probably found his best and most private relaxation by going up to his flat at the top of No 10 and playing his clavichord.

Quite often I might have a few words with the Prime Minister as he escorted his guests of honour past the singers into the dining room. On 6 December 1973, however, there was a surprise summons to see him at ten-past-eight. I had just flown back from America, and thought he might want to know how

I had got on; however, his first words were: "What are you singing tonight?" The dinner in question had been arranged (at very short notice) during the Sunningdale talks about the future relationship between Northern Ireland and the Republic of Ireland. For security reasons none of the Irish guests knew where they were having dinner. As Ted Heath wrote later (in *Music – A Joy for Life*): "to their surprise they soon found themselves at No 10. There had been no gathering like it in Downing Street before. For me it was an emotional moment. I was able to bring together round the same dinner table the representatives of those who had spent so many centuries quarrelling with each other. Now at last a settlement seemed to be within our grasp".

There had not been time to print the details of our programme on the menu, and we had booked the singers (who were sworn to secrecy) at the last minute. Originally, I had had a message from Sally Villiers in the political office saying: "Not too much Irish, and nothing controversial". However, when I showed the PM our somewhat bland programme, beginning with two Elizabethan madrigals, and explained that I had been advised to play safe, he looked disappointed and asked if we had anything more amusing. Had we got two of our favourite encores – *The Mermaid* or *The Londonderry Air?* Alas, no – all the copies were back at our house in Winchester. "That's a pity", he said; "Can't you get hold of some Irish songs? That's what they would like". Rather with my tail between my legs, I trooped off to conduct the first grace.

Given that it was nearly 8pm, all the shops and libraries were closed, and I wondered how on earth we could get hold of the kind of music Ted wanted and be ready to perform it within two and a half hours. I rushed back to St Margaret's to 'borrow' some copies of the *Songs of Praise Hymnal*, which had the tune for *The Londonderry Air*, albeit to different words. Then I spoke to an old friend of my father's, John McCarthy, the doyen of chorus masters and arrangers of light music. He immediately agreed to help saying he would look out what he had got but knew that his copies of *The Mermaid* were locked up at the BBC. So, I arranged for a No 10 chauffeur to drive to John's house in Notting Hill Gate and pick up whatever he had been able to lay his hands on. By 8.45pm six songs had been chauffeured back to Downing Street including *If you're Irish, come into the parlour*, but they mostly needed piano accompaniment. As that evening the PM's piano was in its customary place at the end of the drawing room, and too far away for us to use, I quickly made unaccompanied arrangements of two of the songs and, thanks to the Garden

Girls' photocopiers, the singers were able to rehearse a revised programme. At 9.40pm I had a message passed to the PM, explaining that we had got hold of some lighter music and asking if he would approve the revised programme:

If you're Irish, come into the parlour
The star of the County Down
Brigg Fair (from our original programme)
When Irish eyes are smiling
The Londonderry Air

to which he immediately and succinctly responded: "Agreed EH". (I still have the note.)

By this stage we had sung the second grace and could tell that the mood was very different from usual. There was no sense of formality – several guests were getting up from their seats, signing each other's menus and generally being pretty boisterous. Everyone quietened down, however, for our first song *If you're Irish*, and at the end they applauded vigorously, someone shouting "encore", another looking at the Prime Minister and saying "Now, Ted, it's your turn". When we sang *When Irish eyes are smiling*, many of the guests could not resist joining in and by the time we reached *The Londonderry Air* there was more than one tear. It was one of the most moving and yet relaxed evenings we had ever experienced, all the more exceptional given the political background. As the PM later wrote: "Once the singers started, there was no holding back the Irish ... and by the end of the evening they had taken over completely. The lilt of *When Irish eyes are smiling* went round the room. They went back to Sunningdale feeling better towards each other – and even perhaps towards the British."

We also had some fun when visitors from the Commonwealth were guests at No 10, with the Australian Prime Minister, William McMahon, and his wife (whose appearance had been eagerly anticipated by the press in view of the rather revealing dress she had worn the week before at the White House, but who was that evening a model of decorum) being given a rendering of *Waltzing Matilda*.

The atmosphere was distinctly different, however, when Dr Marcello Caetano, the Portuguese President came to London in 1973 to mark the 600th anniversary of the first Anglo-Portuguese Treaty of Alliance, incidentally, the oldest alliance in the world. Edward Heath decided to give a dinner for Dr Caetano in the Painted Hall at Greenwich, and in honour of the occasion he commissioned the Master of the Queen's Music, Sir Arthur Bliss, to compose a piece to be sung by the Martin Neary Singers. Great care was taken over the choice of a text; one of the Prime Minister's private secretaries, Tom Bridges, grandson of the former Poet Laureate, Robert Bridges, suggested an English translation of a Portuguese poem, *Mar Portugués*, whose subject naturally appealed to the PM. However, things then began to get complicated. Sir John Betjeman, the Poet Laureate, was invited to write the English words, but before Betjeman produced his version, Bliss was sent a translation by Alan Goodison of the Foreign Office, so that he could get an idea of what would be involved.

In the event, Sir Arthur preferred the 'Foreign Office version', "for the purpose of a musical setting", as he tactfully expressed it. Accordingly, both Betjeman's and Goodison's translations, as well as the Portuguese original, were printed on the splendid menu, together with the rest of the music performed before dinner by the Orchestra of the Royal Marines School of Music, and at the Ceremony of Beating the Retreat by the Naval Home Command Band of the Royal Marines. Here is part of the Prime Minister's own description: "In a setting of unsurpassed splendour, it all made for a magical evening. Under the splendid ceiling paintings of Sir James Thornhill, the augmented body of singers sang in two antiphonal groups, on each side of the staircase leading into the hall." In deference to the guest of honour, we began with a *Magnificat* for double choir by the seventeenth-century Portuguese composer, Dom Pedro da Esperanca, then moved on to three English madrigals before giving the premiere of *Mar Portugués*. Sir Arthur had clearly taken account of the hall's reverberant acoustics, and he conjured up some thrilling sounds. However, as his letter to me three days later disclosed, despite his name being on the official table plan, Sir Arthur was not present.

"Dear Martin,
I was sorry I was not able to hear you and your singers in The Painted Hall last Monday evening – (I hope you and your singers did not find it too difficult to get there!).
I have a letter from the PM in which he writes "It sounded splendid and made a fitting conclusion to the musical part of the proceedings at dinner". So <u>many</u> thanks to you and your singers,
Gratefully,
Arthur Bliss

The somewhat cryptic parenthesis at the end of Sir Arthur's first sentence needs some explanation. He had decided, *after* accepting the commission, along with several others to voice his protest against the Caetano regime by declining to attend the dinner. What I had not been prepared for, however, was to have eggs and tomatoes thrown at the car windows as I attempted to drive into the Royal Naval College. This was no doubt the reason for Bliss's concern about our journey and, needless to say, press and TV reporters were there to capture the goings-on.

Inevitably, there were one or two jibes in the gossip columns about Ted Heath's 'grand' style of entertaining; *Back Page* in the *Observer* reported that awestruck visitors are commenting that his style is getting "positively courtly. At a recent dinner for top civil servants, Ministers, their wives and Mr Thatcher, grace was actually *sung* – by the St Margaret's Westminster singers, a sort of middle-aged Group."There was champagne when you arrived and more with the pudding. Over the coffee and brandy the singers offered half a dozen madrigals, including a number called *I gave her cakes* (a catch by Purcell). It was difficult to decide from his face whether John Davies, the Secretary for Trade and Industry, was appalled or just incredulous."

Looking back, it seems amazing just how much music Ted found time for during his premiership. He was bold in not only continuing to direct his annual Broadstairs Carol Concerts but also to conduct the London Symphony Orchestra at the Royal Festival Hall in a performance of Elgar's notoriously tricky overture, *Cockaigne*. And, despite having no time to practise, he allowed himself to be filmed for a television documentary, playing the Harrison organ in the chapel of Balliol that he had known so well 40 years earlier.

After his abrupt exit from No 10, Ted found solace in going to concerts and listening to his vast collection of CDs. For many years he enjoyed attending the Salzburg Festivals and meeting up with the legendary German conductor, Herbert von Karajan. But as became patently obvious, the abrupt end to his premiership caused Ted distress for the rest of his life, and no amount of music could restore this 'Joy for Life', which, in happier times, had been in the title of one of his books.

In the late 1970s and early '80s Penny and I persuaded Ted to come to several concerts in Winchester Cathedral. But, true to form, on most of these occasions he was wary of meeting the opposite sex. I remember my wife telling Ted, before entering the Cathedral, that she had seated him next to the bishop's wife. This did not go down well, and Ted decided to swap seats with his detective so that *he* could talk to the bishop's wife. However, the charming lady in question, Peggy Taylor, leant across to speak to him, and after the interval Ted chose to sit next to her.

Past political differences did not prevent Ted from enjoying friendships with some of his former political foes. I gather that there was a warm exchange of letters between Ted and Harold Wilson, on the death of Harold's father, while towards the end of his life Ted invited Harold's widow, Mary, on a number of social occasions, such as his 85th birthday dinner, when he placed her next to him.

The drawing room at Ted's final home in Salisbury Cathedral Close, with its spectacular views of the Cathedral, was dominated by the Steinway, but towards the end of his life the piano was rarely played, and the signed photographs of Monarchs and Presidents remained in position on the lid. And although Ted often found it difficult to express warmth and gratitude to visitors who took the trouble to visit him, I for one know just what a loyal supporter and friend he could be, as when he expressed his outrage at what happened at Westminster Abbey in 1998 *(see Chapter 20).*

CHAPTER 10

Moving to Winchester, 1972–78

"Painful and dangerous is the position of the young musician who, after acquiring great knowledge of his art in the Metropolis, joins a country cathedral".

In 1969 the Rector of St Margaret's, Michael Stancliffe, was appointed Dean of Winchester, where, within two years, the Dean and Chapter were faced with finding a new Organist. Back in 1968, Douglas Guest (a previous Organist at Salisbury Cathedral, and then Organist and Master of the Choristers at Westminster Abbey) had encouraged me to apply for the vacancy at Salisbury, and I duly did an interview and audition; but quite rightly Richard Seal was chosen. However, in February 1971, after a similar application process, I was delighted to be appointed Organist and Master of the Music at Winchester Cathedral.

Four months before taking up the post, I received a letter from the author, Christopher Booker, who at the time was chiefly known for having co-founded the satirical magazine *Private Eye* and for the equally controversial television programme, *That was the week that was*. He had recently become a regular member of the St Margaret's congregation, having been drawn there by the quality of the preaching. We had become good friends, sharing a love of cricket and music. These mutual interests came into their own on a wet day at the 1976 Oval Test Match when, despite the lack of cricket, we spent an absorbing time with some like-minded fanatics trying to match historic cricket scores with the Mozart work with the equivalent Koechel number. Christopher's encyclopaedic knowledge was exceptional and perhaps I should not have been surprised when, in a note of *'Bon voyage'* for our move to Winchester, he included a typically pertinent passage:

"With tongue in cheek, ... this passage from [your illustrious predecessor] Samuel Sebastian Wesley's *A Few Words on Cathedral Music, and the Musical System of the Church, with a Plan of Reform (1849)*:

"Painful and dangerous is the position of the young musician who, after acquiring great knowledge of his art in the Metropolis, joins a country cathedral. At first, he can scarcely believe that the mass of error and inferiority in which he has to participate is habitual and irremediable. He thinks he will reform matters gently, and without giving offence; but he soon discovers that it is his approbation and not his advice that is needed. The choir is 'the best in the England' (such being the belief in most cathedrals) and if he gives trouble in his attempts at improvement, he would, by some Chapters, be at once voted a person with whom 'they cannot go smoothly' and a 'bore' ….

"The Cathedral Organist should in every sense be a professor of the highest ability – a master in the most elevated departments of composition – and efficient in the conducting and superintendence of a choral body!"

My training and preparation for taking charge of the music at a cathedral had not been entirely conventional. Although I had greatly benefitted from making music with top class musicians in London, I had not served as an Assistant Organist in a cathedral, nor played for daily Evensongs. I had however done some deputising for Douglas Guest at Westminster Abbey, directing the Lay Vicars and playing the organ at the Epiphany services in January 1971. To be in charge of a choir of such quality as I inherited at Winchester was an enormous privilege, and it was now up to me to further develop its undoubted potential. What was I taking on? Little did I realise just what opportunities and challenges lay ahead.

Before I moved to Winchester, David Willcocks and George Guest kindly allowed me to sit in on the early morning practices with their choristers at King's and St John's Colleges Cambridge, when I saw at first-hand how brilliantly they both held the attention of their choristers. David later told me of his own experience as a Westminster Abbey chorister, when Sir Edward Elgar came to conduct. His neighbour said to him: "Do you know he is always looking at me" to which David replied: "He's always looking at me too"!

I knew I had to find a way of gaining the confidence of the choristers and of enabling them to enjoy the demanding routine, which, each week, involved nearly 20 hours of practices and services. Before arriving, I learnt their names (from a photograph) and then at the morning rehearsals I followed the practice of David Willcocks in having a different pair on either side of me each day. This enabled me quickly to discover the boys' individual strengths (and occasional weaknesses). One issue to be resolved was how soon to 'blood' a young chorister with a solo. I decided to take the plunge and give a nine-year-old a small solo at a weekday Evensong (with not many more in the congregation than the proverbial 'two or three gathered together'). I took the line that if he broke down, it was my fault; I had chosen the music and selected the soloist. And, virtually without exception, the boys responded enthusiastically and successfully. In this way, the young singers became used to singing solos as if they were part of the daily routine, and before nerves became an issue. I had already seen the value of a voice-trainer at St Margaret's, Westminster, and it was not long before Ken Tewkesbury, one of the Winchester tenors, who had previously sung in the Covent Garden Opera Chorus, was not only helping with warm-ups but also coaching boys individually with their solos.

I was installed on 15 January during my first Evensong with the Full Choir, when the psalm appointed was No 78 (with 73 verses), and I spent hours trying to learn the five chants. The Choristers and Lay Clerks knew them and, never having accompanied that psalm before, I was mightily relieved to get through without taking a wrong turning. I soon learnt to love the psalms, and very much agreed with the Winchester Lay Clerk, Keith Ross (a former King's College Chorister and Choral Scholar): "if you get the psalms right, Martin, everything else falls into place".

In February 1972 came my first voice-trials (held jointly with Winchester

Evensong in Winchester Cathedral, 1980
(Photo: © Mike Evans).

College, whose Choristers, known as Quiristers, attended the Pilgrims' School). These yielded an outstanding crop of candidates, one of whom had auditioned to be a Quirister rather than a cathedral chorister. The boy in question had laryngitis and, in the octave above middle C, could hardly sing a note. Understandably Raymond Humphrey, director of the Chapel Choir, decided with his colleagues at the College not to take him. However, I was fascinated by his unusually rich lower range, and to general surprise asked if the Cathedral might poach him. Having obtained permission from the College to approach his parents, I discovered that the boy's father, who had been a Wykehamist, was the distinguished music critic and Berlioz authority, David Cairns. He and his wife agreed to accept the offer for their son, Dan, to become a Cathedral Chorister. Aged over 9½, he was already quite old to begin as a chorister, and rather than waiting until the autumn term, we arranged for him to start at the Pilgrims' School in April.

Playing cricket in Pilgrims' School yard in Winchester *(Photo John Crook)*.

Little did I realise at the time, however, just what benefits appointing Dan would bring to the choir, and indeed to Penny and me. Not only did David and Rosemary become some of our most special friends, but David's musical advice on countless occasions over the past 50 years has been beyond measure, and it was thanks to his links with the record industry that the Cathedral Choir made several recordings. And Dan did indeed turn up trumps, although I never heard him sing a note above a top F.

Our 16 years at Winchester coincided with a remarkable team of clergy and musicians: Bishop John Taylor, the Dean (Michael Stancliffe); the Canon Treasurer and Vice-Dean (Alex Wedderspoon); and three Precentors, Tom Gaunt, Anthony Caesar and Roger Job. As well, there were three brilliant Sub-Organists, Clement McWilliam, James Lancelot and Tim Byram-Wigfield, and some quite exceptional singers, outstanding of whom were the baritone, Donald Sweeney, the tenor, William Kendall and the alto, Keith Ross.

However, my arrival came at a time when the Canon Treasurer, Fred Bussby, was understandably concerned about the rising cost of the Cathedral Choir, and I was faced with the prospect of the Dean and Chapter, instead of paying half the Pilgrims' School fees for each boy, being forced to peg their contributions to £300 per annum. This could well have had serious consequences on recruitment, as Winchester College was making no such reduction in respect of the Quiristers, who also boarded at Pilgrims' and whose duties, particularly out of term, at Easter and at Christmas, were so much fewer than those of the Cathedral Choristers. So, I came up with the idea of reducing the number of Choristers from 24 to 20, and in return keeping the 50% ratio; to my relief this was agreed.

My other innovation was to establish a practice before every Evensong for the men and for the boys. I had been amazed to discover that the cathedral choir only had two full rehearsals per week for one hour after Evensong on Mondays and Fridays. After negotiations with the Pilgrims' School headmaster and the Lay Clerks, I was able to persuade the Dean and Chapter to push the time of Evensong on Saturdays and weekdays back to 5.30pm, instead of 5.15pm, with a full rehearsal at 5pm. In return, as it were, for this extra commitment, the choristers were excused singing at Monday Evensongs which was sung by the Lay Clerks, who then had an invaluable practice without the choristers after the service. This made a huge difference, not least in extending the repertoire, and providing time to do justice to the contemporary music that was to come our way.

Mercifully, within a couple of years, the cathedral finances improved considerably, thanks mainly to the newly appointed Canon Treasurer, Alex Wedderspoon's innovation, namely instituting the voluntary Red Gown Stewards, whose warm welcome to the increasing number of visitors resulted in substantial donations. (Soon many other cathedrals followed suit, although 50 years later, most now have admission charges.)

My first months at Winchester were especially challenging, as in July that year we were due to host the Southern Cathedrals Festival (SCF) (for which the programme had to be planned before we arrived). The festival was started on a small scale in the 1920s but was cancelled after a dispute over who should pay for tea! It was re-started in 1960 by the Organists of Winchester (Alwyn Surplice), Chichester (John Birch) and Salisbury (Christopher Dearnley), and their choirs were the main participants (unlike the much older Three Choirs Festival, which was longer and included the large, amateur Festival Chorus). In the 1972 SCF programme, the headmaster of the choir school, Martin Briggs, wrote: "What is a chorister? He is not an angelic, other-worldly being whose first recorded cries in infancy were perfect top Cs, and who seems to have escaped original sin". I had indeed inherited some boys with exceptionally high ranges, not least 9-year-old David Hurley (later to have an illustrious career as a member of the King's Singers), prompting me to put down the Allegri *Miserere* for Ash Wednesday.

The Organist of the home cathedral is chiefly responsible for the festival repertoire, and in some ways my coming fresh to it may have been an advantage, as I assumed all things were possible. My fellow organists, John Birch and Richard Seal, were somewhat shocked at some of my proposals, such as Bach's great motet, *Komm, Jesu, komm*. It transpired that none of the three choirs had ever performed a Bach motet before, and John Birch had serious doubts (to put it mildly) as to whether Chichester would be able to manage it. Despite this however, I went ahead and to their credit all three choirs coped splendidly, as the BBC's recording was later to confirm. As the Bishop of Winchester wrote in his welcome message, "on the eve of our entrance into the European community, it is appropriate that our Festival should have a European 'flavour' and include works from France, Germany and Italy in addition to works representing our rich English Cathedral repertoire".

I wanted to take full advantage of the larger forces, and so the Friday concert, *Five centuries of Cathedral music*, opened with Andrea Gabrieli's *Magnificat for three choirs*, with the choirs placed in separate groups in the nave. We also marked the centenary of the birth of Ralph Vaughan Williams with his setting of Mr Valiant's great speech in Bunyan's *Pilgrim's Progress*, *Valiant for Truth*, and at the Festival Eucharist with his *Mass in G minor* for double choir and soloists.

The SCF had premiered a number of commissions, the most famous being Leonard Bernstein's *Chichester Psalms*. This was at the initiative of the Dean of Chichester, Walter Hussey, who expressed the hope that the new setting should have a taste of *West Side Story* rather than an Anglican anthem; and Bernstein duly obliged. The work has an unashamed lyricism, particularly in the setting of Psalm 23 (*Adonai roi*) for a deep solo soprano, and the haunting melody in 10/4, for Psalm 13. This involved the choirs singing in twentieth-century Hebrew, for which they were given some phonetic guidance, but one sequence in Psalm 2, "shev ba-sha-ma-im", to the choristers' amusement, sounded uncommonly like "Shove your bottom in".

Commissions, one has to admit, are not always successful, and Malcolm Williamson's *Te Deum* for Chichester in 1971 was a case in point. On the other hand, Welsh composer William Mathias' *An admonition to rulers* for the Winchester Festival in 1969 had gone down well but had hardly been performed since the premiere. So, prompted by Clement McWilliam, who had played the important organ part at the first performance, we repeated this setting in 1972.

Here is the composer's introduction: "When invited to write a new work for the Southern Cathedrals Festival, I already knew of the festival's interest in extending the church choral tradition in adventurous ways, and thought it therefore a good opportunity to attempt a setting somewhat different from the traditional type, anthem or motet". That was music to my ears! But who should be invited to write a new work for the 1972 Winchester Festival?

In 1971 my parents had met the young up-and-coming composer, John Tavener, after he had improvised on the organ (apparently very loudly) at a wedding. In the course of conversation, Maman asked John if he would like to meet me, and John duly came to supper. I had little idea of what to expect from a composer who had made a huge hit with *The Whale*, and tentatively asked if he would compose a *Missa brevis*. Quite some days later, John telephoned to ask if we would accept instead *A Little Requiem for Father Malachy Lynch*, an Orthodox priest and a close friend.

As soon as I saw the score, I was intrigued by the way John had constructed this short work. It has a deceptively simple seven-note theme, which is repeated in inversion, i.e. upside down, and then in reverse. The resulting harmonies are beautiful, as was the opening seven-note instrumental chord on which the whole piece was based. To begin with, the choirs found the idiom difficult to comprehend, and it was a challenge to cope with the irregular rhythms of the fast *Dies irae* section, but by the time we reached the performance, we had all gained in confidence, and the work was warmly received with a favourable review in the *Daily Telegraph*.

As well as directing the Cathedral Choir, I was also very fortunate to become the conductor of the Waynflete Singers, which had been founded in 1970, principally to perform sacred masterpieces outside the Cathedral Choir's normal range. In effect, they were the cathedral's choral society, supported

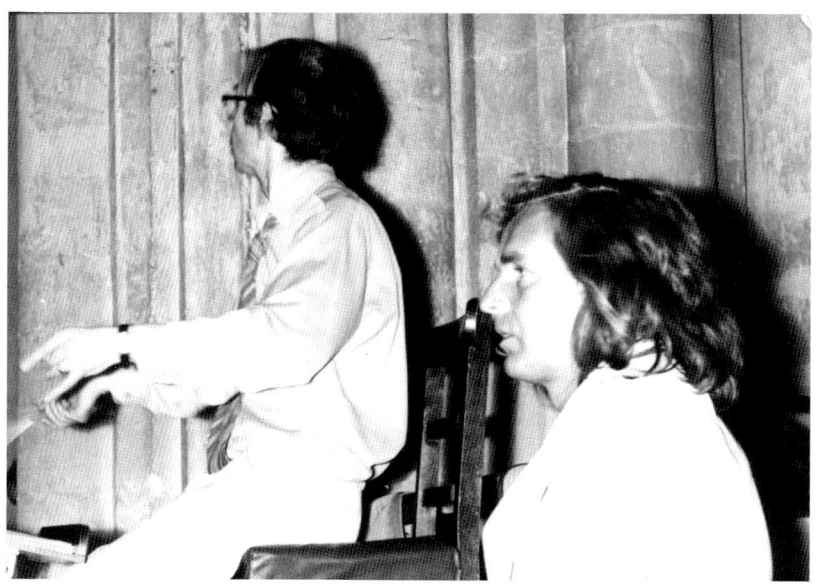
Rehearsing with John Tavener, 1975.

by the Dean and Chapter and conducted by the Organist and Master of the Music. To begin with, the 'Wayns' who numbered around 40 singers, were essentially a chamber choir. My predecessor had attracted some good and keen singers, and I much enjoyed the Monday evening rehearsals. Our first season (1972–73) was devoted to Bach, parts 1–3 of the *Christmas Oratorio* and the *St John Passion* – all in English, accompanied by the excellent local chamber orchestra, the Bournemouth Sinfonietta, sadly long since defunct. I felt strongly that the Cathedral Choristers should also have a chance to sing in at least some of the choruses, which they duly did. The performance of the *Christmas Oratorio* took place one day after the birth of our second daughter, Alice Teresa, and I spent most of the day at the hospital, while supposedly being on hand to help Penny through her labour, glued to my copy of the score. Alice grew up to be a fine cellist.

After the Bach concerts, the next Waynflete programme was very different. Encouraged by the full houses at virtually all the Southern Cathedral Festival concerts in July 1972, Angus Watson (Director of Music at Winchester College) conceived the idea of our holding a series of 'Winchester Summer Concerts' in May and June 1973. I was very much in favour, not least because it provided an opportunity to perform another work by John Tavener, *Celtic Requiem*, in which, as with many of his scores, there is a real sense of music theatre, the visual drama being an integral part of the composer's conception. Scored for clarinet, trumpet, trombone, Aeolian bagpipes, piano, organ, percussion (7 players), timpani, electric guitar and strings, with high soprano, children's choir and chorus, the musical idiom was unusual to say the least, with virtually everything relating to a vast chord of E flat major. Despite its title, the work is not actually a requiem for anyone in particular. Instead, it takes the rough format of a singing game for children. A character, Jenny Jones, is selected by the children, who, at one point, dance around her to ward off evil spirits. But how was this going to work in the cathedral?

In the Spring of 1973 John paid a visit to Winchester with Vicky Maragopoulos, his Greek friend, when we tried to devise a scheme whereby the children's games, an essential component of the work's religious drama, could be seen by the audience. Goodness knows what visitors to the cathedral that day must have thought when Vicky lay on her back in the nave chancel, nor indeed, when we brought in a full-size swing (from the nursery school in the Close). At the performance, the children's games, acted by the splendid choirs of the Pilgrims' and St Swithun's Schools, made a great impact, and I still remember the extraordinarily moving effect as they processed slowly down the central aisle of the longest cathedral in England to the West End, singing "Jenny Jones is dead, is dead", with the evening sunlight streaming in through the Great West Window.

Anthony Payne, in the *Daily Telegraph*, under the headline, "Compelling style of the Requiem", wrote: "It is a healthy and encouraging sign when new British works travel beyond the confines of London and make their way into the provinces.

Certainly, John Tavener's *Celtic Requiem*, which was performed in Winchester Cathedral last night and which has already received a number of fine interpretations in London, achieved on this occasion a poetic atmosphere, a directness and simplicity of utterance which none of the other performances I have heard quite equalled … The most problematic aspect of the work's structure, its reliance on a complex series of sound collages which superimpose contrasted texts and musical textures, was very lucidly exposed under the direction of Martin Neary and the composer. Indeed, in spite of the cathedral's resonance, this was perhaps the clearest as well as one of the most compelling of the Requiem's stagings, and only the stratospherically high soprano line, easily encompassed by June Barton, was sometimes lost in the big *tuttis*."

I was grateful that we were able to have a preliminary rehearsal with the Bournemouth Sinfonietta, which, I later discovered, had been attended by none other than 19-year-old Simon Rattle, who had just been awarded a conducting scholarship by the Bournemouth Symphony Orchestra.

The following season, encouraged and indeed cajoled by David Cairns, we took up the challenge of performing Berlioz's *L'Enfance du Christ*. This was the first time I had conducted a full symphony orchestra (the Bournemouth Symphony Orchestra), and it is amazing to recall that we managed to get through on just one rehearsal with the orchestra.

As already mentioned, I inherited from Alwyn a very talented group of choristers, including the exceptional Tim Wilson, who was fully capable, I thought, of singing the soprano solos in *Messiah*. Tim's performance in May 1974 was remarkable. The only concession we made, because of the length of the phrases, was to have several boys sing the solo in 'Rejoice greatly'.

As happens in most cathedrals, the Organist at Winchester was provided with a house in the Cathedral Close. To begin with we lived in the house of my predecessor; then in 1974 we moved into a remarkable house previously

Nicola (violin) and Alice (recorder) and MN on the practice organ
in the undercroft at their house in Winchester, 1977.

occupied by the cathedral architect, 10 The Close, which, as well as having some beautiful Jacobean glass in the drawing room on the first floor, had an extraordinary Norman Undercroft, with large pillars. This room was big enough to house a mechanical action practice organ of two manuals and pedals, which was specially built by Grant, Degens and Bradbeer. I greatly valued being able to practise the organ in the privacy of our home, and the action made it easier for me to adapt to the different touch of the mechanical action instruments on which I was increasingly being invited to play in England and on the Continent. However, there were some unexpected problems concerning our cat who was scared of dogs, and on one occasion, when a dog came into the house, Magnificat (yes, that was her name) jumped swiftly up into the organ case, knocking over several pipes.

Soon after our move to No 10, our son, Thomas Sebastian, was born. He had to have his blood changed at birth, and we will never know how this may have affected him. But it was not long before Penny suspected that something was wrong because he was very slow to achieve his 'milestones' such as walking and talking. One of the hardest moments in our lives was when we were told by a paediatrician in 1977 that Tom was disabled and would almost certainly be unable to lead a normal life. Everyone connected with the cathedral was incredibly sympathetic and understanding, just one

It soon became clear that Thomas was very musical and it was an added sadness that he would never become a chorister.

example being the Bishop and his wife arriving on our doorstep on a Sunday evening with camomile tea and honey, and the Bishop asking us to think of an opal, which is only so beautifully coloured because it has a flaw in it. By then, it was clear that Tom was very musical – he sang and was fascinated by the notes on the piano – and it was devastating to realise that he would not be able to be a chorister as we would have hoped.

One of the Winchester Summer Concerts the previous year had been given by the Bach Choir, conducted by Sir David Willcocks, which included a fascinating work by Sir Arthur Bliss, *The world is charged with the grandeur of God*, for choir, two flutes and brass. I thought this would be a splendid challenge for the 'Wayns' for the 1974 Christmas concert, along with a rarely performed setting of the Lord's Prayer, *Otcenas* by Leos Janáček.

Moving on to 1975, the most significant event was the arrival of John Taylor, as Bishop of Winchester. For his Enthronement Service Bishop John had asked if I would set some words from T S Eliot's *Little Gidding*. Feeling, however, that we should have a real composer, I persuaded the Dean and Chapter to commission a setting from the composer Jonathan Harvey, a lecturer at Southampton University in the Winchester Diocese. Jonathan (whom I had known when we overlapped at Cambridge) had already acquired a reputation with his distinctly *avant-garde* style, and I have to admit that it was a gamble. I had played one of his organ pieces, *Laus Deo*, on an organ recital tour of America in 1973. It lasts barely four minutes but took me more than thirty hours to learn.

Before starting on the project, Jonathan came to several services and was clearly fascinated by the challenge of the cathedral's resonant acoustics (4½ seconds). His composition, *The Dove descending*, in which he used a sequence of tritones to match the 'pyre on pyre' of Eliot's words, really did test us. But the Dean approved, while admitting that it "may not have been appreciated by the Duke of Wellington."

(See Appendix 1 for an interview I did with Jonathan Harvey for the magazine 'Cathedral Music' in 2009)

By now my mind was working on the music for the Southern Cathedrals Festival, which was returning to Winchester in 1975. Up to 1974 the SCF concerts and services had been sung exclusively by the three Cathedral Choirs. But I felt that, when the cathedral choirs were rehearsing or resting, there were several gaps in the schedule that would present ideal opportunities for some extra events. So, in 1972, we inaugurated the Saturday morning Recitals, which in Winchester were generally given by Winchester College musicians. I also wanted to find a way of including a major work, which would have the benefit of giving the many SCF volunteers a chance to perform.

For understandable reasons, my colleagues at Chichester and Salisbury were not in favour of disturbing the basic pattern of events from Thursday Evensong until Sunday. So, in 1975, I came up with the idea of an 'Eve of Festival Concert' on the preceding Wednesday, at the first of which the works were Schutz's *Veni Creator Spiritus*, for four choirs, and John Tavener's *Ultimos ritos*, also for four choirs and sundry other instrumentalists and speakers.

Over the years Tavener's choice of texts had become increasingly eclectic, but they all shared a deep devotional quality. Many settings composed in the 1970s concerned the subject of death, and 'dying unto oneself', nowhere more profoundly expressed than in *Ultimos Ritos*. In this remarkable work, written in honour of the Spanish Mystic, St John of the Cross, with whom the composer felt a great affinity throughout his life, he deliberately let his own music in the final bars be drowned out by the last four chords of the *Crucifixus* from Bach's *Mass in B minor*. During this last movement *(Coplas)*, the four chords, which have been woven into the texture simultaneously, gradually dissolve into one – an early flowering of Tavener's genius in writing slow-moving but utterly gripping homophonic music.

In 1974 I had attended the world premiere of *Ultimos Ritos* at the Bavokerk in Haarlem, and felt the work could be tailor-made for Winchester Cathedral. This, however, would not only be a challenge musically, but logistically – staging the work as the composer intended with the four choirs in separate groups in the middle of the nave, four sets of tympani (16 in all) at each end, and somehow finding room for the audience. In the event the combination of four *obligato* horn players, seven piccolo trumpeters high up by the choir screen, four percussionists, the strings of the Southampton Youth Orchestra, the Cathedral Choir, the Waynflete Singers and sundry others worked surprisingly well, as the many reviews noted. Peter Heyworth, for example in the Observer, wrote:

> "After a damp and sombre day, a brilliant sun shined through the West window of Winchester Cathedral and flooded that vast nave with light. It would be hard to conceive of a finer setting for the first English hearing of John Tavener's *Ultimos Ritos*, which was composed with a great church in mind; or for that matter to better the impressively confident and well-

prepared performance of this testing score that the augmented Cathedral Choir and the Southampton Youth Orchestra gave on Wednesday under Martin Leary (sic!) at the opening of this year's Southern Cathedrals Festival."

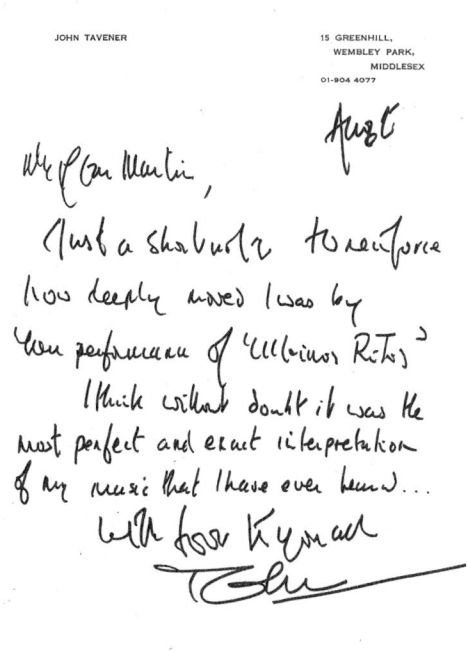

Letter to MN from John Tavener after the performance of Ultimos Ritos in Winchester Cathedral in 1975.

John Tavener wrote me a complimentary letter after the performance: "My Dear Martin, Just a short note to reinforce how deeply moved I was by your performance of *Ultimos Ritos*. I think without doubt it was the most perfect and exact interpretation of my music that I have ever heard."

The rest of the Festival provided a marvellous swansong for Dan Cairns, whose final week in the choir saw him sing the treble solo in Britten's *Te Deum in C*, play the part of the Captain in Britten's *Golden Vanity* – producing the kind of sound the composer had in mind – and give an unforgettable performance of the solos in Bernstein's *Chichester Psalms*.

At the Waynflete Singers 1975 Christmas Concert, we performed the Monteverdi *Vespers*. This was very much thanks to the Dean's two sons, David and Martin Stancliffe, who had become great advocates of 'early' music and persuaded some splendid cornett and sackbut players to take part.

Here is how I previewed our performance in the Winchester Cathedral monthly pamphlet:

"No-one would now dispute that the work known as 'the *Monteverdi Vespers*' is the finest and most substantial piece of church music composed prior to the Passions of Bach and the Oratorios of Handel.

Rather like *Messiah*, however, the Vespers have been the recipient of widely contrasting interpretations. David Stancliffe, whose edition we are privileged to be using, has to my mind succeeded scholastically, dramatically and above all liturgically in his arrangement of the work. He has been particularly sensitive in his scoring of the instrumental parts, revelling in both simplicity and colour; and we hope that, with the help of the London Cornett and Sackbut Ensemble, the sounds which dazzled the Italians in the seventeenth century will come alive again in Winchester in 1975."

I concluded by saying that the Cathedral heating would be on!

One of the unexpected pleasures of moving to Winchester was getting to know more of the music of Samuel Sebastian Wesley, who was Organist of both Winchester Cathedral and Winchester College between 1849 and 1865. He was clearly quite a character, and seems to have fallen out with successive Deans and Chapters at Hereford, Exeter, Winchester and Gloucester Cathedrals as well as with the clergy at Leeds Parish Church. Nevertheless, he was at the heart of the revival of church music in the mid-nineteenth century, and 100 years later the Winchester choristers used to love singing his longer anthems, even if they made them late for tea.

Thanks to the initiative of the BBC producer, Hugh Keyte, the BBC broadcast a concert entirely devoted to Wesley from Winchester Cathedral in May 1976, on the 100th anniversary of his death. For this Centenary Concert we were joined by the Choir of New College, Oxford, the Waynflete Singers and by the Academy of the BBC (the BBC's training orchestra, based in Bristol) with Brian Rayner Cook as baritone soloist and James Lancelot (who had succeeded Clement McWilliam) at the organ. Sir David Lumsden and I shared the conducting.

With these forces and thanks to Hugh's researches, we were able to perform Wesley's orchestral arrangements of two of his greatest anthems, *Ascribe unto the Lord*, and *The Wilderness*. Probably the most unexpected work was the *Symphony*, composed by Wesley in his early twenties. As Hugh wrote in the programme notes, "For all its youthful thoughts, this is a work which is truly symphonic in conception and is unique among the composer's surviving music. After the concert the Dean wrote a most appreciative letter, saying what a revelation it had been; and it was thrilling, thanks to David Cairns, that Pye Records agreed to our including *Ascribe* with its orchestral accompaniment (played by the Academy of the BBC) in our next recording with them.

Another notable, albeit smaller, event in 1976 was the recital celebrating the completion of the restoration work in the Quire. For the best part of a year, services normally sung in the Quire had had to be moved to other parts of the cathedral, often, a long way from the organ console – how James Lancelot, who had succeeded Clement as Sub-Organist, managed to accompany the choir so sensitively was quite amazing. But were we glad to be back in the stalls! The recital programme included the first performance of Jonathan Harvey's *I love the Lord*, which the composer had kindly given me after Evensong one Sunday afternoon, saying he had a little present which he hoped I would like. Jonathan had become a regular at Sunday Evensong, as by then his son, Dominic, had become a chorister. This is how Jonathan described *I love the Lord* (or the *Chord*, as it became known): "This anthem is the fruit of listening to the Choir in the liturgy week after week. The profound impression they have made, in the context of the services and the building, provided the inspiration for the music."

I too occasionally had a stab at composing, usually for specific occasions, the first being a set of *Preces and Responses*, dedicated to the Precentor, Anthony Caesar, and first sung at the Evensong when he was installed and "upgraded" from a minor canonry, to becoming a fully-fledged member of the Dean and Chapter. These *Responses*, which begin with an uncanny resemblance to the opening of the *Gloria* in Stanford's *Magnificat in C*, have one feature of which I was also unaware at the time, namely the first note of every soprano entry is a G.

I had also begun to make some carol arrangements, designed specifically for Winchester and its exceptionally long nave. The most successful was a setting of *We three Kings*, which we sang as we processed from the West End to the front of the nave, with the "Three Kings" (tenor, baritone and bass) in the centre aisle, singing the verses, and the refrains being sung alternately by *Decani* and *Cantoris* in the side aisles. This was all unaccompanied until we reached the last verse "Glorious now behold him arise", when the congregation joined in, accompanied by full organ. In due course *We three Kings* was published by Encore Press, and it has been broadcast on Christmas Eve by the Choir of King's College, Cambridge and included in their CD marking the centenary of the Service of Nine Lessons and Carols.

The 1976 Christmas Concert with the Waynflete Singers was unexpectedly poignant. The main work was Schütz's *Christmas Story*, with the part of the narrator sung most movingly by the great tenor, Peter Pears, just ten days after the death of his partner, Benjamin Britten.

Needless to say, we had some narrow escapes, and none more so than at the 1977 Christmas concert with the Waynflete Singers, which was being broadcast live. I had spared the choristers from having to learn John Tavener's demanding *Canticle to the Mother of God* for unaccompanied choir (singing in modern Greek) alternating with a solo soprano (Elise Ross singing in modern Hebrew). The harmonic language is very dissonant, and the Waynflete Singers were struggling to find their notes from the soprano soloist's cues. At the balance test the BBC producer, Philip Moore, and I really wondered what on earth to do. I then remembered that a nine-year old chorister, who had arrived just two terms earlier, had perfect pitch, so I rushed over to Pilgrims' and found him in the playground. I asked him to stand with the sopranos, gave him a copy of the Tavener and told him to hum the sopranos' note before every entry. The performance was transformed, and the BBC producer couldn't understand how this had happened. The chorister's name was Stephen Layton!

I first met Stephen in 1976, when he was nine years old and his father, an organist in Derby, brought him to Winchester to sing to me some weeks after the regular voice trials had been held. I was so impressed with his musical ear that within a matter of minutes I said that we had better go over to the choir school to see if there was a bed available. He became an exceptional chorister, standing out for his musicality and his beautiful voice. He studied the organ with James Lancelot and played for Evensong while he was still a Chorister. Stephen has become one of the finest choral conductors in the world. For 17 years he was Fellow and Director of Music at Trinity College Cambridge. Other former posts include Chief Conductor of the Netherlands Chamber Choir, Chief Guest Conductor of the Danish National Vocal Ensemble, and Director of Music at the Temple Church, London. Stephen's recordings have consistently broken new ground, and I was delighted when he was awarded the prestigious medal by the Royal College of Organists in 2024 in recognition of his supreme gifts as a choir director. His range of repertoire and the sound world he creates are unique.

Within a month we would find ourselves on a very different mission. Out of the blue came an invitation to sing in Notre Dame in Paris during the Week of Prayer for Christian Unity. We would be the first Anglican Cathedral Choir to sing *Vêpres*, i.e. Evensong. But this did not meet with universal approval, and a few noisy protesters were bundled out of the cathedral by official bouncers. Before we sang Evensong, a message from the Archbishop of Canterbury was read in English and French, commemorating this 'important, historic and encouraging event". After Evensong we rehearsed for our recital, given in front of the nave altar. As a prelude to the recital, I climbed the 85 steps to the console of the famous organ at the west end and played Wesley's *Choral Song* and Bach's 'great' *Prelude in C minor*. At the recital the choir was on top form and the atmosphere quite electrifying as the huge congregation heard the sounds waft down the nave. One could sense a fervent desire to share in the best of another church's tradition. We were amazed at the silence until

MN with Stephen Layton, after Stephen received the medal of the Royal College of Organists, 2024.

deafening applause broke out at the end of the recital. However the transport arrangements in Paris left much to be desired, and I was taken aback to see the choir matron, Thelma Ellis-Jones, standing on top of the choir bus loading the suitcases, assisted by the Head Chorister, Christopher New.

On our return, there was another significant development, once again encouraged by the Stancliffes, who persuaded some of their friends to join us to give one of the earliest performances in the UK of the *St Matthew Passion* with period instruments.

1978 was also notable (I nearly said notorious) for the premiere of Jonathan Harvey's canticles at the Southern Cathedrals Festival combined Evensong. Perhaps inadvisably I had told Jonathan not to feel restrained, and he took me at my word. I can still remember the agonised looks on the faces of my Chichester and Salisbury colleagues, John Birch and Richard Seal, when I showed them the score. But the choirs pulled it off, with a wonderful solo from Don Sweeney in the *Nunc dimittis* and brilliant accompanying by James Lancelot.

In his programme note, Jonathan wrote: "I have always envied cultures such as the Middle Ages and various Eastern cultures for the natural and integrated way much of their music sprang out of ritual. Our music-making, dominated by the box office and everything that 'buying' implies, also by apprehensions of career failure, seems light years away from those ceremonies in which music is not judged as a commodity, but as an agent, more or less effective, for a spiritual tendency within a society. My *Magnificat* and *Nunc dimittis* was commissioned to be part of a ritual, and should perhaps be thought of in terms of its contribution to the worship of a congregation. To be invited to contribute to this worship is a great joy and privilege.

Anyone who knows both the world of avant-garde music and the world of Anglican church music cannot fail to be struck by the sad fact that much exciting music of spiritual import hasn't a hope of entering those time-honoured and notoriously conservative portals. Or has it? The vision of our great cathedrals as once again the spearhead of all that is adventurous, imaginative and sacred in our torn culture helped me write this piece, by no means 'adventurous' by avant-garde standards, but certainly exploiting vocal possibilities rarely if ever encountered in liturgical Anglican Evening Canticles before. It embodies a hope."

Apart from the trip to Paris, during my first six years at Winchester there were no foreign choir tours, though we travelled over southern England, to

Chichester and Salisbury to take part in the Southern Cathedrals Festivals, and in 1975 for the Chichester Festivities. These included remarkable works commissioned by the Dean of Chichester, Walter Hussey, including Benjamin Britten's *Rejoice in the Lamb* and Leonard Bernstein's *Chichester Psalms*. In 1977 we gave a recital at Westminster Cathedral in aid of its music fund.

CHAPTER 11

900th Anniversary of Winchester Cathedral, 1979

"Calling all knitters"

As far back as November 1975, the Dean had called a first meeting to consider how we might best mark the Cathedral's 900th anniversary in 1979. The founding of the cathedral goes back to the days of William the Conqueror, who appointed one of his cousins to be Bishop of Winchester. In 1079 this royal relative began building his cathedral on the site of a large Saxon church founded by St Swithun and, with many additions and alterations over the centuries, this is the cathedral as we know it today.

I was coming to the end of a recital tour in the USA and Canada and feared that I would not be back in time for the meeting, as my final recital, at the Cathedral of Christ the King in St Louis Missouri, was on the previous day. There was a flight leaving very soon after the recital, so that morning I made an advance trip to the airport to check in my baggage. The afternoon recital went well, and I felt obliged to play an encore, but after taking a bow I returned to the console in my overcoat, in the hope that the audience would get the message that I had to leave. I made the flight, and also the British Airways connection in Chicago. And a few hours after I arrived home in Winchester, I was present at the 1979 meeting, albeit somewhat jet-lagged.

I was particularly keen to flag up the possibility of a choir tour to North America, and to my delight this idea was warmly received by the Dean and Canon Treasurer, Alex Wedderspoon. In the course of my organ recital tours in 1973 and 1975, a number of American organists had strongly encouraged me to bring the Cathedral Choir to North America. I had made some preliminary soundings about possible venues, but it was clear that the tour could only take place if substantial sponsorship were found, principally to meet the travel costs. I can state categorically that, without the bold initiatives of Alex Wedderspoon, the tour would never have happened, nor would we have found ourselves giving high-profile concerts in major concert halls. Alex was married to a Canadian, Judith Plumptre, and on his annual summer visit to Canada and the East Coast of the USA, he succeeded in meeting three hall managers and persuading them to include a recital by the Winchester Cathedral Choir in their 1978–79 season. The first was at the National Arts Centre in Ottawa, the second, which was televised as a TV documentary by NBC, was at the new Kennedy Center in Washington, and the third at Carnegie Hall, New York City.

Planning a workable itinerary was not the only challenge; another was assembling the choir. Several of the lay clerks had teaching jobs, from which they needed to be granted special leave to come on the three-and-a-half week tour. So, I wrote to their employers, all of whom agreed, but of course the singers needed to be compensated for loss of earnings. This brings me to Alex's final *coup*, namely that Barclays Bank in New York would guarantee the tour against loss up to $25,000. This and the revenue from the NBC TV programme transformed the tour finances. There were also health issues; one of the choristers was diabetic and needed daily injections. Thanks to the choir matron, and to the boy's father, Humphrey Clucas, who came on the tour as an excellent additional tenor, all went well.

In nearly all of the cities we visited we sang a service as well as giving a concert. The presence on the choir tour of the Bishop and Dean of Winchester with their wives, as well as the Precentor, was I think unique, with the Bishop and the Dean both contributing sermons and lectures. At our opening Evensong in Ottawa, two days after our arrival, despite many of the choir still suffering from jet-lag, we duly sang the psalm appointed for that day, Psalm 78, as we would have done in Winchester. What most of the congregation at Christ Church Cathedral made of it I am not sure, but apparently Sir William McKie, the former Organist and Master of the Choristers at Westminster Abbey, then retired and living in Canada, was moved to tears.

Another hazard was the extremely cold weather, which in Canada was at times 30 degrees below freezing, and I instructed the boys not to speak when outside to save their voices. We were most grateful for the bright red, woolly hats, kindly knitted for every member of the entourage by 23 women members of the Cathedral congregation and a retired colonel, following an appeal from the Dean in the Cathedral monthly pamphlet, "Calling all knitters". Not only did these keep everyone's ears warm, but they also provided a ready means of identification, especially at airports.

All the concerts had been pretty well sold out, but since the final concert at Carnegie Hall was our own promotion, we had to find a way of attracting

900th Anniversary of Winchester Cathedral, 1979

MN and Penny outside Carnegie Hall
in New York, 1979.

publicity to help draw an audience. With this in mind, and thanks to the ingenuity of two staff at Winchester College, Tommy Cookson and James Sabben-Clare (later to become head), the words of the 1970s pop song, 'Winchester Cathedral', were adapted as follows:

"Winchester Cathedral you're bringing me down.
It's nine hundred years and you're still around.
Who would have believed
You'd see nine centuries pass
From Norman Kings, Tudor Queens
Until you get down to people like us,
Winchester Cathedral we've come to call,
Have you got your tickets for Carnegie Hall?"

We sang this as an encore at the British Embassy in Washington and in the United Nations building in New York, and it paid off as we had a good audience at Carnegie Hall. However, all was not plain sailing. Thirty minutes before the concert was due to start, the house manager told me that there was a problem with the (electronic) organ, which was fundamental to the programme. Ten minutes later, came the news that the organ was broken, would not work and could not be fixed in time. As half the programme was accompanied, this meant that we had to think quickly. Carnegie Hall produced a grand piano, but for most of the programme this was not a suitable substitute. So, I dispatched the tour manager and one of the altos by taxi to the choristers' residence (nearly forty blocks away on East 95th Street) to fetch as much music as possible, which, as we were returning home the following day, had already been packed in the boys' suitcases.

We sang most of the first half as planned, but I could not play the Mozart *Fantasia for a Mechanical Organ*. Instead, we inserted Mendelssohn's *I waited for the Lord* and *Lift thine eyes*. Before Purcell's *Jehovah quam multi sunt hostes*, I told the audience what had happened, and how it was likely we would sing the words, translated as *How many there are that vex me*, with unusual fervour.

When we went off at the interval, we still did not know what we could sing in the second half. Fortunately, we had found enough copies of Benjamin Britten's unaccompanied *Hymn to St Cecilia* to replace Wesley's *The Wilderness* (one of our show pieces with superb soloists). I enjoyed talking to the audience about Britten's *Hymn to St Cecilia*, quoting words from the refrain: "Blessed Cecilia appear in visions to all musicians". We then substituted a shorter Wesley anthem, *Thou wilt keep him in perfect peace*, before closing with two unaccompanied motets by Stanford, *Justorum animae* and *Coelos ascendit*, and our by now obligatory encore, *The Turtle Dove* by Vaughan Williams.

Next morning, we were up early to catch the day flight back to London, which was chiefly memorable (at the request of the pilot) for grace being sung before lunch at 35,000 feet. The choristers then had two days off to recover at home before returning in time for the Sunday services.

When Penny and I were both away, her mother or my parents would often move down to Winchester to look after the grandchildren. This was a great blessing, and over the years they made lots of new friends in the Cathedral Close.

900th Anniversary of Winchester Cathedral, 1979

MN's parents, Leonard and Jeanette, in Winchester Cathedral Close.
They often came to help with the children, 1984.

Our next major event in Winchester was the Royal Maundy Service at which we were joined by the Chapel Royal Choir, taking me back to the seven Maundy services at which I sang as one of the Children of the Chapel Royal.

Then, at the end of June, came a two-week Festival of Music, which surveyed 900 years of English and Continental church music, ranging from the 11th Century *Winchester Troper* to the premiere of a newly commissioned work by Jonathan Harvey, *Hymn*. From the later centuries of the Middle Ages came the *Play of Daniel* performed by the University of California Early Music Ensemble (they even brought their own organ with them), and King Arthur's legendary connection with Winchester was marked in a specially devised production of Purcell's *King Arthur*, given by Winchester College in New Hall. The College also combined with the Winchester Music Club in a performance of Britten's *War Requiem*. The heritage of English Cathedral Music was represented by four recitals in the quire and one in Winchester College Chapel, each including music from the so-called Golden Age (1550–1640). The Festival was preceded by a charity concert when Cleo Laine and the John Dankworth Quartet presented 'Wordsongs' – a fascinating collection of poems, many of them set to music by John Dankworth.

The opening concert of Winchester Cathedral's 900 anniversary celebrations when MN conducted the Berlioz *Te Deum* with 500 voices and the London Symphony Orchestra.

900th Anniversary of Winchester Cathedral, 1979

The Festival's opening concert was one of the most extraordinary events during our time at Winchester, both for its repertoire and for the staging. The programme began conventionally with Mozart's *Kyrie in D minor K341*, followed by Messiaen's *Et exspecto resurrectionem mortuorum* (And I look for the resurrection of the dead), for woodwind, brass and percussion. With its complex rhythms it was by far the most difficult work I had ever attempted to conduct, and I was most grateful to the members of the London Symphony Orchestra for their help and patience, particularly at the first orchestral rehearsal in the Royal Albert Hall. They even asked if we could play it through again.

The original plan had been for Sir Colin Davis to conduct this concert, but he had had to decline, and it was David Cairns who persuaded me to take his place. David had proposed that the principal choral work should be the Berlioz *Te Deum* and insisted that we should perform it as Berlioz had specified, with the separation between the choir and orchestra at one end and the solo organ at the other. To say that this was another challenge would be a gross understatement since, in order to accommodate over 500 performers at the west end of the nave, we needed a huge amount of staging. For a long time, it looked as if the costs would be prohibitive, but then two of our good friends from Southern Television, Dave Heather and Angus Wright, came to the rescue by persuading their bosses to televise the concert, and they then picked up the cost of the staging.

The following review by Sandrey Date appeared in *Classical Music Magazine*

"The celebrations for the 900th anniversary this year of the building of Winchester Cathedral included last month a two-week festival which surveyed a panorama of English and continental church music, with several visiting choirs ad orchestras participating, Director Martin Neary's greatest coup took place at the opening concert on 28 June when he conducted a stunning performance of Berlioz's *Te Deum*, With a choir of 500 voices, the LSO and tenor John Treleaven at the west end of the nave, and James Lancelot on the organ at the other end, this performance must have come close to realising all Berlioz's requirements. Neary rose to the challenge of controlling these vast forces with admirable energy and enthusiasm; although his sometimes jerky beat looked somewhat difficult to follow, there was no sign of this in the eagerness and vitality of responses from the performers. The gigantic surge of sound which climaxed the *Judex crederis* was overwhelming: what a pity that no one laid on any flags so that the *Marche pour la présentation des drapeaux* could be included."

CHAPTER 12

Bicentennial Fellowship

"... drink in the spirit but use your instinct"

The day after our arrival back from the North American tour, I had an interview for a British Council UK/USA Bi-Centennial Fellowship. This was part of an exchange scheme whereby each country nominated artists and musicians to spend a year developing their skills in the other's country. In the case of English musicians, most of the applicants had been composers, and I was the exception. My application was almost certainly helped by a telegram recommending me, sent to the British Council by Lyon Rousell, the British Consul-General in Washington, who had attended our Carnegie Hall concert. I was offered a fellowship, and, thanks to the willing support of the Dean and Chapter, I was able to accept.

But where should we live in America? In October 1979, on the recommendation of our friend, Jim Litton, Director of Music at Trinity Episcopal Church, I made a short visit to Princeton, New Jersey, to see if living there for six months would be practical. Thanks to Jim, it most certainly was. He introduced me to one of the men in his choir who was in the real estate business, and as a result we were able to rent a house belonging to one of the Princeton University Faculty who was on Sabbatical. He and his family stayed in our house in the Close at Winchester during a trip to Europe. Secondly, Jim put me in touch with the local school, who agreed to take our two daughters, and he also found excellent instrumental teachers for them. Most important of all, he arranged for me to meet the head of The Eden Institute, a specialist school which had a remarkable programme for autistic children – different from anything available in the UK. And we will always be grateful that Thomas, by now aged five, had the benefit of attending there.

On top of all this, Jim welcomed our daughters into his choir, giving them an opportunity to sing at a time when there were no girls in English Cathedral Choirs. Jim was always so encouraging, and the girls loved his rehearsals – not least because of his habit of rewarding correct theory answers with a generous supply of dimes!

So, three days after Christmas, the whole family, including Thomas and Justine (our au pair) flew to New York, where we were met and driven to our new home by Freeman Dyson (the world-renowned scientist son of the composer George Dyson), who was a professor at the Princeton Institute of Advanced Studies. We all settled in very quickly. I was granted use of the University Library and tennis courts and the girls, within days of starting at Johnson Park School, began to speak with American accents.

I also attended fascinating lectures on *Giulio Cesare* by Merrill Knapp, a world authority on Handel. Princeton was in relatively easy reach of New York and not that far from Philadelphia and Washington, which enabled me to sit in on rehearsals, as well as accepting opportunities to guest conduct choirs and play some organ recitals. Above all, I had time to learn scores more thoroughly, and to think about how best to recreate the kind of sounds the composers from earlier periods would have heard. I gave a lecture about performing *Messiah* at the University of Maryland, discussing the advantage of period instruments and articulation, with advice to "drink in the spirit but use your instinct" – with which the Professor of Music, Howard Server, fortunately agreed. In an appreciative letter, he jokingly acknowledged that truly 'echt' performances of Baroque music are no longer possible. "We can't create the ambience of an unheated church in the dead of winter packed with Saxons, none of whom have bathed for some time". But that should not stop us trying. (I have to admit however that the winter temperatures in Winchester Cathedral were at times quite authentic.)

The British Council allowed me to return several times to the UK, the first occasion on Concorde. This was thanks to the generosity of Southern Television, for whom I was conducting the Fauré *Requiem* with the Winchester Cathedral Choir and the English Chamber Orchestra. The flight lasted 3 hours 11 minutes, causing the pilot to remark as we approached Heathrow that he hoped we had not had to rush our lunch.

The Cathedral Choir had in my absence been extremely well prepared for the Fauré by my colleague, James Lancelot, as had the Waynflete Singers for a performance of the *St Matthew Passion*. This was the second time we had been accompanied by period instrumentalists, and it felt much more comfortable, with the choir's articulation more closely reflecting that of the orchestra.

It was a busy time, as two days after returning to Princeton (not on Concorde), I was off to Gloucester, Massachusetts (on my 40th birthday) to give an organ recital. I then flew directly to Washington, where I was playing at Bradley Hills Presbyterian Church.

Then came another trip back to London. Not to play or conduct, but to be interviewed for the position of Organist and Master of the Choristers at Westminster Abbey. However, on the way out from my interview, whom should I run into but Simon Preston, who, once again, was chosen over me. It was however an "ill wind that blew nobody any good", as my further period at Winchester was wonderfully fulfilling.

Back in the USA, I took part in the Aspen Music Festival, where I directed a performance of Handel's *Acis and Galatea* and conducted William Schuman's *Carols of Death*. The American composer was complimentary about the choir's performance, but in a letter complained about my indecipherable handwriting.

For our last two months in America we moved to Connecticut, exchanging houses with another family, after which we returned to England, Justine flying back with Thomas, while Penny, Nicola, Alice and I travelled home on the QE2. Sailing out of New York on a brilliantly sunny Saturday evening was unforgettable. On the Sunday, the Captain invited me to play for the morning service, when one of the hymns was *Eternal Father, strong to save*, with the refrain *O hear us when we cry to thee for those in peril on the sea*. Later that afternoon these words took on a particular relevance when Hurricane Charlie caught up with us. The ship was diverted to try and avoid the storm, but many of the passengers were seasick – a notable exception being Nicola, whom we found playing (and winning) at bingo.

Throughout our time in America, I kept in touch with Jonathan Harvey. For a recital at the Church of the Ascension in New York Jonathan wrote *Toccata for Organ and Tape*, which I premiered. The piece demanded metronomically accurate timing by the organ soloist in order to coordinate with the pre-recorded tape – with Jonathan as always brilliantly combining live and electronic sounds. This was after spending a week at St Thomas's, Fifth Avenue, where I had stood in as guest director of the post-Easter choral conductors' course.

Jonathan was also in touch about whether it might be possible to stage the premiere of his church opera, *Passion and Resurrection* in Winchester Cathedral. This had originally been intended for Canterbury Cathedral, but they had reluctantly decided not to proceed. I can still remember the committee meeting of the Waynflete Singers when I put forward the idea

MN With Jonathan Harvey, 1981.

of performing *Passion and Resurrection*, and how, to begin with, this seemed pretty unlikely to gain approval. But I was immensely helped by two factors: first, Bishop John Taylor agreeing to be the producer, and secondly securing the interest of the BBC. Amazingly this came about thanks to a chance remark by the bishop's wife after a broadcast Choral Evensong, which was overheard by the BBC producer, Chris Mann. Peggy Taylor asked me if there was any news about the *Passion*. Chris was intrigued, and wanted to find out more, so he stayed to tea. Quite soon afterwards, we heard that he had persuaded his colleagues to consider filming preparations for the opera, treating the project as a documentary. The BBC was particularly interested that there was to be so much local involvement – making it, in a way, a Winchester Oberammergau. So, before Christmas, we did a trial run for the BBC in the cathedral, with Jonathan accompanying on the piano. The reaction was very positive from the BBC, who to our immense relief took over the cost and control of the lighting, effectively allowing us to go ahead.

Nevertheless, it was a huge commitment for the Waynflete Singers; for three weeks there were rehearsals almost every evening, and the singers not only had to memorise their notes but learn how to act their parts, this last discipline proving perhaps the most challenging of all. The bishop had ingenious ideas for the production, such as when the women's chorus, in their blue and white nuns' costumes, lay on their backs kicking their legs in the air to represent the Sea of Galilee. Most of the solos were sung by Lay Clerks from the Cathedral Choir, including the incomparable Donald Sweeney as Jesus. The audience (or congregation) joined in singing several plainsong hymns, and the programme was broadcast on BBC1 on Easter Day 1982.

The work was received with almost unanimous critical acclaim. I cannot do justice to the power of Jonathan's musical inspiration, the genius of his conception or the thrill of his orchestral writing. I do know that those of us who were privileged to take part in *Passion and Resurrection* will remember it for the rest of our days and I believe this also to be true for many in the audience.

"*Noli me tangere*" from Jonathan Harvey's *Passion and Resurrection*. Mary Magdalene (Rosemary Hardy) approaches Jesus (Donald Sweeney) *(Photo © Clive Barda)*.

Martin Neary: Time to declare

The crucifixion scene from *Passion and Resurrection (Photo © Clive Barda)*.

For an article about *Passion and Resurrection* by Stephen Walsh, which appeared in *The Observer* on 29 March 1981, see Appendix 2.

CHAPTER 13

Winchester, 1981–87

"The lay clerks were splendid and carried the day."

After my Bicentennial Fellowship, it was a joy to be back to the routine of daily Evensongs, and to find the choir in such good order, thanks to James Lancelot's excellent work in my absence. There were also some more exciting events on the horizon.

Until recently the Channel Islands were part of the Diocese of Winchester. During my first years as Cathedral Organist, I paid several visits, giving recitals in Guernsey, Jersey and Alderney. The Dean and Chapter decided that, to mark the 900th anniversary, the choir should, albeit one year late, spend a weekend in Jersey and Guernsey, taking part in services and giving concerts. We numbered nearly 40 and it took three (admittedly very small) planes to fly us from Guernsey to Jersey. Over the years we made some very good Channel Island friends, one of whom, Lloyd Warry, generously gave us his grand piano.

There was another Winchester Southern Cathedrals Festival to plan for July 1981, when Richard Seal and I would be joined by Alan Thurlow, who had succeeded John Birch at Chichester. This gives me an opportunity to say what a pleasure it was to make music with my cathedral colleagues and their choirs in their respective buildings – Chichester with its intimacy, Winchester with its imposing grandeur and extremely long nave and Salisbury with its unique spire and open space – I remember particularly thrilling performances of Tallis's 40 part motet, *Spem in Alium* there, with eight choirs of five parts placed in the nave aisles on either side.

Speaking of choir personnel, on Easter Day 1981 the much-revered alto, Eric Owen, retired after singing in the Winchester Choir for more than 30 years. He started in 1950 when the choir's duties included singing at Mattins on three weekdays and at a Eucharist on Saints' Days, and the choir salary was usually the principal source of a Lay Clerk's income. He took all the fresh initiatives in his stride, welcoming the new young singers and choral scholars (and beating them at table tennis on the 1979 American tour). As reported in the 1981 Southern Cathedrals Festival programme, Eric had a dry sense of humour and a fund of anecdotes, one being a "crisis" during the 1966 SCF's combined choirs Evensong which clashed with England's appearance in the World Cup Final. On that occasion the Organist of the day saved the situation by surreptitiously keeping in touch with the score in the organ loft and conveying the unfolding drama by signs to the choirs below.

As before, we included an Eve of Festival Concert, this time with the London Symphony Orchestra accompanying Michael Tippett's *A Child of our Time*, which was another challenge for the Waynflete Singers and their conductor, who were joined by the Reading Bach Choir. The oratorio uses a traditional three-part format based on that of Handel's *Messiah*, and is structured in the manner of Bach's *Passions*. The work's most original feature is Tippett's use of African-American spirituals, which carry out the role allocated by Bach to chorales. Tippett justified this innovation on the grounds that these songs of oppression possess a universality absent from traditional hymns.

In the *Sunday Times*, Felix Aprahamian wrote that it was "... among the most moving performances I have heard since its unforgettable wartime premiere ... Mr Neary was indeed as fortunate in his soloists (who included Wendy Eathorne, David Thomas and Elizabeth Stokes) as in the choral and orchestral (LSO) forces he controlled with such skill and fervour." Two days before our performance, following an intense morning rehearsal at the Albert Hall with the LSO, I returned home to Winchester to discover that, to everyone's amazement, England, led and inspired by my school friend, Mike Brearley, had beaten the Australians in the Test Match at Headingley, with Bob Willis's astounding 8 for 31. And at the evening rehearsal of the Tippett with the Waynflete Singers and the Reading Bach Choir, I felt as if I was walking on air! The 1981 Festival also included more commissions and premieres; Jonathan Harvey's *The Tree* for trebles and organ and John Tavener's *Where shall I make my beginning?* as well as performances of Jonathan's *I love the Lord* and his controversial *Magnificat and Nunc dimittis*.

The following year we gave another performance of the *St Matthew Passion*, and, as was noted in the reviews, the choirs had clearly become more adapted to the style of the period instrumentalists.

1982 also brought an unexpected invitation from Air Canada for the choir to tour Western Canada, to mark the launch of direct flights from London to Vancouver. No English Cathedral Choir had been in this area since 1927, when there was a tour by the Lay Clerks of St George's Chapel, Windsor combined with the choristers of Westminster Abbey. Once again, we were accompanied by the Bishop and Dean of Winchester and their wives, and once again we were greatly indebted to Vice-Dean Alex Wedderspoon, who, with the help of friends of his wife, Judith, persuaded the Orpheum Theatre in Vancouver to promote a concert which became a sell-out, with an audience of 2800.

However, just a week before departing we had a blow; our tour manager, Surgeon Commander Tony Revell, had to withdraw when all naval leave was cancelled in anticipation of the Falklands war. He was much missed, but his principal duties were handled most efficiently by two of the lay clerks, Roger Lowman (travel) and Allan Mottram (daily timetable).

On Easter Monday we flew to Calgary and from there the tour took us to Vancouver, Victoria, Edmonton, Saskatoon, Regina, and Winnipeg. The reviews were complimentary, one referring to Winchester's 'liquid tenors'. There were many highlights, not only musical ones, beginning on our first day with a visit to the hot springs in Banff, where most of the party bathed in the open air surrounded by a countryside still deep in snow.

At our last stop, Winnipeg, it has to be admitted there were two hiccups. As described already, the tour was sponsored by Air Canada, but this had not prevented a rival airline, Ward Air, from placing an advert in the concert programme. I won't describe the look on the face of the Air Canada representative when he saw it, nor what he did to his copy of the programme. The Dean though took the opportunity of publicly thanking Air Canada for their generous sponsorship and expressing the hope that any members of the audience thinking of flying to London would do so by Air Canada.

The following morning there was a further problem when the coach, due to transport us to catch a very early morning flight to Toronto, had not appeared as scheduled. In a moment of panic, I called two taxi firms requesting as many cabs as they could muster to take us to the airport. Yellow cabs started to appear in droves from all directions, and we duly made the flight, allowing us just enough time to visit Niagara Falls, before flying back overnight to London, in the course of which Air Canada ran out of gin. I wonder why?

Concerts given by the Cathedral Choir and Waynflete Singers continued to attract the attention of the BBC, and in 1982 we were delighted to be invited to share a BBC Prom with Christopher Hogwood and the Academy of Ancient Music; in the second half we performed Bach's *Magnificat* with the rarely heard *Christmas Interpolations*. The concert was on 31 August, towards the end of the Summer holidays, during which I had not only spent time at

Winchester Cahedral Choir at Niagara Falls, 1982.

our holiday cottage in Dorset working on the score, but had also taught the first soprano part to our two daughters, 13-year-old Nicola, and nine-year-old Alice, who sang next to their mother with the Waynflete Singers in what Felix Aprahamian described in the *Sunday Times* as his "pick of the week".

There was another anniversary to observe, 1984 being 1000 years since the death of Bishop Ethelwold of Winchester (one of a trio of monastic bishops, who oversaw a major reform of the Benedictine movement in England). He was also a musician and was probably indirectly responsible for the copying of some of the first music ever notated in manuscript in this country. On Low Sunday, thanks to advice from the distinguished scholar, Dr Susan Rankin, we inaugurated the Saxon Festival by including in the Liturgy, as had happened 1000 years earlier, the *Visitatio Sepulchri*, a short enactment of the visit by the Three Marys to the empty tomb. As the Dean later wrote in the June *Monthly*

Pamphlet, "the Precentor and three Lay Clerks carried out their instructions so well, not only singing their parts impeccably but also 'acting them' with such impressive, stylized deportment and gestures, so that they seemed like figures from the Bayeux Tapestry or the Winchester Bible come to life".

Then in December the Cathedral Choir gave a concert of Anglo-Saxon choral music at St George's Church Bloomsbury, in conjunction with The British Library. The programme included *Threefold Litany* for two solo men and full choir, *Responsories (for Swithun)* men's voices and *Agnus Dei* with tropes for two solo men and full men's voices. The plainchant idiom (known to some as 'stone-age' music!) was to say the least unfamiliar, and I have to admit not very appealing to the choristers, so I let them off pretty lightly. But the lay clerks were splendid and carried the day.

In 1985 we celebrated the 300th anniversaries of the births of Bach and Handel, with performances of the *St Matthew Passion* and *Dixit Dominus*. Of all the music I gave the Winchester choristers to sing, the Handel was vocally and musically the most demanding, principally because of the predominantly instrumental writing, with long passages of semi-quavers and no time to breathe. In October and November 1984, when I was Artist-in-Residence at the University of California at Davis (during another, shorter Sabbatical), I had worked intensely at *Dixit* with the College Choir, who were somewhat puzzled at the first rehearsal by my spending 30 minutes on the opening word.

Back in Winchester, at most of the early morning choristers' practices from January 1985 onwards, I allotted 10–15 minutes for *Dixit*, and by the time of the concert and recording for EMI, the boys were in good shape – our recording coming out at the top in the *Gramophone* and on the BBC's *Record Review*. This was the last recording we made with James Lancelot, who after ten years as Sub-Organist at Winchester, was appointed as Director of Music at Durham Cathedral. It is impossible for me to do justice to his huge contribution, principally as a superb accompanist, but also when taking over when I was away, not to mention being such a supportive colleague. James was succeeded by Timothy Byram-Wigfield, Organ Scholar of Christ Church, Oxford; and once again we had picked a winner.

Tim's first overseas trip with us in 1985 was very special. For some time, the Dean had been developing strong ties with the Benedictine Community of Fleury at St Benoit-sur-Loire, and over the half-term weekend the choir travelled to France with the whole Dean and Chapter (apart from the Canon

Winchester Choristers in the side aisle in 1985 *(Photo: © John Crook)*.

in Residence) to St Benoit. Our programme included on the Saturday a recital in the Basilica followed by Evensong with the monks, and on the Sunday morning High Mass.

In 1986 the choir had two overseas trips. The first was to the USA, including concerts on the West Coast, in San Francisco and Los Angeles, where we were accompanied by members of the LA Philharmonic Orchestra in Purcell's *Funeral Music* and Mozart's *Missa Brevis in F, K192*. On a day off, the boys thoroughly approved of their visit to Disneyland. Secondly there was a short visit to Vienna, where we had the privilege of singing Britten's *Ceremony of Carols* with harpist, Jane Lister, in the beautiful Musikverein, as well as combining with the Vienna Boys Choir. The concert was recorded and later broadcast across Europe.

At Disneyland, Los Angeles, 1986
(Photo: © John Crook).

Winchester Choristers with harpist Jane Lister at Musikverein, Vienna, 1986
(Photo: © John Crook).

Earlier in 1986 we had marked the 900th anniversary of *Domesday Book* with a concert series in the cathedral spanning the development of English Church Music from pre-Norman times to the present day. Three of the programmes – *The Ancient Art of England*, given by Gothic Voices, *Troubadour Songs* by Emma Kirkby and Anthony Rooley and *Ten Centuries of Cathedral Music* by the Cathedral Choir – reflected the astonishing musical art which flourished in medieval England and included part of the *Lament for the death of William the Conqueror*, dating from the eleventh century. How the *Lament* was performed remains conjectural, and we experimented with different interpretations, Gothic Voices singing just a single line, while the cathedral choir attempted an organum effect, with the melody sung at the fifth and octave.

We were also invited by the English Chamber Orchestra to take part in their 1986 Christmas Concert at the Barbican, specifically to perform Arthur Honegger's *Une Cantate de Noël*, which, by a stroke of good fortune, I had conducted (albeit in a simplified piano arrangement) at Cambridge 25 years earlier. This unusual and rarely performed work, with parts for a boys' semi-chorus as well as full choir, was tailor-made for our Winchester vocal forces. As Richard Morrison wrote in his *Times* review, "it must be the only Christmas cantata to begin with a dead march: a groaning sound which develops from sombre organ clusters ... and a penitential psalm setting, depicting 'the people that walked in darkness'. Suddenly a boy's chorus interrupts with a cry of rejoicing, and the whole texture erupts into a multilingual pageant of folk-carols, woven into a glorious polyphony". Richard wrote that "The Winchester Cathedral Choir, the Waynflete Singers and the English Chamber Orchestra gave a delightfully fresh-toned performance", but he was less complimentary about Parts One and Two of Bach's *Christmas Oratorio*, which he thought were "rather politely interpreted ... so one was grateful to that exciting counter-tenor, Christopher Robson, for injecting some high-ranging vigour in *Bereite dich Zion*".

In Winchester Cathedral the following evening, we included Part 3 of the *Christmas Oratorio* (hopefully with more verve). We also repeated the Honegger *Cantata*; everyone was most enthusiastic about the piece and, thanks to generous sponsorship from my Chapel Royal contemporary, Michael Wilkinson (by now a highly successful steel magnate), we managed to persuade EMI to record it. This they did, together with some stunning Poulenc pieces, his *Mass in G* and *Quatre Motets pour le temps de Noël*, for

Christmas at Winchester Cathedral, with Alice, lantern bearer for the Dean, Michael Stancliffe, and Nicola for the Bishop, John Taylor, 1983.

which the cathedral choir was on top form – not least the treble soloist, Mark Harris, who sang a series of perfect top G's in the *Agnus Dei*. We recorded the Poulenc at the east end of the Cathedral by St Swithun's Shrine, and were greatly indebted to the producer, Andrew Keener, for capturing the resonant acoustics so well.

Then, for the next Waynflete concert, it was back to my beloved Handel and his oratorio *Samson*. Philip Langridge sang superbly in the title role, as did the other soloists Gillian Fisher, Michael Chance and David Thomas in theirs. The programme booklet quoted *Music in London 1890–94* by George Bernard Shaw, another devotee of Handel: "The first four bars of 'Fix'd in His everlasting seat' are alone worth getting up a performance on the festival scale for; and if it were possible to get an English tenor and an English chorus to catch the ring of pagan joy-worship in 'Great Dagon has subdued our foe', that too would be a memorable experience". Thanks to our soloists, chorus and orchestra (leader Roy Goodman), I like to think we would have satisfied GBS.

That year (1987) the repertoire at the Festival Hall 5.55 pm Organ series was expanded, and Winchester Cathedral Choir was invited to perform the

Duruflé *Requiem*. This was no mean undertaking in the notoriously dry acoustic, and we were much indebted to Tim Byram-Wigfield for his excellent organ accompaniment, and to the soloists in the *Pie Jesu* movement, ex-Winchester Chorister Timothy Wilson (alto) and 14-year-old Alice (cello).

Dean Michael Stancliffe retired in 1986 and moved with Barbara to Pickering in North Yorkshire, but very sadly he died there on 26 March 1987. For more than 20 years he had been an inspiration to me at St Margaret's and at Winchester. As a preacher he was a master of words, which made his comment that "music could go beyond words" all the more powerful. He and Barbara loved the psalms, and on their summer holidays in Greece they listened to the recordings of the Winchester Choir singing the psalms for the day which one of the vergers, Ray Godfrey, had recorded for them. They were both much loved and respected in Winchester.

Thereafter it was a pleasure to work with Michael's successor as Dean, Trevor Beeson, a Canon of Westminster, who had also been Rector of St Margaret's.

I was very touched that Jonathan Louth, the long-serving secretary of the Winchester Old Choristers' Association, who had left the choir a few months before I arrived, should have commissioned John Tavener to compose a piece marking my period at Winchester. *A Christmas Proclamation "God is with us"* was clearly written with the cathedral acoustics in mind. John adapted the text from the Orthodox service of Great Compline, which is sung on Christmas Eve. Beginning tranquilly, the piece is a radiant and joyful celebration. There is a prominent tenor solo, powerfully sung at the premiere by Willie Kendall, and a shock in the final section when *fortissimo* chords on the organ, in the most foreign key imaginable, dramatically punctuate the choir's *"Christ is born!"*.

My last services as Organist and Master of the Music were on Christmas Day, 1987. The Evensong anthem was Vaughan Williams's *Fantasia on Christmas Carols*, with Alice playing an expanded cello part.

Being interviewed by Christopher Pollard, Head Chorister at Winchester Cathedral, 1986.

CHAPTER 14

Andrew Lloyd Webber *Requiem*

*"Freshly composed pages would be chauffeured
to Winchester almost every week"*

As already noted, Winchester Cathedral Choir occasionally strayed from the regular diet of cathedral music. In the mid-1970s, the local TV station, Southern Television, broadcast a series of programmes, *Come Sunday*, for which we recorded a number of pieces. These recordings were led by two ITV producers, Angus Wright and Dave Heather, who in 1977 were planning a Christmas programme featuring Cleo Laine, Johnny Dankworth and the Cathedral Choir. To my delight, the Dean and Chapter agreed to the recording being made in the Cathedral, and the readings were shared between the Bishop of Winchester, the Dean and the renowned actor, Andrew Cruickshank (well-known for his role in *Dr Finlay's Casebook*). There were some stunning sequences, one of my favourites being Cleo singing the Beatles' *Eleanor Rigby*, followed immediately by the treble duet *Pleasure it is* from Benjamin Britten's *Ceremony of Carols*.

However, seven years later in April 1984, I was completely unprepared for a telephone call from Andrew Lloyd Webber's office asking if Winchester Cathedral Choir might be able to run through, hopefully at his Sydmonton Festival in July, a *Requiem* he was in the process of writing. My first reaction was to ask if Andrew really wanted the pure sound of a cathedral choir. I was assured that he did, and that he had heard many of our recordings, but to make sure we were on the same hymn sheet I persuaded him to come to Evensong in the Cathedral the following Sunday, to hear us at first hand.

And so, in company with Sarah Brightman, whom he was about to marry, Andrew duly came, trying (unsuccessfully) to avoid being recognised by the choir parents, who were of course rather intrigued. Over tea, and my asking about the kind of setting he was proposing to compose, Andrew mainly talked about architecture; he was fascinated by our house in the Close, with its Norman undercroft.

To familiarise the choir with the kind of idiom we could expect, in the next two weeks we tried out a couple of Andrew's pieces, after which I broached the subject with the Pilgrims' School Headmaster, Michael Kefford, who was immediately enthusiastic, and with the Dean and Chapter, who as always were very supportive. One of my anxieties was whether there would be sufficient time for the boys to learn the new work, when we already had a demanding programme for the upcoming Southern Cathedrals Festival, including a typically challenging Jonathan Harvey premiere, *Come, Holy Ghost*.

Alongside Sarah Brightman, who had an amazing range reaching up to a top D, Andrew was keen to involve a solo boy treble, and, after hearing 12-year-old Paul Miles-Kingston, he decided to give him an important role. A few freshly composed (or, in some cases, revised) pages would be chauffeured to Winchester almost every week; and after Andrew himself had come to Winchester to see how things were progressing, he decided to go ahead with the initial run-through on Friday 13 July at All Saints Church, Old Burghclere. As well as the two upper voice soloists, the try-out version had tenor and bass solos, originally sung by two Winchester Lay Clerks, Willie Kendall and Donald Sweeney. The accompaniment was provided by

Cleo Lane with the Winchester Choristers when they took part in a Southern Television programme, 1977.

a small group of Andrew's favourite instrumentalists, with James Lancelot playing the specially imported electronic organ.

The performance went down well with Andrew's guests, and recordings were sent to potential recording companies. Immediately, Peter Andry, head of the classical wing of EMI, offered to record it. The work, however, was not completely finished, and after the world-renowned Placido Domingo had agreed to be the tenor soloist, Andrew decided to give the tenor a bigger role and to take out the bass solos. He wanted to have the Winchester Cathedral forces as the choir, but who would conduct the recording? I understand that unsuccessful approaches were made to Andre Previn and Simon Rattle, but Lorin Maazel accepted – tempted, it was rumoured, by the offer of flights on Concorde.

Lorin Maazel, Paul Miles-Kingston and MN discussing the recording of the Lloyd-Webber *Requiem (Photo © Clive Barda)*.

As was his custom, for much of the orchestral scoring Andrew relied on the arranger, David Caddick, but when all the forces joined up for the first time at the Henry Wood Hall, the recording engineers became worried that the violins were drowning the boys' voices; and so all the English Chamber Orchestra violinists booked for the recording at the Abbey Road Studios were released on full pay.

Recording of Andrew Lloyd Webber's *Requiem*: Placido Domingo, Sarah Brightman, Paul Miles-Kingston (soloists), Andrew Lloyd Webber and Lorin Maazel, 1985 *(Photo © Clive Barda)*.

The score certainly had some tricky moments, such as the syncopated rhythms for the tenor soloist in *Hosanna in excelsis*, and, as the composer was quoted as saying, Paul, the treble soloist, was "kind enough to assist Maestro Domingo in finding some of his notes". It was extraordinary to see how Paul kept his cool, and Maazel commented that he was not just a fine musician but already a fine artist. Paul's fame was quickly spreading, and the following weekend he found himself singing at the former Prime Minister, Edward Heath's, 40th annual Carol Concert in Broadstairs. Sir Edward had asked Andrew to write a special piece for the occasion, and Andrew responded by offering the *Pie Jesu* from the *Requiem*. When Ted telephoned to ask me if he could borrow Paul for the following Sunday, I had to explain that Paul was due to sing at a Winchester Cathedral carol service that evening, and jokingly said that I was afraid it would be impossible unless, of course, Ted would like to lay on a helicopter – which he duly did.

By this time Andrew had decided to fly Paul and the choir to New York for the televised world premiere of the *Requiem* at St Thomas's Church on Fifth Avenue. Also taking part were the St Thomas' Choir and the Orchestra of St Luke's.

Winchester Choristers with the Choristers of St Thomas, New York City, 1984.

Thinking back nearly 40 years, what really impressed everyone was the way Paul handled this extraordinary year. One moment he was standing between Sarah and Placido in the full glare of television lights, and the next he would be relaxing with his mates in the playground.

I later learnt that it had been Humphrey Burton of the BBC who had first asked Andrew, six years earlier, at the time of the troubles in Northern Ireland, to compose a *Requiem*. Andrew thought it was "a wonderful idea", but with the opening of *Evita* in New York, plus *Cats* and *Starlight Express*, he had too much else going on. However, the death of his father, William Lloyd Webber, caused him to think again, as did the death of a young journalist who had recently interviewed him, Phil Geffes, killed by the IRA bomb at Harrods.

The New York performance on 24 February 1985, for the benefit of The Holy Apostles Soup Kitchen for the Poor and Homeless of New York, was widely praised, although some of the reviews of the new *Requiem* were decidedly critical – one of the more complimentary being by Edward Heath in the *Financial Times*.

Then came the UK premiere in Westminster Abbey, in aid of the victims of the Brighton bombing, at which we were joined by the Winchester College Quiristers. Among the audience was the Prime Minister, Margaret Thatcher, who kindly invited the choir to a post-concert reception at 10 Downing Street. She was most hospitable, and took the boys into the Cabinet Room, where she placed the youngest chorister in her chair. Later she asked if she could be sent a score of the *Requiem*, as she was learning to read music.

Talking of music, how would I describe Andrew's score? To be honest (and not just because I had been the conductor), I preferred the simpler chamber-like version which we gave at Sydmonton. But the full version had some thrilling moments, such as *Hosanna in excelsis*, even if the syncopated rhythms, as already noted, sometimes caused problems. For a short while *Requiem* was exceedingly popular, every performance drawing full houses, and in recognition of sales in the United Kingdom of over 100,000 copies of the EMI album, Paul Miles-Kingston and I received Golden Discs. The release of *Pie Jesu* as a single pushed it up the charts, and for several weeks Andrew telephoned us each Tuesday morning with news of its latest position. But when it reached No 3, it was overtaken by *Frankie goes to Hollywood*, and Andrew no longer called.

I rather lost touch with Andrew, until 1992, when I took some Westminster Abbey Choristers to Bridgewater House (opposite St James's Palace) to sing at a fund-raising dinner in aid of the restoration of the Henry VII Chapel at the Abbey. At 4.30pm on the day, I was informed that one of the guests would be Andrew Lloyd Webber, and my immediate reaction was to try to find something by Andrew for the boys to sing as a surprise encore. But there were less than three hours to sort this out. Having dug out an old copy of *Pie Jesu*, I went over to the Choir School and found 13-year-old chorister, Michael Jennings, who not only had a beautiful voice, but was also a fast learner. Within a matter of minutes, he had mastered the opening solo in *Pie Jesu* and the other boys then quickly learnt the chorus part. When it came to the encore, young Michael enchanted his audience, which again included Margaret Thatcher, while Andrew Lloyd Webber was moved to tears.

CHAPTER 15

Arrival at the Abbey

"You turned me down at Winchester"

As in 1980, there was much speculation about who would be appointed as the next Organist of Westminster Abbey. In July 1987, I was invited to meet the Dean and Chapter in the Jerusalem Chamber, and they were joined by their music adviser, Sir David Willcocks. I was interviewed by the Dean and Canons Harvey, Charles and Gray, but can't remember much of what was said, apart from my expressing surprise that there was not a Sung Eucharist at the Abbey every Sunday (which I later learnt went down quite well). There was then a gap of a week until 9 July, when the Dean telephoned, inviting me to become the Organist and Master of the Choristers – to which I responded, "with the greatest pleasure". The news was not being made public for several days, and we had to keep quiet about it until the official announcement. However, a member of the Winchester Evensong congregation, the Revd Mark Potts, later told me that he had detected a wry smile on my face that evening at the opening words of Psalm 47: "O clap your hands together, all ye people: O sing unto God with the voice of melody".

My first services at Westminster Abbey, starting on the Feast of the Epiphany, were sung by the Lay Vicars (adult singers), as the choristers were on their post-Christmas holiday. It was not until 22 January that the full Abbey Choir appeared. It was quite a challenge to produce an interesting repertoire for such a lengthy period of Men's Voice services, and I introduced some mediaeval carols, such as *Of a rose sing we* and *Alma redemptoris mater* to vary the menu. I gave the boys a demanding first weekend with their new choirmaster, including Britten's *Festival Te Deum in E*, and they responded very well.

Arrival at the Abbey

Westminster Abbey Choir with Gordon Roland Adams (Headmaster) and MN in front of the Abbey's high altar, 1988.

At Evensong on Saturday 6 February, Accession Day, I was installed as Organist and Master of the Choristers. The service began with the Introit *I was glad* by my Winchester predecessor, Alwyn Surplice (sung in the nave). The psalm was 91, to the Alcock chant, which had made such an impression on me in 1949 at my first Maundy Service as a Chapel Royal boy, The Canticles were Herbert Howells's *Gloucester Service* and the anthem William Byrd's *O Lord, make thy servant Elizabeth*. We also sang the *Accession Responses*, arranged by William McKie (Abbey Organist 1941–63), the Hymn: 'We have a gospel to proclaim' (including my descant) and the National Anthem. For the voluntary I played César Franck's *Pièce héroïque*.

MN at the Westminster Abbey organ, 1988.

After the service, it was lovely to meet up with many Winchester friends who had come up for the service – Evensong in Winchester Cathedral that day was said (i.e. there was no choir) – but it was revealing to hear comments from a Winchester friend, an educational psychologist, about the way the Abbey choristers were singing. His view was that the boys looked scared. I had heard that my predecessor's regime had been exciting but also at times extremely demanding, and there were stories, later confirmed, of the boys being reprimanded if a service had not gone well.

A few months earlier, I had met the senior boys informally including Adam Aitken, about to be my first Abbey head chorister. He took me by surprise by asking: "Do you remember me, Sir? You turned me down at Winchester". I can't remember how I answered his question, other than by saying that I was delighted to have the benefit of his singing now.

As well as a change of Organist, there was also a new Headmaster, Gordon Roland-Adams (GRA). He and I immediately hit it off, and we resolved to encourage a more relaxed approach. That did not mean, however, reducing the level of concentration. There had been a system of "rewards" for the boys who would start each term with a credit of £10, to which would be added or deducted 'plusses' or 'minuses' (+ 10p or – 10p), or 'goods' or 'bads' (+50p or –50 p). I decided to adapt the system and to start with a smaller amount of £5, and to be more generous with the plusses, hoping that this would save any of the boys from being in debt at the end of the term!

One of GRA's great attributes was that he knew what the pressures of being a chorister could be like from his time as a chorister at Worcester Cathedral, and he appreciated that the boys needed time to unwind and let off steam after a big service. He also loved music and had been such a regular 'Prommer' at the BBC Proms, that early on in our time he was chosen by the Prommers committee to put the wreath around the bust of Sir Henry Wood (founder of the Proms) on the last night of the Proms – as is traditional. It was agreed that the boys should stay up to see this on television, even though they could not understand why they were not being sent off to bed at the usual time. Finally, GRA appeared on the TV screen – producing a great cheer.

We decided to drop the practice of calling the boys by their surnames – if there were two brothers, they had been known as "Smith major" and "Smith minor" – and we also restored the morning practices to 8.20am instead of at the end of the morning before lunch. This had the advantage of not interrupting the boys' academic work in the middle of the day and enabled me to be free to attend the numerous meetings concerning special services.

Another innovation was to arrange for the boys to have individual voice training lessons on Saturday mornings with a qualified voice teacher, Sheena Wolstencroft. This was to make an enormous difference, particularly with breathing. I often sat in on these training sessions, and learnt a lot, not only about vocal technique, but also how to help the boys gain confidence with their solo singing. Without having all their fellow choristers listening to them, the boys were often more relaxed.

The school could accommodate 36 boys, but there was room for no more than 24 in the choir stalls. When they first arrived at the Choir School, the boys generally spent a year as probationers, without singing at services. It seemed to me that we should do something to get the older probationers singing at the occasional service. And so, within a month, to begin with on Thursdays, we gave the top group of choristers the evening off, and Evensong was sung by the younger boys and the Lay Vicars. I deliberately chose simple music – the first trial Evensong had *Dyson in F* and Hilton's *Lord, for thy tender mercies' sake*; we just about got away with it, but it was tough going. And I soon realised that the balance would be better if the junior choir Evensongs were on Mondays when only six (instead of 12) Lay Vicars normally sang.

Under my predecessor, Simon Preston, the Abbey Choir had made some outstanding recordings, but it was felt that a popular CD could be a winner at the Abbey Bookshop, and so in March we made a recording of "Music for Royal Occasions". Despite concerns that recording in the Abbey would be impossible because of the traffic noise from Parliament Square, we went ahead, only to be interrupted during the first session by firemen charging down the nave, answering what transpired to be a false fire-alarm call. Fortunately, we were not disturbed during the remaining sessions. Recording in the Abbey enabled us to be accompanied (beautifully by acting Sub-Organist Iain Simcock) on the Abbey organ. I also recorded the Widor *Toccata*.

I have to admit that my attention span at sermons was not always 100 per cent – it was important to be ready for the next piece of music. However, the sermon at Matins on Mothering Sunday, 13 March, 1988 left me with an enduring memory. The preacher was Jane Asher, the actress who was also Campaign Chairman of the National Autistic Society. She began by asking us to think of those mothers whose children were not able to express their love. This was almost too much for me to bear, because what she said rang so true, reminding me of experiences with our autistic son, Thomas. I only just managed to play the next hymn.

The following day, Monday 14 March, there was a different kind of occasion to play for – The Commonwealth Observance. The custom was for the Abbey Choir not to take part in this annual ceremony, which in those days was deliberately not called a service, but an Observance, at which all of the most prominent of the religions practised in the Commonwealth countries were accorded an equal space. The musical content was also wide-ranging, and instead of an organ voluntary there was often a performance by a steel band, beginning very quietly. This was appreciated by Prince Philip, who one year asked why I had not played the organ quietly like the steel band, which he much preferred. I took the liberty of responding by saying that, with nearly 2000 people in the Abbey, there was a need for a strong organ accompaniment in the hymns, and that he had not been sitting in the 'cheap seats'. Luckily, he accepted the explanation and laughed.

Soon we were into Holy Week and the Easter Services. In former times, the Abbey Special Choir had performed an oratorio, but this had lapsed. However, I felt there should be some extra music, and so on the Tuesday evening the choir gave a recital: *Music for Passiontide*. And a Holy Week concert became a regular feature, including, in due course, broadcast performances of the Bach *St John Passion* with a group of excellent period instrumentalists.

On Easter Day we sang the Mozart *Missa Brevis in D K.194* with orchestra. All the musicians were up in the organ loft, which was fine for sound, but not good in that few could see the choir. So, in subsequent years we moved the choir and orchestra to the lantern crossing, enabling those people in the transepts and the quire to have a much better view. But it did little for those in the nave, because of the organ screen. This was something that had worried me, not least because in the nave the sound of the organ almost inevitably drowned the choir. So, after some experiments, two microphones were installed above the choir, and I think this made a significant improvement, although this extra amplification was removed after my time.

At the end of April, acting Sub-Organist, Iain Simcock, left to become Assistant Organist at Westminster Cathedral, and in his place, we welcomed Andrew Lumsden, whom I had first come across when he was head chorister at New College, Oxford, and the New College choir had come to sing at the Wesley Centenary Concert in Winchester in 1976. Andrew's accompaniments were often spectacular, not least when we were on tour.

Another innovation was to set up a scheme of permanent deputies for the Lay Vicars. One of the challenges for the director of a London choir is coping with the inevitable absences of many of the adult singers, because of outside solo work. When booking a deputy the Lay Vicars were asked to sound out first the two permanent deputies in their parts. The scheme meant that there was more consistency in the attendances, which certainly helped if there were new repertoire that needed rehearsing prior to the day of the performance.

A challenging development during my first year at the Abbey was establishing a regular Sung Eucharist at 11.15am each week, instead of on just the second and fourth Sundays in the month. The extra service inevitably increased the amount of music we were singing each week, and after some quite long negotiations with the Headmaster and the Lay Vicars, a formula was agreed whereby at Mattins the Choir left during the hymn after the Third Collect, to allow time for a short break and an extra practice before the Eucharist. In keeping with the current liturgical thinking, the Creed was normally said, but for the Gradual we would sing a psalm or a seasonal motet.

Another regular annual service in September is the Battle of Britain Service, dating back to July 1947, and the Unveiling and Dedication of the Battle of Britain Memorial. In 1990 the service included Vaughan Williams's *The Souls of the Righteous*, specially composed for the occasion in 1947. This was the first notable national event for the newly established choir after the war, and it was attended by the King and Queen. Over the years, the format of the service had hardly changed, but by the 1990s it was clear that some of the wording needed adapting, and the Dean succeeded in changing the title from 'A Service of Thanksgiving for Victory granted in the Battle of Britain 1940' to 'A Service of Thanksgiving and Rededication on Battle of Britain Sunday'. As he wrote in the introduction: "Today we record our continuing sense of gratitude for what was achieved in the darkest moments of war, and we rededicate ourselves to strive untiringly for peace, justice and freedom in the world today".

I have mixed memories of the annual service for the Inauguration of the General Synod because In 1990 I made a significant miscalculation. I had been asked to choose a short setting and selected *Darke in F*. But it transpired that the *Agnus Dei* was far too short. The custom was for The Queen to walk on her own from her stall by the organ screen to the altar rail to receive Communion, and then to walk back as the choir sang the *Agnus Dei*. Unfortunately, not to say embarrassingly, we finished this well before Her Majesty was back in her stall. I tried my best to signal to Andrew to continue playing, but understandably he did not grasp the problem. At the post-service reception, Her Majesty asked the Dean why no music had been sung when she walked back after receiving Communion. The Dean then turned to me, saying, "Yes, why was there no music, Martin?" I replied, saying "M'am, I think my head may be for the chop". The Queen was very understanding, and I promised to do better next time. This service alternated in turn between the 1662, 1928 and 1980 rites, and I remember hearing from the Queen's Lady-in-Waiting, Dame Susan Hussey, how in 1995, during the drive from Buckingham Palace to the Abbey, Her Majesty had asked if they would be exchanging the peace. After arriving at their places and looking at the Order of Service (1662), she had whispered, "We're all right!".

There were also regular annual events linked with Westminster City Council, including, on the Sunday after their election, a service for the new

Mayor of Westminster. For these, too, there were special service meetings, which were not always straightforward. I remember a discussion about hymns with Dame Shirley Porter, who was Jewish. She was very keen to have "Fight the good fight". I expressed some surprise because of the text. She said, "don't worry about that" but when I read out the second line of verse 1: "Christ is thy strength, and Christ thy right", and the last two lines of verse 4: "Only believe, and thou shalt see that Christ is all in all to thee", she had second thoughts.

The Remembrance Sunday service was particularly poignant in 1990, when it marked the 50th anniversary of the bombing of Dresden. The fine Dresdener Kreuzchor paid a short visit to England, and on that Sunday in the Abbey, following the two minutes' silence and the *Last Post* and *Reveille*, they sang the closing chorale, *Du heilige brunst*, from the Bach motet, *Der Geist hilft*. The service concluded with the Dresden and Abbey Choirs joining together in the last movement of the Brahms *Requiem*, *Selig sind die Toten*.

MN with Junior Abbey Choristers, 1990
(© *John Crook*)

The two great festivals of Easter and Christmas are very special and, along with the regular services of Choral Evensong and Choral Eucharist, provide the backbone of the Abbey's worship and the *raison d'être* of the choir. But the Abbey is unique in that it is often the scene of other special events including memorial services for public figures from the world of politics, the arts and entertainment. And for me many of them are especially memorable.

CHAPTER 16

Special services and events

"I wish to be imposed upon"

In my ten years at the Abbey, I must have been involved in at least two hundred "Special Services", ranging from relatively small-scale funerals to great national occasions, such as the Service of Thanksgiving for the life and work of Laurence Olivier OM. I regarded advising the families on the choice of music as an important part of my responsibilities. The repertoire would be discussed at a Special Service meeting and generally the discussions went smoothly. But at one point during a meeting for the Olivier Service, I felt the need to express my views quite strongly. I began by saying "I don't want to impose myself", to which Lady Olivier (Joan Plowright) immediately responded: "I wish to be imposed upon".

As the Dean, Michael Mayne, said in the Bidding, "exactly 84 years after Sir Henry Irving was buried in Poets' Corner, we come to honour the greatest actor of our time". The choice of music reflected the close links Lord Olivier had had with Sir William Walton, and the service began with London Brass playing, from the organ loft, the fanfare from Walton's film score for *Hamlet*. Then, during the processional hymn, nine items symbolic of Lord Olivier's life were carried by a glittering list of actors to the Sacrarium and laid on the High Altar. The actors included Douglas Fairbanks, Michael Caine, Maggie Smith, Paul Schofield, Derek Jacobi and Jean Simmons. The Choir sang Stanford's setting of Psalm 150 and Vaughan Williams's *Valiant-for-truth*, after which Dame Peggy Ashcroft read an extract from *Lycidas* by John Milton and Sir John Gielgud *Death be not proud* by John Donne. Sir Alec Guinness's delightful address was followed by an inspired improvisation by Andrew Lumsden on the Agincourt Song, before the recorded voice of Laurence Olivier was heard reading an extract from Act 4 of *Henry V*, which rose to a tremendous climax at "upon St Crispin's Day". All then joined in singing *Jerusalem*, during which the choir processed to the organ loft. After the prayers, the choristers sang two verses of Vaughan Williams's setting of *Dirge for Fidele*, from *Cymbeline*, accompanied on the harp by Jane Lister. Jane also played in Christopher Palmer's specially commissioned (and thrilling) arrangements of Walton's *Coronation Te Deum*, for choir, brass, organ and harp and *Crown Imperial*. Lord Olivier had been a chorister at All Saints Margaret Street, and it was there that he made his first stage appearance. In his autobiography, which included a reference to his final solo, "O Trinity, O Unity" from Stainer's *I saw the Lord*, he emphasised the extrovert qualities we still look for (in reasonable measure!) in choristers today.

I had become increasingly conscious that a relatively small proportion of the vast number of visitors to the Abbey were attending any of the sung services. And so, in 1990 I suggested to the Dean and Chapter that, twice a week, on Tuesdays and Thursdays, some of the Junior boys should sing for five minutes in the nave during their morning break. This also had the advantage of giving the new recruits a chance to sing in the Abbey, rather than their having to wait, sometimes for as long as a year, until there was a vacancy in the choir stalls. These "Weekday concerts at Westminster", as they were described in *The New York Times*, proved popular not only with the tourists, but also with the Abbey staff. Unfortunately, however, we had to stop the scheme in 1994, when the Abbey Choir School was being refurbished, and the choristers were staying overnight at a hotel off Gloucester Road. How the headmaster, staff and boys coped with that was pretty miraculous.

Another memorable special service celebrated the 150th anniversary of the British Deaf Association in 1991. Although most of the congregation were completely deaf, communication, thanks to the sign language of the 'leaders' standing on platforms around the Abbey, was amazingly good. An unforgettable moment was when the Abbey choristers joined the choir of the Royal School for Deaf Children in Margate to sing together.

Here is a description of the service, sent to me by Glyn Martin, one of the Honorary Stewards:

"This was not one of the great musical presentations of your time in charge but in every way, it was supremely memorable. The Abbey was packed with profoundly deaf people. The service was to have a short piece performed by a choir of 14 totally deaf children with their teacher playing the piano accompaniment. During the rehearsal it became obvious that this would not work, and you were called from the Song School for advice. There was a quick discussion, and you went back to the Song School and returned with the Abbey boys. They stood in an arc around the fourteen deaf children and sang from sight:

> *"Let there be peace on earth and let it begin with me,*
> *Let me walk with my neighbour in perfect harmony"*

The service itself was remarkable. The hymns and anthem were all translated into sign language by wonderfully skilled people with an expressiveness and grace which was quite new to me. As Dean Michael Mayne said in his book *Pray, Love, Remember:* "The deaf children sign the words and make what noise they can and are surrounded by our boy choristers who sing with them. The integration of able and disabled singing those words is especially poignant."

I was a steward in the North Transept with Brigadier Ian Gray, and at the end of the item by the deaf children and the Abbey boys I turned to Ian to find him wiping tears from his eyes. It was a memorable moment! So, there we are! There were many equally memorable days for me, but it is this which has stayed with me most strongly".

I could not help thinking of that verse from Psalm 137: "How shall we sing the Lord's song in a strange land?" and realizing how alien the world would be for the deaf, were it not for the courage of those afflicted and the work of the British Deaf Association.

At the Service of Thanksgiving for the Life and Work of Dame Margot Fonteyn de Arias in July 1991, there were five addresses, the final one by Dame Ninette de Valois. Before the Blessing, the Abbey Choir sang *In paradisum* from the Fauré *Requiem*, accompanied by the Orchestra of the Royal Opera House.

As at Winchester, my time at the Abbey coincided with several musical anniversaries, the first in 1991 being the 200th anniversary of the death of Mozart. The English Chamber Orchestra devoted their entire season of concerts at the Barbican to pieces composed in a particular year and the Abbey Choir was allocated 1774, when 17-year-old Mozart composed two beautiful Masses for choir, two violins and continuo. 1774 also yielded the *Bassoon Concerto* and *Symphony No 29 in A*, which I directed. I have to confess that it was somewhat daunting to discover that the previous concert in the series had been conducted by Sir Colin Davis.

There was a wide variety of music at the Service of Thanksgiving for the Life and Work of Dame Peggy Ashcroft in November 1991. Before the service, members of the Royal Shakespeare Theatre Band played music from productions of *The Wars of the Roses* and *All's well that ends well*, directed by former Abbey chorister, Guy Woolfenden, Director of Music at the Royal Shakespeare Company. These instrumentalists also accompanied the Abbey Choir in Guy's *Gloria in excelsis Deo*, from the RSC's 1970 production of *Henry VIII* in which Peggy Ashcroft played Queen Katherine. Julian Bream played an *Etude* by Villa-Lobos, which he had often performed at poetry readings with Dame Peggy. Then came an impassioned address, particularly about Peggy's concern for human rights, by Harold Pinter, a reading from *Cymbeline* ("Fear no more the heat o' the sun") and the second movement of Mozart's *Piano Concerto in C, K 467*, played exquisitely by Murray Perahia and the English Chamber Orchestra. A second address by Sir Peter Hall was followed by *Laudate Dominum* from the Mozart *Vespers*, with Felicity Lott as the soloist. After the prayers, which ended with the Abbey Choir singing William Harris's *Bring us, O Lord*, all remained seated for portraits of some of the Shakespearean heroines played by Dame Peggy as described by their counterparts. Following the hymn *Let all the world* (for which I had been encouraged to compose a descant) and the Blessing, Sir John Gielgud read an extract from *Antony and Cleopatra*, and "Our revels now are ended", from *The Tempest*.

Our next musical anniversary was in 1992, marking the centenary of the birth of Herbert Howells. Howells, or "Holy Herbert" as he was affectionately known by his contemporaries, was an unusually modest man. He would have been moved, and perhaps surprised, to discover that, to mark his Centenary, almost every Collegiate Chapel and Cathedral Choir in the UK sang one or more of his settings during the birthday weekend, 17 and 18 October. At Westminster Abbey, which towards the end of his life he came to regard as his spiritual home, the Dean and Chapter, in association with the Herbert Howells Society, presented the Herbert Howells Centenary Concert, including the world premières of three of his works which had been completed by Christopher Palmer: *Threnody* for cello and orchestra, *By the waters of Babylon*, for baritone, violin, cello and organ and *Michael* – A Fanfare setting. The programme opened with Hubert Parry's *Blest pair of Sirens*, and the second half was devoted to Howells's masterpiece, *Hymnus Paradisi*.

My own experience of Howells's music dates back to 1953, and singing *Behold, O God, our defender* at the Coronation of Queen Elizabeth II. As it happens, this anthem is the first work analysed by David Maw in his Introduction to *Paradox of an Establishment composer*. He writes: "If the muted tone and warm sound-world of the piece seem to manifest the respectability expected for such an occasion, they sit oddly with the ecstatic turn the music continually takes". Dr Maw's analysis of the harmonic sequences of the three clauses from Psalm 84, and how they are stretched, is complemented by his conclusion that there is also something "highly personal and emotionally raw". I very much agree. David Maw also refers to the orchestrated version used at the Coronation, which inevitably is rarely heard, but which represents Howells at the height of his powers, as does the sweeping phrase: "For one day in thy courts is better than a thousand".

As Patrick Russill, Director of Music at Brompton Oratory, has written, Howells's musical language "is simultaneously nostalgic and hopeful, personal and corporate. In addition to his uniquely evocative exploitation of voices in architectural space, Howells manages to encapsulate not just the ethos of the service, typically progressing from introversion to proclamation, but also to suggest the continuum of tradition – spiritual, cultural and musical – of which the worshipper is a part".

In *The Music of Herbert Howells*, edited by Phillip Cooke and David Maw, the impact of the heart-breaking death of his son, Michael, is also discussed perceptively, providing the most informed account we are likely to have of what actually happened. There is an intriguing chapter, 'Musical Cenotaph: Howells's *Hymnus Paradisi* and Sites of Mourning' in which Byron Adams suggests, supported by strong evidence from Howells's daughter, Ursula, that "in the process of trying to hold on to the memory of his son, Howells tended to idealise away any real and personal characteristics, so that *Michael* became a metaphor for the grief itself". Adams also acknowledges that investigating Howells's personal convictions can be unsettling to many who only know him as a composer of church music. In other words, the title of 'Holy Herbert' may be somewhat misleading.

It has become clear that many more of Howells's works were affected by the tragedy than had been previously appreciated, including the unfinished *Cello Concerto*. Howells continued to work on this concerto "for Mick" throughout his life – as he wrote to Arthur Bliss: "I keep pulling to pieces and remodelling". The scholar, Jonathan Clinch, has now completed (with invaluable advice from John Rutter) the last movement, of which Howells had left considerably more than previously thought; and fine recordings have been made by Guy Johnston and Alice Neary.

The Service of Thanksgiving for the life and work of Sir Geraint Evans had a distinctive Welsh flavour, two of the hymns being sung in Welsh, with which we were helped with phonetics by Welshman Tony Rees, of the Abbey's Chapter House. The main musical items however were extracts from operas, performed by the orchestra of the Royal Opera House. Bernard Haitink conducted *Tutto e disposto* from *Le Nozze di Figaro*, sung by Thomas Allen; Sir Georg Solti conducted the trio *Soave sia il vento*, with Amanda Roocroft, Anne Howells and Stafford Dean, and the Monologue from Verdi's *Falstaff*, with Bryn Terfel; Sir Colin Davis conducted Elizabeth's greeting from *Tannhäuser* with Dame Gwyneth Jones, who 'added an amazing descant in *Land of my fathers*, the quintet from *Die Meistersinger*, with Gywneth Jones, Elizabeth Bainbridge, Arthur Davies, Ryland Davies and Gwynne Howell, and *Wach Auf*; and Sir Edward Downes conducted *Una Furtiva Lagrima* from *L'elisir d'amore*, sung by Dennis O'Neill. Understandably, the Abbey Choir's contribution was smaller than usual, namely the Croft *Burial Sentences* in procession, and, after the Blessing, Benjamin Britten's *Antiphon*, "Praised be the God of love". With three boy-angels singing from the organ loft, this made quite an impression, not least on Sir Georg Solti, who asked: "Ven did he wrote it?", and Jeremy Isaacs, the General Director of the Royal Opera House, who kindly invited the choristers to go to an opera. Subsequently they much enjoyed going to Covent Garden and seeing *Turandot*.

Among other moving services, I must mention one in 1991, after the invasion of Iraq by the USA and its allies, including Great Britain. The BBC decided not to transmit their pre-recorded *Songs of Praise* on the next Sunday but asked if they might broadcast a live edition from the Abbey. The Westminster Christian Council Service (part of the Week of Prayer for Christian Unity), planned for that Sunday was transferred from the Central Hall to the Abbey, and the large congregation encompassed many different faiths and denominations. During the intercessions, the Abbey Choir sang the *Sanctus* from Walton's *Missa brevis* and a short Taizé chant to the words of the *Kyrie*. The whole service was bound together in a most remarkable way by the presenter, Dr Colin Morris, who voiced strongly, both in the Abbey and through the medium of television, people's pent-up feelings on that first weekend of the war.

In February 1993, there was a Service of Thanksgiving for the life of Sir Kenneth MacMillan. Afterwards, I received a very appreciative letter from Peter Brownlee, General Manager of the Royal Ballet, singling out the "angelic voice of Simon de Baat", who sang the *Pie Jesu* solo from the Fauré *Requiem*, accompanied by the Royal Ballet Sinfonia. The choir's main contribution was the opening movements of Britten's *Rejoice in the Lamb*.

Evensong on the Feast of the Annunciation, 25 March 1993, was followed by the Dedication of a Memorial to Anthony Trollope: Novelist, Public Servant, Pioneer of the Postal Services and the Creator of Barsetshire. At Evensong we sang the *Magnificat and Nunc dimittis in D minor* by Trollope's contemporary, Thomas Walmisley, and Robert Parsons's *Ave Maria*. At the Dedication, attended by the Prime Minister, John Major, who had been a strong supporter of the Memorial, the readings by Victoria Glendinning and Jack May included an account of Trollope's fictional Mr Harding attending a service in Westminster Abbey and not being very inspired. They also described the final years of Mr Harding's life, and how "in his last weeks, he would sometimes open his cello case and pass his fingers over the strings, producing a single sad sound. In earlier, happier times he had played his beloved cello daily to anyone who would listen, and sometimes to no-one at all". At this point, our daughter, Alice, played the *Allemande* from Bach's *4th Cello Suite in E flat major*. I cannot help having been biased, but it was very reassuring to hear the Prime Minister tell Alice at the reception afterwards how he had been nervous for her beforehand, but as soon as she started playing, he relaxed.

With the blessing of the Dean, we had a number of special services which showed these were no longer confined to royalty, senior parliamentarians, high achievers in the arts or other senior dignitaries.

The first, on 28 June 1993, was the Service of Thanksgiving for the Life of Bobby Moore, Captain of the winning English Football team in the World Cup, 1966. As Michael Parkinson wrote in his column in the *Daily Telegraph*: "When we gathered at Westminster Abbey to pay tribute to Bobby Moore, it was only the second time in the Abbey's history that there had been a thanksgiving service for an athlete. You could win some money on who the other one was. I said W G Grace, C B Fry, Jack Hobbs. The answer was the West Indian cricketer, Sir Frank Worrell". The service was attended by an astonishing number of former English sporting stars, including Sir Bobby Charlton who gave one of the addresses – the other was by the comedian

Jimmy Tarbuck, an ardent cricket fan. The choir's main contributions were the Croft *Burial Sentences* and Mendelssohn's *O for the wings of a dove*.

In February 1994, there was another Thanksgiving Service which broke new ground – a service commemorating the life of the comedian, Les Dawson. It began with the Croft *Burial Sentences* leading into the Bidding, in which the Dean caught the spirit of the occasion, remembering Les Dawson's sense of fun and his hatred of rehearsals, and ending with verse 2 of Psalm 126: 'Then was our mouth filled with laughter, and our tongue with joy'. The Order of Service included the following note: "Members of the congregation are asked to understand that extensive maintenance is being carried out on the organ, and therefore only part of the instrument can be used at today's Service". So, it was very helpful to have an orchestra, consisting mainly of musicians who, before the Service, played a number of pieces from Les Dawson's television series.

In May there was a Service of Celebration of the Life of Brian Johnston, the cricket commentator. I could hardly believe my luck when, before the Service, I found myself escorting my childhood cricket hero, Denis Compton (on crutches after a hip operation), and having one of my most prized conversations on the long walk to the Abbey quire. Nearly everyone was complimentary about the singing and in particular about the treble soloist in *O for the wings of a dove*. Christopher Martin-Jenkins, the distinguished Test Match Special commentator and journalist, said he thought singing a solo in front of such a gathering would have been more nerve-wracking than opening the batting in a Test Match. I have to confess however that the first words Brian's widow, Pauline, said to me after the service were: "You gave us the wrong tune for 'All things bright and beautiful'. The tune on the service paper was *Royal Oak*, whereas Pauline had been expecting the traditional tune by W. H. Monk.

In July 1994, there was a Memorial Service for John Smith, the Leader of Her Majesty's Opposition, who had died suddenly of a heart attack. The service reflected not only John Smith's integrity but also his devout faith, and there was a simple response (from the Iona Community) "Watch, watch and pray, Jesus will keep to his word" for everyone to sing between the prayers; however, as *The Times* reported, the "solemnity of the tribute was leavened by the Grimethorpe Colliery Band playing with gusto before and after the Service – including, at the end, the Processional Music from *Lohengrin*. It was one of the most moving services in my time – a day when, as reported in the

Evening Standard, "Westminster forgot politics and remembered John Smith". For the Introit we sang Vaughan Williams's *O taste and see* and, as an anthem, his *Valiant-for-truth*.

A month later, there was another historic event in the Abbey, namely a Service to welcome South Africa back into the Commonwealth. The service did not gloss over the issue of apartheid, nor the evil it had perpetrated. The South African actor, Janet Suzman, read an extract from Alan Paton's *Cry the beloved country*, Bishop Trevor Huddleston led the Prayers of thanksgiving, and the inspiring, heart-rending address was given by Archbishop Desmond Tutu. I was very keen that some traditional music from South Africa be included. In the event there was a moving contribution from the Elite Swingsters, who were flown over specially from Soweto to perform a Peace Song (which, due to a misprint in a fax, emerged on the service paper as a 'Peach Song') and the two South African National Anthems, *Uit die blou van onse hemel* and *Nkosi Sikelel' iAfrika*. These were sung by the Abbey Choir in their original languages of Afrikans and Xhosa respectively. To say that the pronunciation was challenging would be an understatement, but we were greatly helped by the famous journalist, Donald Woods, whose exposure of Steve Biko's death and his own escape from South Africa were the subject of the film *Cry Freedom*. The Abbey Choir sang Handel's *Let their celestial concerts all unite*, and the unexpected highlight was the spontaneous applause after Chief Emeka Anyaoku, the Commonwealth Secretary-General, received the new South African flag from the Deputy President and placed it among the other flags of the Commonwealth.

On, 5 December 1994, we marked the 150th anniversary of the birth of Sir Frederick Bridge (Abbey Organist from 1882 to 1918), with a special Evensong, attended by several of his descendants, among them some of the John Stainer family who were related. Bridge directed the music at two Coronations: of Edward VII in 1902 and of George V in 1911, the first of which, like the Coronation of King Charles III, took place more than 50 years after the previous one.

I cannot remember how we received the invitation to sing at the Naming Ceremony of the cruise ship *Oriana*, but I do know that as a result the Abbey received a substantial donation towards the costs of the Choir School refurbishment. The boys certainly enjoyed the experience of sleeping on board, although it was disappointing that the planned early morning trip around the Isle of Wight had to be abandoned because of bad weather. The singing duties, although unusual, were not too onerous. On the Tuesday evening the choir sang a grace before dinner; then on the Wednesday morning at the Naming Ceremony we sang John Hilton's madrigal, *Fair Oriana*. For the rest of the music, we were accompanied by the Band of the Royal Marines; the choir was some distance from the band which made things tricky. Nonetheless, Vaughan Williams's *O clap your hands* seemed to go down well, and as Her Majesty passed by on her way out, she said, "We do meet on some extraordinary occasions!"

During dinner aboard the *Oriana*, Major Michael Parker, who was in charge of the forthcoming VE Day Celebrations, asked if it might be possible for the Abbey Choir to take part in the Opening Ceremony in Hyde Park on 8 May 1995. I undertook to explore this with the Dean and Chapter, who readily agreed. The main questions to be resolved were what we should sing and with what accompaniment. This turned out to be a massed tri-Service Band of 150 plus 60 Mounted Band and, to overcome balance problems, the choir was amplified. We sang the National Anthem, the hymns *O worship the King* and *O God, our help in ages past* and Douglas Guest's setting of *For the fallen*.

In July 1995 the choir sang at the Service of Thanksgiving for the former Prime Minister, Lord Wilson of Rievaulx. His family were very musical, and at the Special Service meeting, attended by Lady Wilson, her daughter-in-law, Joy Crispin-Wilson and Lady Falkender (Marcia Williams), produced a list of suggestions and requests. Including some Sullivan was a "must"; Lady Wilson told me later that his favourite opera was *Iolanthe*, whose words as well as music he particularly relished, especially "The House of Lords throughout the war did nothing in particular and did it very well!" The family also were keen that the Wilson's twin granddaughters, Jennifer and Catherine should take part, possibly singing a duet, such as Mendelssohn's *I waited for the Lord*, with the Abbey Choir. These and other musical matters were discussed, but not completely resolved at the Special Service meeting, the minutes of which noted that "a final decision on musical elements would affect the order of the service and would be left to the Abbey authorities". The main issue was the participation of Jennifer and Catherine, and so I arranged to have a private session with them in the Abbey, behind closed doors, to see what might work best. My inclination was to find a spot in the service where they could sing a duet on their own, standing in front of the Sacrarium. This experiment worked well, and we decided on a short duet by Richard Dering, *Gaudent in coelis*, which I accompanied on the chamber organ. Catherine and Jennifer's beautiful singing impressed everybody, including Prince Charles, who made a point of telling Lady Wilson that he did not know how her granddaughters could have done it. This was not the first time that the Prince of Wales had expressed both his pleasure and astonishment at the way young singers had coped with solos on big national occasions. Jennifer and Catherine's contribution was greatly appreciated, as was Christopher Robinson's organ playing before the service of the *Overture, In Memoriam* by Arthur Sullivan.

Of all the anniversaries which were marked in 1995, one of the most poignant was the 75th anniversary of the laying to rest of The Unknown Warrior on 11 November 1920. In the presence of the family of the Rev'd David Railton CF MC, who conceived the original idea, the choir sang Douglas Guest's *For the fallen*. David's daughter, Dame Ruth Railton, founder of the National Youth Orchestra, became a great fan of the choir. Besides those who died in the war, innocent victims were also remembered, and to reflect the multi-religious traditions of our visitors, the Dean and Chapter commissioned a work from John Tavener, *Innocence*, for which he used Jewish, Muslim and Hindu as well as Christian texts. The 25-minute piece, scored for soprano, tenor, bass, choir, cello, organ and bells, which received its premiere on 10 October, was also the principal work on the choir's Tavener recording, about which the *Gramophone* critic wrote: "If I had to recommend a single disc to convince anyone of the mastery of John Tavener, this would be it".

On 19 October 1995 there was a Service of Thanksgiving to celebrate the completion of the Restoration of Westminster Abbey. Ten minutes before the service, the Choir began a procession from the Lady Chapel to the West End, singing the *Te Deum* in Latin to plainchant. The service included the unveiling by the Queen of the new west window of the Lady Chapel. This was followed by the choir singing, from the Shrine of St Edward, John Tavener's *Hymn to the Mother of God*. We then moved back to the Quire stalls to sing Psalm 122 ('I was glad when they said unto me'), to the marvellous chant for double choir by Walter Parratt, and after a Prayer of Rededication, the final section of Edward Bairstow's anthem, *Blessed City*: *To this Temple, where we call thee*.

All choristers know just how much time is consumed with extra practices in the run-up to Christmas. During my years at Westminster Abbey, I was often asked in radio or TV interviews how the choristers coped with all the music to be learnt. So, on one occasion I took along a chorister, Philip Stopford (later a Cathedral Organist) to speak, unscripted, on behalf of the 'workers'. To the first question, "Don't you get bored, learning and singing so much music at this time of year?" he replied: "No, as long as it's not *bad music*".

"And what constitutes *bad* music?"

"Well … anything before Handel!"

The chorister's reaction was not untypical, but I like to think that, by the time he left the Abbey Choir, he had begun to take more seriously Handel's own verdict on one of his greatest predecessors at the Chapel Royal. After receiving congratulations on one of his oratorios, Handel responded: "If Purcell had lived, he would have composed better music than that". The eighteenth-century historian Charles Burney went further: "Purcell is as much the pride of an Englishman in music as Shakespeare in productions of the stage". Perhaps it was as well that the chorister who made the remarks about "bad music" had left the choir before 1995, when we marked the 300th anniversary of Purcell's death in a series of services and concerts. This began with a televised programme on 5 March – the 300th anniversary of the funeral of Queen Mary in 1695. The first half included music from the Coronation of William and Mary in 1689 and the Birthday Ode: *Now does the glorious day appear*, written for the Queen. We were joined by the New London Consort and a fabulous group of soloists, Emma Kirkby, Evelyn Tubb, Michael Chance, Ian Bostridge, Stephen Richardson and Simon Birchall. The second half was devoted to music performed at Queen Mary's Funeral, including marches by Thomas Tollett and James Paisible, which were played on Flatt Trumpets in procession.

Then on 30 June, as part of BBC Radio 3's *Fairest Isle* season, we gave a recital, *Purcell and the Abbey Line*, dating back to the 14th-century *Litlyngton Missal* and the plainchant antiphon *Unxerunt Salomonem Sadoc Sacerdos*, and the *Sanctus* and *Benedictus* by John Tyes (Master of the Lady Chapel Choir 1399–1402). The Golden Age was represented by Robert White's *Christe qui lux es et dies*, Edmund Hooper's *Behold, it is Christ* and Orlando Gibbons's *Organ Fantasia in A minor* and the eight-part *O clap your hands*.

From the Restoration era came Henry Lawes's setting of *Zadok the Priest* (which, understandably, has rather disappeared since being superseded by Handel's incomparable version for the Coronation of George II in 1727). On the other hand, there were impressive settings by John Blow, such as *God is our hope and strength*, which were a revelation. To my mind however, it was once again anthems by Purcell, *They that go down to the sea in ships*, with its virtuoso bass solo, splendidly sung by Simon Birchall, and the eight part *O Lord God of Hosts* with its beautiful verse sections, which stole the show.

The celebrations reached their climax on 21 November with a Purcell 300 event for which the BBC used three separate areas of the Abbey for the performers and audience. The ambitious programme, designed by Nicholas Kenyon, Controller of Radio 3, had some surprises, and I remember being taken aback to discover that Nick was planning to include Elgar's orchestral arrangement of Purcell's *Jehovah, quam multi sunt hostes*. Nick stuck to his guns, and after I had asked him if Elgar had kept Purcell's original harmonies and dissonances at *Ego cubui*, he proudly produced a score which showed that he had. This was splendidly performed in the nave by the BBC Symphony and Chorus, conducted by Andrew Davis, who also directed Britten's *Young Person's Guide to the Orchestra* – the *Rondeau* in the original version having already been played by the New London Consort in front of the High Altar. They also accompanied the Abbey Choir in Purcell's Coronation anthem *My heart is inditing*, and I conducted Handel's *Zadok the Priest*. There were two premieres, the first being Michael Tippett's *Song for Caliban*, with Andrew Davis directing the Nash Ensemble in the South Transept. In totally different ways the opening and closing settings also made their mark, Jonathan Dove's *Fairest Isle Fanfare* abounding in Purcell quotations. Tess Knighton in *The Times* considered that "perhaps the crowning glory was James Bowman's powerful account of Purcell's *Evening Hymn*". After all the musical excitements, I found the single line of the bass violinist, Catherine Finnis, as she played the introduction and then James's beautiful entry so moving, that I could barely play the organ continuo.

There was little time to linger, as on the following morning we had the Festival of Saint Cecilia Service organised by the Musicians Benevolent Fund (now called Help Musicians). Since 1990, when St Sepulchre's, Holborn had been declared unsafe, the annual service had been held in turn at Westminster Cathedral, St Paul's Cathedral and Westminster Abbey, and sung by the three choirs. In 1995 we were joined by the Chapel Royal Choir and by the Royal College of Music Baroque Orchestra. The service began with Purcell's setting of Psalm 122, *I was glad*, sung by the Abbey Choir in the nave in front of the screen. There were two other anthems by Purcell, *Blow up the trumpet* and *O God, thou art my God*, and after the address by the Reverend Professor Henry Chadwick, the orchestra played Purcell's *Chacony in G minor* as a procession moved through the North Lantern to the grave of Henry and Frances Purcell. There Sir David Willcocks (chairman of the Council of the Musicians Benevolent Fund) laid a wreath under the Memorial on which is engraved: "Here lyes Henry Purcell Esq. Who left this Life, And is gone to that Blessed Place Where only his Harmony can be exceeded". The Gentlemen and Children of the Chapel Royal then sang *Thou knowest, Lord* – which we now know Purcell wrote for Queen Mary's funeral, and after the Intercessions all the musical forces joined together for Purcell's *Te Deum*, including the wonderfully expressive counter-tenor solo, "Vouchsafe, O Lord", movingly sung by Simon Gay. This was the only Musicians Benevolent Fund service in my time that did not include a new commission. In 1989 we premiered Jonathan Harvey's *Thou mastering me God*, and in 1992 John Tavener's *Annunciation*.

Henry Purcell's memorial on a pillar above his grave in the 'Musicians' Aisle'(© Dean and Chapter of Westminster).

Speaking of premieres, I also initiated a series of commissions for the Abbey Eucharist, starting with Francis Grier's *Missa Trinitatis* followed by masses by Jeffrey Lewis, Bryan Kelly and Jonathan Harvey. We included Francis's *Mass* on a CD, *Millennium*, and after I had left the Abbey, James O'Donnell directed a superb recording of Jonathan's *Mass*. Not surprisingly this was the most adventurous of the new settings. And there were more in the pipeline.

Encouraged by the Dean, we tried to ensure that services of thanksgiving reflected the personal qualities and tastes of the person for whose life we were giving thanks, while at the same time retaining a degree of dignity appropriate to the Abbey. The service for Lord Home of the Hirsel (Prime Minister 1963–4) in January 1996 seemed to me to capture the warmth and integrity, which had shone throughout his life. On the first page of the Order of Service, there was a quotation from Cyril Alington, Elizabeth Home's father: "We live in two worlds already, and the less visible is not further from us than the visible. Indeed, every act of pure love, every kind word, every thought of good belongs to both worlds. They have an undying and eternal worth; even if we forget them, God does not; they proceed from and belong to His own world, His own spirit." This set the mood for the whole service, and after the choir had sung the first 12 verses of Psalm 139, *O Lord, thou hast searched me out and known me*, the Prime Minister, John Major, read extracts from Lord Home's autobiography, affirming the strength of his Christian faith. Among the letters of thanks after the service, I particularly treasure those from Lord Home's son, David, and from Lady Wilson of Rievaulx.

The year 1996 saw the 70th anniversary of the BBC's *Choral Evensong*, which was first broadcast from Westminster Abbey on Thursday, 7 October 1926 on the National Programme. Choral Evensong eventually moved to the Home Service and then switched to Radio 3. Only the Sunday appeal, *This Week's Good Cause*, had been running longer (by just a few months). The records showed that among the choristers who sang at the first broadcast and who were still alive in 1996 were Harry Abbott, Wilfred Chappell, John Cruft, and Edgar Alder. The service opened with an Introit, composed by the BBC producer, the late James Whitbourn: *Glory to thee, O Lord* – part of the opening prayer of the Byzantine daily office. In former years, Evensong was broadcast every Thursday from the Abbey, and David Willcocks who attended the Choir School from 1929 to 1934, used to tell the story of how, after the Dean had finished reading the Second Lesson and before the choir sang the *Nunc dimittis*, he would make a loud cough so that his mother in Cornwall would know that he was all right.

The Service of Inauguration of a Memorial Stone to Innocent Victims, outside the West door of the Abbey, commemorated the many victims of violence and war. The opening hymn sung to *Eventide* (the tune associated with *Abide with me*) was a translation by Alan Gaunt of words set by Dietrich Bonhoeffer, the German Evangelical pastor and theologian, who was hanged by the Nazis in April 1945, just 21 days before Hitler committed suicide. After the Address by the Dean, the choir sang *O vos omnes* by Pablo Casals to the text from Lamentations: "Is it nothing to you, all you that pass by? Behold and see if there be any sorrow like unto my sorrow". The service also included part of Psalm 10 to plainchant, and after Her Majesty and His Royal Highness the Duke of Edinburgh had laid a wreath of white flowers at the memorial stone, the choristers sang *A Litany to the Holy Spirit* by Peter Hurford.

On 11 November 1996 Evensong included *Stanford in G* and Balfour Gardiner's *Te lucis ante terminum*, and was followed by the Unveiling and Dedication of a Memorial to Sir John Betjeman. At the Dedication, apart from the hymn *The day thou gavest*, the repertoire was less conventional. After the Blessing, the Abbey boys sang a short setting of a verse from John Betjeman's 'Christmas' beginning *'No love that in a family dwells'*, which I had composed over Christmas 1961, when an undergraduate. By chance, I had kept the one and only copy, so nearly 35 years later, it received its first performance! I was rather relieved to receive an appreciative letter from Prebendary John Gaskell about the setting, as the choice of music at the dedication had been a matter of some dispute – I had resisted pressure from Mervyn Horder, who had proposed one of his own Betjeman settings. One reason for John Gaskell's approval was the choice of text, "which brought out John as a believer". However, we went along with the request for the outgoing organ voluntary to include a medley of "appropriate melodies" much loved by Sir John.

In February 1997, the Service of Thanksgiving for the life and work of Douglas Guest, Organist and Master of the Choristers 1963–81 and Organist Emeritus, was attended by many of Douglas's colleagues and former choristers, some dating back to his time as Organist of Salisbury and Worcester Cathedrals. Before the service, Christopher Robinson played the *Allegretto* from Elgar's *Sonata in G* and at the end Stephen Cleobury played Bach's *Fantasia in G* and the *Allegro con brio* from Mendelssohn's *Fourth Sonata*. Two works by Douglas were sung by the Abbey Choir: the Introit (sung in the Nave) was the beautiful *Sanctus* from his comparatively unknown *Missa brevis Sarisburiensis*. It made a great impression, and several choir directors, including Richard Seal, Organist of Salisbury Cathedral, asked to see a copy. We also sang *For the fallen* composed in 1971 for the annual Service of Remembrance to words by Laurence Binyon. The Abbey choristers clearly remembered him fondly, and I liked hearing that at his first choir practice, he told the boys that any misbehaviour would result in a "reign of terror, which would make the French Revolution look like a children's tea party". The boys quickly got the message and soon grew to respect and feel genuine affection for him – indeed at his last service several were in tears. In his address, as well as praising Douglas for all he achieved at the Abbey, including directing the music at the State Funeral of Earl Mountbatten, Sir David Willcocks also spoke warmly about Douglas's contribution in the wider field of music, and not least to the National Youth Orchestra. He was much respected by the choral societies he directed, even when he was moved to say on at least one occasion: "To think the public is being asked to pay money for this!" He had high standards, and I knew it was high praise when, after a performance I had directed of *Ye now are sorrowful* from the Brahms *Requiem*, with head chorister, Joe Crouch, the outstanding soloist, he commented: "Just as I would have done it."

In 1997 there had also been some thrilling concerts, including a performance of Handel's *Jephtha*, which raised £29,000 for the Handel House Museum. Then on Sunday, 17 August, as part of the BBC's Benjamin Britten weekend, the boys interrupted their summer holiday and took part in two Proms at the Albert Hall on the same day – is this a record? The afternoon concert opened with *A Ceremony of Carols*, and after a superb performance of the solo oboe piece, *Metamorphoses after Ovid*, by Nicholas Daniel, the whole choir, with Martin Baker brilliant at the organ (making it sound brighter and clearer than one thought possible) sang *Hymn to St Peter, Hymn to the Virgin* and *Rejoice in the Lamb*. Then in the evening the boys sang from high in the gallery in Britten's *War Requiem* with the BBC Symphony Orchestra and other choirs conducted by Andrew Davis.

At the Abbey I was thrilled when the Dean and Chapter agreed that a service in memory of Denis Compton, my cricketing hero from childhood, could be held there in July 1997. I did wonder however what the musical requests might be. At the planning meeting I asked Denis's widow, Denise, if there was any specific music she would like and she replied: "Could there

Special services and events

be something by Whitney Houston?" We did not manage that, but after the Blessing, the choir sang *Pie Jesu* from Andrew Lloyd Webber's *Requiem* which seemed to be much appreciated. The boys were delighted to receive an invitation to watch some cricket at Lord's, which they did (including a visit to the Pavilion) when they came back in the middle of August to sing at the two Proms. The address was given by Compton's one-time Middlesex teammate, J J Warr, who produced some delightful anecdotes, such as Denis's CBE medal having been last seen round the neck of his Old English sheepdog.

On 6 September 1997, the funeral of Diana, Princess of Wales was seen by several billion people round the world. It was the highest-profile service during my time as Organist. The story of how it was planned in less than a week after she was tragically killed in a car crash in Paris, illustrates how the Abbey has to hold itself ready for any eventuality. It shows how the Abbey's long experience of dealing with such events makes it unique. I was heavily involved in the planning and was responsible for organising the music. It was a huge privilege, and I have often been asked if I was nervous or panicky. My usual answer is that there was simply no time to panic; one just had to get on with it *(see Chapter 17)*.

Before the summer break in 1997, plans for the Golden Wedding anniversary service of Queen Elizabeth and Prince Philip on 20 November had been taking shape. Over a period of months there were several alterations reflecting the wishes of the Queen and Prince Philip, who had clearly considered the service in great detail. Compared with other royal services, much of the music was their personal choice, including two hymns sung at their wedding in 1947 and Benjamin Britten's *Jubilate*, composed at the request of Prince Philip. But, because of the death of Princess Diana, it was clear that the format would need some adjusting. The Intercessions were expanded, one of the most moving moments being a prayer "for those for whom this thanksgiving occasions sorrow, as we remember with gratitude the life of Diana, Princess of Wales".

It was also decided that the Abbey Choir should sing a short anthem while the Archbishop of Canterbury gave a private blessing to the Queen and Prince Philip. On such occasions it is customary for the Abbey Organist to write a new work, so during the preceding summer, while on holiday in Dorset, I selected some familiar words from the Anglican hymnal, *May the grace of Christ our Saviour*. My aim was to compose a setting which would complement what was happening in the liturgy but not be too predictable.

I wanted to find a simple rhythm, which felt natural for the words without being four-square, and this led me to a 7/4 meter. The four-line structure is quite simple, although in the soprano part the second half of the tune is almost a replica in inversion of the first two lines. I called the tune 'Studland'. I realise now that the rhythmic pattern is quite similar to a passage in Manuel de Falla's *El amor brujo*, which had made a great impression when I heard it at Tanglewood in 1963.

There was a strong desire for less pomp, and it was decided that, at the end, William Walton's *Coronation Te Deum* would be replaced by the *National Anthem*, during which the Queen and Prince Philip would process to the West End. But how was this going to work? The plan was for them to reach the Nave at the beginning of verse 2, but as verse 1 was not long enough, I was charged with writing a short interlude for brass, leading into verse 2 and a new descant. But this was still not long enough for the royal party to reach the West Door, so I made an arrangement for brass and organ of Handel's *March from Scipio*. Despite the sad memory of Princess Diana's funeral, the service turned out to be a joyful and heart-warming occasion – a lovely touch being the way other couples, representing all those celebrating their 50th wedding anniversary in 1997, were invited.

The Service of Thanksgiving for Sir Georg Solti in March 1998 brought together a host of outstanding singers, instrumentalists and conductors with whom he had made music. Once again, there was a considerable discussion about the musical content, and not least about where to place the instrumentalists; but the final choice of guest musicians could hardly have been bettered. Matthias Goerne sang Mozart's *Mentre ti lascio*, Dame Kiri Te Kanawa sang *Morgen* by Richard Strauss, while three stars from the Royal Opera House, Sarah Walker, Robert Tear and Gwynne Howell, were the soloists in the *Gloria* from Kodaly's *Missa Brevis*, Lady Solti having been very keen to have some Hungarian music played or sung. It was thrilling to have the Abbey Choir augmented by singers from London Voices, and I could not remember ever hearing a louder choral sound at the Abbey. The music after the Blessing was also memorable, when all the forces plus a goodly number of Sir Georg's family and colleagues, joined together for the triumphant final chorale from Bach's *St John Passion*. Valerie Solti was most appreciative of what she was kind enough to call "a sublime triumph". Little did I realise that this would be my last major service as Organist and Master of the Choristers.

Special services and events

Sir David Willcocks presented the Willcocks medal
to Chorister Alexander Wall, 1992.

CHAPTER 17

Funeral of Diana, Princess of Wales

None of us can ever say again: "We don't do that sort of music here!"

On Sunday 31 August 1997, Diana, Princess of Wales, was killed in a car crash in Paris. News of her death went round the world in seconds and triggered a state of mourning in Britain unlike anything seen in our lifetime. It reached its climax a week later with Diana's funeral in the Abbey on 6 September. For senior members of the Royal Family, draft arrangements for their funerals are prepared well in advance of the event. But for Diana, nothing had been prepared. Apart from her being so young and healthy, she was no longer strictly a member of the Royal Family since her divorce from the Prince of Wales. Nevertheless, that Sunday I began to think of what music might be requested, should the decision be taken in favour of an Abbey funeral.

I watched on TV the Prime Minister, Tony Blair's, moving tribute to the 'People's Princess' and became convinced that the music at the service should somehow reflect this. Was there anything written in the 1990s which might be suitable? In the early afternoon I phoned John Tavener to ask which of his pieces might be worth considering should the families agree to something of his. John's music has a spirituality and yet an approachability, which seemed to me to be as ideal as we could find. I talked to him about *The Lamb* and said in passing that it was a pity that *Song for Athene* was not shorter. He said that, strangely enough, he had been wondering whether he dared to ring me as the idea of *Song for Athene* had also occurred to him. I asked him to hold on while I looked at the text. It was perfect, opening with the Hamlet quotation, "May flights of Angels sing thee to thy rest" and including "Give rest, O Lord, to your handmaiden who has fallen asleep" from the Orthodox funeral service.

The next day, Monday, I was informed by the Receiver General that the service would be held in the Abbey in five days' time, the following Saturday. I received many telephone calls, not only from choir parents, wondering if their boys would be needed, but also from numerous others, offering their services – singers, composers, and members of the public with musical suggestions. I took the view that we would only decide about the choir when we had a clearer idea of what was going to be sung.

By lunchtime the guidelines for the service had been established and I asked the school secretary, Helen Ingmire, to recall the boys from their holidays. I decided to take the risk of not inviting the three boys who had left the school the previous month, although they would have undoubtedly made a great contribution. They would all have started at their new schools by the day of the funeral and if they came we would have had to exclude some of the younger boys from that year's choir, which would have been hard. But it was not an easy decision. The Press were already putting it about that Elton John would be singing, although at this stage this had not yet been agreed. In fact Elton and I had several conversations that day and I told him that whether he took part would depend a lot on what he proposed to sing. *Candle in the Wind* was completely unknown to me but I felt that, as the lyrics were written in memory of Marilyn Monroe, that would rule it out. I asked him if he could sing a different song or perhaps write some more appropriate new lyrics for *Candle in the Wind*. Within six hours Elton's lyricist in California, Bernie Taupin, had faxed over *Goodbye England's Rose*. Having been dubious at first, I began to feel quite strongly that unless something like this were included, the service would fail to reflect the personality of the Princess or to meet the needs of vast numbers of people.

The next day, Tuesday, there was a special meeting of the Abbey's Lay Chapter at which it was decided that the organ recital scheduled for that night would have to be transferred to St Margaret's because of the preparations in the Abbey by the BBC and ITV. Unfortunately I missed the recital because of a lengthy telephone conversation with Princess Diana's sister, Lady Sarah McCorquodale who told me she had been "put in charge of the music" by the Spencer family. We discussed in detail the organ music before the service, about which she had strong views, and I promised to include as much as possible. I put forward Tavener's *Song for Athene* as the final piece in the service, but she needed convincing. Later that evening I received a summons to the Deanery, where I also found the Precentor, Barry Fenton. As the deadline for printing the service paper drew closer we put together our recommendations for the Dean to refer back to the Palace, including the newly revised *Candle in the Wind*.

By Wednesday lunchtime everything, including the Tavener and Elton John, had been agreed by the two families, but we were being asked to find room also for something from the Verdi *Requiem*. I listened to a recording at the Deanery, and we wondered whether the *Libera Me* would be possible, though with organ, of course, not orchestra (The Royal Philharmonic Orchestra had offered their services earlier in the week but there was not room for them). In any case our brilliant Sub-Organist, Martin Baker, who was still in the USA on holiday, would be able to play an organ transcription of it if anyone could. The Dean asked: "Where do we put it, Martin?" and I replied: "between the two readings by Princess Diana's sisters".

Lynne Dawson was my first choice for the soprano solo, and her husband got a message to her in Berlin where she was singing Pamina at the Staatsoper. She rang me, apparently in a state of shock, but said she could do it and would be back on Friday morning, the day before the funeral. We discussed the extract and the fact that we were cutting out 120 bars. To my relief no one castigated me for this later. Inserting the Verdi between the two readings brought a different dimension to the service, moving it on from the strictly liturgical Anglican tradition to something more dramatic, and so paving the way for what might be the controversial appearance by Elton John. I telephoned Stephen Ashley King, manager, of the BBC Singers, who were broadcasting choral evensong at St Brides, Fleet Street that afternoon. He quickly asked the singers whether they could sing at the Saturday service and the Friday rehearsal and was able to ring me back within a couple of hours to confirm that most of them could. I realised that, given their presence in the organ loft for the Verdi, we could also use them in the Tavener *Song for Athene*, antiphonally with the Abbey Choir in the stalls. That evening all twenty-four boys, including Jonathan Kirk and Sebastian Roberts who had flown back from Brazil and Canada respectively, were back in the school by 6:30pm.

I began our Song School rehearsal that evening by asking the boys to think clearly about how they would feel if their mother had died, Prince Harry being the same age as some of them, adding how important it was that we did all we could to make the music as good as possible both out of respect for Princess Diana and also to try to help the millions who were mourning her death. We sang through most of the items apart from *Make me a Channel of your Peace*, the arrangement of which had yet to be written. Mercifully the boys remembered the Croft *Burial Sentences* better than I had expected, and all except Sebastian were in good voice.

On the following morning, Thursday, Sebastian still had a terrible cough, and we called in the school doctor, after which I decided, most reluctantly, that he would not be well enough to sing at the service. I had had an early start as I had to write the arrangement of *Make me a Channel of Thy Peace* for the boys to begin learning at the 9.00am Song School practice. At the end of this we tried out the sentences in procession in the Abbey, having already walked it in time around the stalls in the Song School. This would be essential if we were to keep together. The boys found it somewhat amusing. Because poor Sebastian would not be able to sing at the funeral, we managed to track down the mother of another boy, Jack Knight. She took the call while she was shopping and quickly drove him to the Abbey. For a boy who had only been at the School since January, he did extremely well, but I decided to put him close to where I would be standing. Meanwhile the headmaster and staff had taken the boys swimming. While they were away, I went to Church House to sit in on a press conference at which everyone was given an advanced draft copy of the Order of Service. There were questions as to why no member of the royal family was taking part and why Elton John was. The Dean responded quickly: "Because I invited him". Back to the Abbey for the 5.00pm full choir rehearsal, which included walking the course for the sake of the BBC. I ran into Tom Fleming, who would be commentating in the Abbey for the BBC and who came round to our house to discuss the service. Throughout the day there had been many more phone calls, offers of help and requests for interviews, and we had a problem, quickly resolved, of finding a hotel for Lynne Dawson.

The next day, Friday, the day before the funeral, we had a substantial practice in the Song School and Abbey, and as things were going well, I cancelled the boys' practice planned for later in the morning. Lynne arrived from Berlin, and we had a piano run-through of her solo. She had hardly slept a wink the previous night, but immediately radiated confidence. At 1.00pm the BBC singers arrived and I showed them their places in the organ loft, where there was just enough room for them, and explained the order of service, including their part in the Tavener, stressing the need for tremendously dynamic and articulated singing in the second half of the Verdi. The extra television monitor and speakers, which the singers needed to see me and hear the sound of the Abbey choir clearly, had at last been installed. The full dress rehearsal started at 2:00pm after an inevitable list of last minute instructions.

The Croft *Burial Sentences* sounded fine but were too long, which presented a serious problem – should we omit the last section, "I heard a voice from heaven" which was printed in the service paper, or could we start processing from further back in the nave? We tried two alternative starting points, but neither worked satisfactorily. I assured the Dean that we would get it right by the next day. The other critical timing was that of *Song for Athene* as the coffin was carried out. At the first rehearsal it was about right, save for the final pianissimo 'Alleluia'. The Dean proposed that we omit this section, both for the sake of the timing and also so that the piece would end with a huge triumphant chord immediately before the Nation's one minute silence. We then tried it with some organ reinforcement, to which the composer later gave his blessing, and finally achieved a last verse which was incredibly powerful. The Abbey Choir was then finished for the day, while I had another session with Lynne, Martin Baker and the BBC singers. The Abbey was then closed for a private rehearsal for those reading and speaking, and for Elton John, whose technical team had spent the whole day fixing up synthesizers and other equipment in the south choir aisle. The quality of sound on the Abbey's speaker system was at first very distorted but after a great deal of skilful adjustment by the sound engineers, a much improved sound emerged. Everyone prayed that it would be as good the following morning. Back at the office my wife, Penny, was doing a final and correct version of *Make me a Channel of Your Peace*, since at the rehearsal we found that some of the words on the copy did not agree with those in the service paper.

  On Saturday, the day of the funeral, I was wide-awake at 4:30am, so got up and paced around the drawing room. How could we solve the problem of the Croft Sentences being too long? If we walked with much smaller paces, but still in time to the music, we would cover less ground and fit in more music. It was obvious, perhaps, but would it work? At 7:30am I went into the Abbey and asked the Abbey Beadle how slowly he could walk – not easy while carrying a heavy mace, but the principle was established. At 8:45 Lynne arrived at our house to change and warm-up. She deliberately avoided watching the TV coverage of the funeral procession. At 9.35 we had a short rehearsal in Cheneygates (a large room off the Cloisters) with the BBC Singers, checking the opening of the Verdi and particular points of intonation in the Tavener, then on to the Song School. All 24 boys were fit. We paced out the procession again with smaller steps this time, and spent some time familiarising ourselves with the corrected version of *Make me a Channel of your Peace*. At 10.15 the Lay Vicars arrived, and in addition to the obvious points, we tried out particular sections for balance and improved some of the boys' vowel sounds.

At 10.48 we left the Song School and became part of an extraordinary ritual as the service unfolded.

34b The coffin bearing the body of Diana Princess of Wales arrives at the Abbey for her funeral.

The timing of the Croft *Sentences* worked as well as we could have hoped, and it was soon time for me to mount the organ loft steps for the Verdi extract. I felt relief and gratitude as Lynne soared effortlessly up to the top B flat. All would now be well. The Prime Minister's lesson from Corinthians was followed by Elton John's song; the sound system was fine, and everyone listened intently – as indeed they did to Earl Spencer's address. Outside the Abbey we heard applause, which was gradually taken up to an extraordinary degree by the congregation inside. When should we begin the next hymn? Eventually I signalled to Martin Baker to start *Make me a Channel of your Peace*, and this was followed by the Archbishop's prayers, during which the choristers sang the *Londonderry Air* (using the words "I would be true ...."). We then had a rousing version of *Cwm Rhondda* (Guide me, O Thou Great

Redeemer), although I had to hold back the start of the last verse until the pall-bearers had appeared under the organ screen.

The Commendation led directly into *Song for Athene*. The Chaplain and Sacrist, Jonathan Goodall, had noticed at the rehearsal the day before how the pall-bearers virtually walked in step with the pulse of the music and, as they passed the choir stalls I found myself beating in time with their measured tread. The sound of their footsteps added an extraordinary intensity in a totally unexpected way. I was able to see the procession reach the tomb of the Unknown Warrior and then the Great West doors opened as we reached the climax, with both choirs and organ at *fortissimo*.

In the days before and after Princess Diana's funeral, there was a huge amount of press comment about the musical content of the service and indeed about the power of the music itself. In the *Classic FM Magazine* Henry Kelly began his account by quoting Oscar Wilde, who described music as "the art which is most nigh to tears and to memory", and "how we were reminded of this quality in music in that terrible week of mourning following the death of Princess Diana.

> "It would not be an exaggeration to say that music played a dominant part in the service, reflecting the unbearable emotions of the occasion. I include without hesitation Elton John's magnificent singing …
>
> "At the end of the day what I am trying to underline is that when we realise what a crucial part music can play in our mourning and grief, maybe we will understand better what a crucial part it plays in the rest of our daily lives".

In the *Sunday Telegraph* John Simpson noted "the way in which the most formal of people, uniformed and robed and elderly, wiped away tears at the words of Elton John; even though, beforehand, many of them must have been against the idea that he would sing".

John Simpson continued: "The demand for new ways of doing things was in the air, and the sound of it had reached into Westminster Abbey."

By no means everyone wrote supporting the inclusion of *Candle in the Wind*, but I think the editorial in the November 1997 issue of the *BBC Music Magazine* reflected the feelings of many, save possibly for its conclusion about the defining moment of the funeral: "Unlike Paul McCartney, no-one has accused Elton John of being the modern equivalent of Schubert."

Funeral of Diana, Princess of Wales

The *Evening Standard*'s columnist, Brian Sewell, described *Candle in the Wind* as an "interruption" by a "minor entertainer", wondering if "the People" would have wanted Elton John if they had been asked. But he acknowledged that "For many people ... Elton's contribution was the defining moment of the funeral. Where 'classical' and 'popular' music meet on common ground, it doesn't matter a jot as long as the music is good."

Brian Hunt, writing in the *Daily Telegraph* a day before the funeral, also had reservations about *Candle in the Wind*, and called it "the jarring note", but acknowledged that "the rest of the programme had been chosen with a care that becomes more apparent the deeper one looks.

"The overt patriotism of the hymn *I vow to thee, my country* may stick in some throats, but the community feeling that has spread through the nation this week needed expression."

Make me a Channel of your Peace had a childlike simplicity, which also felt right, and a month later I received a letter from the author and composer, Sebastian Temple:

"Dear Mr Neary:

It is with great pleasure that I am writing you this letter, long overdue. It has always pained me that I couldn't read or write music, but each time I tried, something came up to stop me until I thought that the Lord did not want me to be musically educated.

"The truth is that I didn't even like the song when it flowed through me. But to hear what you did with it delighted me, so I changed my mind, and now I am happy to have been the instrument of God's peace in the composition of that song. You made it sound so right and so perfect. How can I not be grateful to you for the privilege of hearing it as it should sound?

"I must admit that the whole funeral service was totally unforgettable. All the music thrilled. Princess Diana's death certainly stirred a universal archetype within us all."

It was fascinating to see how the wide-ranging and contrasting musical settings in the service drew differing responses, but how virtually everyone recognised the value and wisdom of including a variety of styles, by no means all of which were to their individual taste."

Anthony Payne, the composer and critic, reviewed the music in *The Independent*:

"It was populist but never cheap in content, and it was the reworking of Elton John's famous *Candle in the Wind*, bravely sung by its composer under great emotional stress, that captured the imagination of most of the people interviewed on BBC1. This was understandable, but no less keeping in tune with the occasion were the closing sequence form Verdi's *Requiem*, John Tavener's *Song for Athene*, whose almost Holstian climax brought the service to a majestic close, and Holst's own *I vow to thee, my country*, one of the Princess's favourite hymns".

"In *Song for Athene* the combination of the closing lines from *Hamlet*: 'May flights of angels sing thee to thy rest' and the words from the Orthodox Funeral Service, which affirm so strongly our belief in the Resurrection, and how even in that moment of utter grief there is hope, made a statement which few could not have been moved by, as everyone stood silently to mark the Nation's one minute silence."

In the weeks following the funeral I received a vast number of letters (nearly all positive) about the choice of music especially the Tavener, including an extremely appreciative one from Princess Diana's sister, Lady Sarah McCorquodale, who graciously apologised for ever having questioned the suitability of *Song for Athene*. Many requested information about how to get hold of the music, including my "arrangement" of *I would be true (The Londonderry Air)*, for which I had done nothing except keep the tune unaccompanied!

There was also a very heart-warming and over-generous fax from my good friend, John Bertalot, at that time Director of Music at Trinity Church in Princeton, New Jersey, which ended:

"You realise, of course, that by your gracious acceptance of a full variety of music at that service, none of us can ever say again "We don't do that sort of music here!"

"As Earl Spencer, by his address, changed the course of the Monarchy, so you, by embracing such a wide spectrum of musical offerings, have for ever changed the nature of music which will be offered in places of worship from this time forth, but at the same time, you have given us a standard of perfection to aim for which few will be able to approach and none surpass. Thank you!
John"

And the following editorial in the *Daily Telegraph* on 8 September meant a great deal to all of us at the Abbey. "The Service had been a huge challenge, especially to the Abbey, and once again, the Abbey seems to have successfully pulled it off." Under the heading, "Luckier than we know", it continued: "It was a fine funeral, almost everyone agrees – moving and fitting, but does anyone realise quite how extraordinary an achievement it was? In sheer logistics alone, it was a prodigious feat. The task of choosing and rehearsing the service, of relaying the ceremony to the whole world beyond in so short a time and with no precedent or ready plan was the hardest ever undertaken in Britain. Not the crustiest courtier, nor the most pomaded dress designer, nor the most committed charity worker could have complained that the service failed to speak to him or her. Nor could the people who clapped outside, or the many millions more who watched it at home. None of them did".

In November that year, I received a letter from the Secretary of the Royal Victorian Order, informing me that it was Her Majesty's intention to appoint me Lieutenant of the Order in the forthcoming New Year Honours List. This was in fact the third honour to come my way in 1997, for earlier in the year I had become a Fellow of the Royal School of Church Music and been awarded an Honorary Doctorate of Music by the University of Southampton.

When the news of the LVO became public I was swamped with generous letters. At the Investiture, when presenting me with my medal, the Queen was very kind about the music at Princess Diana's funeral and told me how much she had wanted me to give me the award. One of the other recipients that day was Elton John. We had a lengthy chat before the ceremony, at which he was announced as "Sir John Elton"!

CHAPTER 18

Foreign tours

The choir members, young and old, were beaming

1988, North America

Before I arrived at the Abbey in January 1988 there had been a provisional plan for a choir tour of America in October that year, and it was decided that this should go ahead. As well as planning the programmes and teaching the boys some new repertoire, this also necessitated preparing the junior choristers who were not touring to sing at the weekday evensongs during our absence.

Except for New York, Toronto and Garden Grove, California, the boys stayed with families of choir members from local churches. Invariably they had a brilliant time, and several spent a day at an American school, providing a chance to teach their American hosts how to play soccer. On several occasions Joe Crouch, the head chorister, was interviewed on radio or television and singled out "staying with hosts" as one of the most enjoyable aspects of the tour.

The coast-to-coast tour had two basic programmes – one including delightful readings by the Dean, Michael Mayne, who, with his wife Alison, accompanied us on the tour.

Our first concert took place at The Cathedral of the Incarnation, Long Island, on 21 September. The programme was called 'Music for Royal Occasions', and began with Parry's *I was glad*, which had been composed for the Coronation of King Edward VII in 1902. At that Coronation Parry sat in the Nave next to the actor Sir Henry Irving. They did not know each other. After the anthem, Irving apparently turned to Parry and said, "Well, I don't think much of the music so far". Parry's reply is unrecorded.

Our second concert was in Worcester, Massachusetts, where the boys had their first experience of singing in a concert hall. It was perhaps not surprising that the first reviewer of the tour – in the *Worcester Telegram* – thought "the choir looked somewhat vulnerable as they took to the stage in their bright cassocks, but by the end the choir members, young and old were beaming".

Giving concerts is different from singing at services. A concert audience expects more expression from performers, and it took some time for the well-disciplined English reserve to melt. But by the end of the tour the boys were not only smiling more easily (this never hurts the vocal sound) but were also taking compliments from their hosts quite naturally and handling the hugs of their surrogate mothers with not a little charm and grace.

After Worcester we had an intense period, first before an audience of 2,500 in Roy Thomson Hall in Toronto, then in the enormous 'Gothic' National Cathedral in Washington, followed by a concert in St Thomas, Fifth Avenue in New York, which was described by the *New York Times*, as "exquisite", with Britten's *Rejoice in the Lamb* "the most ravishing performance of the evening".

In Minneapolis, we had been asked to sing a new work, *The Last Invocation* (words by Walt Whitman), by the local composer, Carol Barnett. Her setting sounded particularly effective in the resonant Basilica, and we repeated it at All Souls-tide in the Abbey. From Minneapolis we flew to Milwaukee where we found the Dean, who had left the tour to preach at Harvard, on crutches. He had sprained his ankle badly when stepping onto a boat, but mercifully he recovered quite quickly.

Soon after the 1988 tour, I flew to South Africa to direct a course for the Royal School of Church Music at Grahamstown. I nearly did not make it as, after arriving at Johannesburg and going through Passport Control, I was summoned to a separate room for questioning. This was because on my entry form, under occupation, I had written "church musician", and the authorities were clearly under orders to check the credentials of anyone with church connections entering the country. Eventually I was allowed in, but it was a sharp reminder of the kind of police state the country had become. By far the majority of those attending the course were against apartheid, although I gathered that one or two objected to sharing a dormitory with those of a different ethnic origin. After the course I stayed on to play organ recitals in Cape Town and Johannesburg, where the area by the cathedral of Christ the King was notorious for violence and robbery. On a day off I was driven through the Soweto township, when the terrible conditions that people were living under made a lasting impression.

In 1989 our first extra commitment was to record some Christmas music with the phenomenal Danish recorder player, Michala Petri, including several delightful arrangements by a former Abbey chorister, David Overton. Then, out of the blue, we received an invitation to take part in a Music Festival in

February at Nantes (Brittany). We gave two concerts; the first a programme of English Church music, and the second, a choral and orchestral concert with the London Virtuosi, consisting of Mozart's *Missa brevis in D*, K.194, Schubert's *Unfinished Symphony* and the Fauré *Requiem*. The church, Notre Dame de Bon Porte, had a glorious acoustic – it resembled a smaller version of Brompton Oratory – and with a fine French romantic organ, the setting could hardly have been more appropriate for the Fauré.

Apart from services, the rest of our work in the Spring term 1990 was principally devoted to preparing for a recording of the psalms and for a live transmission of our performance of Bach's *St John Passion*. This was a memorable event for us all, and very much part of the Abbey's offering for Holy Week. There was no applause, and the congregation joined in one of the Chorales. For the boys it involved much hard work in familiarizing themselves with the German. In this they were helped, indeed inspired, by an expert coach from Westminster School, Richard Stokes. There was also the thrill of singing with an excellent Baroque orchestra using period instruments and listening to an outstanding team of soloists.

1990, Hungary and Switzerland

Our next foreign tour (in 1990) was to Hungary and Switzerland with the City of Oxford Orchestra. After flying to Budapest we had a 160 mile coach journey to Nyiregyhaza in North East Hungary. Out first concert was given in nearby Nyirbartor, but before this the boys visited the school of the Cantemus Choir (mostly girls), who gave a brilliant account of *This Little Babe* from Britten's *Ceremony of Carols*, followed by a haunting folksong by Bela Bartok. The Abbey boys were given copies, and were soon being taught to sing in Hungarian. The sight-reading ability of the British seemed to impress our hosts, even if our linguistics did not. In fact the only word we managed in Hungarian was "kissenham" – thank you. Before leaving, we all joined together in a round of *London's Burning*. It was a most happy and moving experience, and I was not surprised to see addresses being swapped.

Our main concert was in Budapest at the magnificent Coronation Church, the Matyas Templon, where the church was sold out for our programme with the City of Oxford Orchestra. Handel's *Foundling Hospital Anthem* was much applauded, but it was Britten's *Hymn to St Cecilia* which perhaps made the greatest impact. The following day was free, and after a visit to the zoo, we moved on to the 19th century Thermal Baths, where we had a lovely swim, and watched games of chess. with the participants basking in the warm water as they played!

We then flew to Switzerland. The contrast between rural Northeast Hungary, with its horse-drawn carts, and prosperous metropolitan Zurich could hardly have been greater. The Choir gave a concert at the Liebfrauen Church in Central Zurich and on the following evening they sang in the nearby small town of Jona. From German Switzerland we then travelled by train through wonderful scenery to Lausanne, where we were based for our last three concerts, two of them in Geneva at the Cathedral of St Pierre. Exceptionally clear weather enabled us to have a spectacular view of Mont Blanc on our first drive into Geneva.

Here are two of our tour programmes:

Programme A

Handel:	Zadok the priest
	My heart is inditing
Gibbons:	See, see the word is incarnate
	O clap your hands
Handel:	Organ concerto, Op. 4 No.2 in B flat
Britten:	Hymn to St Cecilia
Handel:	Blessed are they that considereth the poor and needy. (Anthem for the Foundling Hospital)

Programme B

Byrd:	Laudibus in sanctis
	Ave verum corpus
	Carman's whistle (harpsichord solo)
Humphrey:	Hymn to God the Father
Purcell:	O Lord God of Hosts
	Hear my prayer, O Lord
	O God, thou art my God
Harris:	Faire is the heaven
Tavener:	Hymn to the Mother of God
Harvey:	I love the Lord
Bach:	Prelude and Fugue In A major (harpsichord solo)
Bach:	Der Geist hilft

1991, Halle, Leipzig and Berlin

With Common Entrance safely negotiated, all seemed set fair as we made our final preparations in the Song School on Friday morning 9 June 1992 for a short choir tour of Germany. But at 11.00 I had a nasty shock when John New, our chief baggage-master Lay Vicar, rang to say that he had discovered that instead of leaving from Heathrow (as stated on our tickets), the Lufthansa flight that evening was from Gatwick! With only a few hours to go, and some of the Lay Vicars due to meet the party at Heathrow, some quick work was needed to contact everyone. Luckily, we all caught the plane. The invitation had come from the Halle Handel Festival for the choir to give a concert in the Marktkirche, where Handel learned to play the organ. With support from the British Council, we were able to combine this with performances in Berlin and Leipzig.

Everywhere we sang had until November 1989 been part of the German Democratic Republic. The political and economic effects of reunification were widely reported, and it was very moving for us to witness some of the more personal aspects of this. For example, I found myself introducing organists from neighbouring East and West Berlin to each other who had not met before.

With the new freedom, attendances at services had dropped considerably, and interdenominational differences had surfaced more prominently. It was therefore particularly valuable that we were accompanied on the tour by Canon Anthony Harvey, not just because of his skill as interpreter, but also for expressing so cogently in his introductions to the programmes our feelings towards our fellow Christians in Germany. On each occasion Canon Harvey's remarks were warmly applauded – never more so than when he spoke at the end of the Roman Catholic Mass at St Hedwig's Cathedral in Berlin on the Sunday morning. I still remember the deep spirituality of this service – the magical setting of 'Et in terra pax' at the opening of the Gloria in Vaughan Williams's *Mass in G minor*, with the measured tread of the G major chords, acquiring a special significance. The service concluded with a specially requested performance of John Tavener's *Hymn to the Mother of God*. We had already sung this anthem on the previous evening in the Marienkirche, where the extremely resonant acoustics reinforced the rich sonorities of this extraordinary piece. As usual our programmes were drawn mainly from the English Cathedral repertoire, old and new, but I could not resist including the Bach motet *Der Geist hilft*, which in the Thomaskirche in Leipzig we sang by his grave.

It would have been good to include a substantial amount of live Handel in our programme in Halle, but the position of the main organ at the West End of the church rather ruled that out. However, Andrew Lumsden accompanied the boys on a small modern chamber organ in the charming duet from the Foundling Hospital anthem, *The people will tell of their wisdom*. His richly deserved appointment as Organist and Master of Music at Lichfield Cathedral robbed the Abbey of one of Britain's finest service accompanists, as can be heard on the two CDs of the Psalms we recorded for Virgin Classics. We were extremely fortunate, however, in Andrew's successor as Sub-Organist, Martin Baker, whose route to the Abbey was, I suspect, unique – Martin had been Organ Scholar at Westminster Cathedral, and then Assistant Sub-Organist at St Paul's Cathedral. He was and remains one of the finest improvisers of his generation.

1992, Halle, Karlsruhe and Berlin

In 1992 we were invited back to Halle to perform the four Handel Coronation anthems with the London Handel Orchestra. We also took part in a Festival of English Music in Karlsruhe and at an ecumenical service in East Berlin.

The Halle programme, which we repeated in the Abbey at a concert in aid of the Florence Nightingale Museum, ended with the Hallelujah Chorus. In this, the 250th anniversary year of the first performance of *Messiah*, we sang the 'Hallelujah' on several occasions, including a television production for the Japanese company NHK using their High-Definition Technology.

1992, North America

Our second coast to coast tour of North America was designed partly to help publicise the work of the Abbey Trust and the restoration of the Henry VII Chapel. We started and ended in New York, beginning with Evensong at St Thomas Church on Fifth Avenue, and finishing with a concert at Alice Tully Hall, where three choristers (Alastair Brookshaw, Simon de Baat and Christian Wilson) gave us a magnificent start with their solos from a high gallery in Britten's *Antiphon*. Alastair and Simon also sang the lament in Walton's *The Twelve* with great presence and understanding.

1993, France

In the summer term of 1993, the choir made a short tour to France, beginning with a concert at St Claude, a small town in the Jura mountains. The title of the programme had, rather charmingly, been translated as *Un Voyage de Pâques à la Trinité*. Next morning, after a coach trip through beautiful scenery, we caught the Train Grand Vitesse at Bourg en Bresse, and in under two hours had arrived in Paris for a concert at St Denis. The Basilica was completely packed, and the audience of 1700 insisted on two encores and then applauded the choir all the way down the vast nave. Our final port of call was Sully-sur-Loire, where, as well as giving a concert, we took part, with Canon Harvey, in a Mass at the Roman Catholic Church of St Stephen. The parish priest was extremely welcoming, and we sensed that our contribution of music by William Byrd (arguably the first great composer of the Church of England, though he remained a catholic throughout his life) fitted alongside the Mass (said in French) without any awkwardness or incongruity. Everyone was invited to receive Communion, at which Canon Harvey assisted with the administration. He also preached the sermon (in French), concluding: "This celebration is much more than simply a gesture of ecumenical friendship, rather an experience, short-lived perhaps, but authentic, of a more profound unity – the unity which God alone is able to create among us when, altogether, we offer him our liturgical, musical and spiritual resources".

1994, Moscow

As a follow-up to the Queen's visit to Moscow in 1994, the Abbey Choir was invited to perform there by the British Council, who felt we would be able to bring something uniquely British.

At our first concert we were joined by a fine team of young Russian string players, who accompanied the boys most musically in the duet *The people will tell of thy wisdom* from Handel's *Foundling Hospital Anthem*. At concerts in the Tchaikovsky Hall and the Bolshoi Hall, it was the twentieth-century works by Britten, Harvey and Tavener which seemed to make the greatest impression, one of the highlights being Britten's *Rejoice in the Lamb*, with outstanding solos, none more so than Head Chorister Alex Martin's *For I will consider my cat Geoffrey*. The sound of the trebles was much admired and commented upon, and after Schubert's *Ave Maria*, there was such stamping of feet that we had to repeat it. I was frequently asked about our methods

Foreign tours

The boys in Moscow on a tour following the Queen's visit in 1994.
It featured on the cover of the *Westminster Abbey Chorister* magazine.

of voice-training, which gives me an opportunity to acknowledge and thank Sheena Wolstencroft for her invaluable individual work with the boys. As our main encore, we sang Rachmaninov's *Hymn of the Cherubim* in Russian, or rather in a phonetic version, thanks to our former organ scholar, William Whitehead, who had read Russian at Oxford.

We were the first foreign choir to perform at the Patriarch's Palace within the Kremlin. Our concert there was attended by many famous Russian artists, including Nikita Kikhailkov, who was so moved that he kissed me, but (to quote Peterborough in the *Daily Telegraph* the next day) "when it came to the choristers, he restrained himself to handshakes". In a short speech he said he was sure that Russian children would soon have the same beautiful expressions on their faces as the Abbey Choristers, through the experience of singing such wonderful music – a most moving testimonial.

Wherever we went we were shadowed by three security guards, Boris, Sasha and Sergei. Their presence was very necessary on a short foray into the Moscow Metro, with its huge, highly decorated stations, terrifyingly fast escalators and crowds of passengers. Few of us were able to read which station we were at anyway, save for ten-year-old Nicholas Richardson, who had been teaching himself Russian. We were very dependent on a team of interpreters, whose command of English was exceptional, though we were amused at the description of an ancient instrument at the Glinka Museum, constructed '2000 years Before Christmas'! There were no language problems however at the Moscow State Circus, where we were entranced by some remarkable jugglers and trapeze artists, nor at the British Embassy, where, after lunch, a group of Lay Vicars gave a hilarious rendering of *The Mermaid* by John Whitworth (a former Lay Vicar).

Martin Neary: Time to declare

President Clinton laid a wreath at the Tomb of the Unknown Warrior
(Photo: © Tariq Chaudry).

The Choristers do not normally sing when a visiting head of state lays a wreath at the Tomb of the Unknown Warrior, but an exception was made when the President of the United States, Bill Clinton, and Mrs Clinton visited the Abbey in December 1995. As they and their escorts moved towards the quire, the boys sang my short arrangement for trebles of *Morning has broken* to the well-known tune, *Bunessan*. President Clinton stopped to listen and then encouraged us to sing some more – which we did. When Nelson Mandela visited the Abbey, he insisted on shaking hands with every boy making it quite difficult for them to hold their music, follow the beat and

Nelson Mandela shook hands with all the boys when he came to lay a wreath at the Tomb of the Unknown Warrior.

keep singing! Another occasion when the boys sang was when the President of Ukraine visited the Abbey. Canon Colin Semper and I told him about the choir's visit to Moscow, and how we hoped one day to perform in Ukraine. President Kuchma seemed distinctly interested, but we thought no more of it until the Ukrainian Ambassador, HE Sergio Komissarenko, telephoned me to invite the choir to fly to Kyiv to take part in the events marking the tenth anniversary of the Chernobyl disaster – just eight weeks away.

1996, Kiev

It was hard to believe that the necessary arrangements (not least financial) could be made in the time, but the Ambassador was quite determined and when, during one of several visits to our house, I said that a lot of details still seemed to be up in the air, he remarked: "Yes, but getting closer to the ground". Thanks to his dynamism, to the support of the Dean and Chapter, and in particular to the generous sponsorship from Wogen Resources (whose managing director, Colin Williams, was an Honorary Steward), what seemed an impossibility became a reality.

The principal event in the Kyiv Opera House was both spectacular and poignant. It was divided into three parts, depicting the building of Chernobyl, the explosion and aftermath and the future, with a screen showing films and pictures of those who died. A speech by the President was followed by an extraordinary variety of performers, including a conjurer/fire eater, an army band, Cossack dancers, poetry, ballet dancers and, in the final part, the Abbey Choir. The boys sang Peter Hurford's *Litany to the Holy Spirit* and then the Lay Vicars joined them for the *Kontakion of the Faithful Departed* to the Kyiv melody. We then moved on to music from *Messiah*: *Since by man came death* and the *Hallelujah Chorus*, after which a ten-year-old Ukrainian girl, born on the day of Chernobyl, came through the Choir to sing a beautiful, unaccompanied Ukrainian song. All then stood for the Ukrainian National Hymn.

Once again Michael and Alison Mayne travelled with us – I am not sure however if our Ukrainian hosts knew how to treat a Dean. Michael had a televised half hour audience with President Kuchma, while our party was given a rather terrifying police escort, with any cars in our path being cleared out of the way.

Our second concert was at the Tchaikovsky Conservatoire, when during the organ introduction to *Zadok the Priest* a ginger cat (looking remarkably like the Abbey's own Eric) appeared on the stage. Martin Baker, as always, coped brilliantly with the organs of variable quality he had to play, and he received a great ovation for his performance of the transcription of Mussorgsky's *Great Gate of Kyiv*, which we had seen the day before on a sight-seeing tour.

At our final concert the Dean spoke very movingly, telling the packed audience in the House of Organ and Chamber Music that all those who died at Chernobyl would be remembered when he dedicated a memorial to all innocent victims outside the great west doors of the Abbey later in the year. This concert also included Richard Farnsworth's outstanding rendering of the first soprano part (with the top Cs) in the Allegri *Miserere*.

1996, Cologne

In September 1996, through Steven Abbott, who had set up our recordings with Sony Arc of Light, we were invited to give a concert in the Kirche St Kunibert in the Cologne Convention for Classical Music. The schedule was pretty tight, and the situation was not helped when our flight was delayed. We lost virtually all our rehearsal time in the church, and it was a relief that the programme, drawn from our recordings, went off without mishap.

1996, North America

"Five standing ovations out of five" was chorister Toby Dunham's comment after the opening concerts on our 1996 tour of North America. Our visit to Toronto was particularly special, as we sang at the same church (St Paul's) as twelve Abbey choristers and eight St George's Chapel Windsor Lay Vicars had sung in 1927. Here are extracts from reviews of our concerts in Washington and Minneapolis:

> "As the Choir of Westminster Abbey demonstrated in Sunday's concert at Washington National Cathedral, great choral singing involves more than just beautiful sound, though it had it in spades. What the Choir of Westminster share with their Oxford and Cambridge counterparts is an ability not simply to ride an acoustic like the Cathedral's but to project into it and fill it … Crowned by penetrating unearthly singing from its

matchless boy sopranos, the choir offered clarity and seamless blend in equal measure." *The Washington Post*.

"The House of Windsor may be tottering on the throne, but some English institutions are flourishing as never before. The Choir of Westminster Abbey stands at the summit of discipline and musicality under the direction of Martin Neary ... The Choir has shed the languid English tone and style of decades past and taken on a continental tang. The boys' voices are strong and sweet, and the men's well cultivated and perfectly balanced." *St Paul Pioneer Press*.

1997, Oslo

'Small singers – big sound'. This was the headline in the newspaper review of a concert *(A Millennium of music from Westminster Abbey)* which we gave during a memorable visit to Oslo in 1997. We were guests of Oslo Cathedral as part of their 300th anniversary celebrations. Our first engagement was a spectacular ceremony with the adult Oslo Cathedral Choir in the City Hall (where the Nobel Peace Prizes are presented). After the Oslo Choir had sung Duruflé's *Tu es Petrus* from a high gallery, we processed down a vast staircase chanting the fifteenth-century carol *Angelus ad virginem*. Between the musical items an actor delivered most dramatically in Norwegian, a series of addresses which unfolded the history of Oslo and its cathedral from the time of the Vikings. The choir listened with great decorum, and later joined in singing in Norwegian the hymn *The Church's one Foundation*, with a beautiful descant by the Oslo Cathedral organist, Terje Kvam, who incidentally has done much to bring the English Cathedral repertoire to Norway. Speaking of organists, we were delighted to meet the Englishman, John Carroll, who was still in post after 39 years, having just been appointed to St Edmund's Church in 1958 when the Abbey Choir with Sir William McKie and Osborne Peasgood had sung in Oslo and Bergen. Our visit was shorter, with a pretty tight schedule, but there was time for some sight-seeing, including the Kon-Tiki Exhibition and the Olympic ski-jump site at Holmenkollen, when the intrepid among the party braved a thrilling/terrifying simulator.

CHAPTER 19

Some honorary positions

The newly installed President found himself looking for new accommodation and a new Clerk.

The Royal College of Organists

In 1960, when I became a member of the Royal College of Organists (RCO), it was housed in Kensington Gore (next to the Royal Albert Hall) in a magnificent building that still bears its name. In due course I was elected to the Council and became one of the examiners for the College diplomas, and in 1987 the President, Sir David Lumsden, nominated me to be his successor for 1988–1990. By then the Council was becoming increasingly concerned about the College's future in Kensington Gore, because the 99-year lease was soon to expire, and the peppercorn rent of £1 per annum would then be increased to a figure in the region of £60,000 per annum.

The lease had been granted by the Royal Commission for the Exhibition of 1851, and I couldn't help wondering why its length (99 years) compared so unfavourably with that of the nearby Royal College of Music (999 years). Could it have been a slip of the pen? In any case, the situation meant that much of my presidency was spent in searching for a new home for the College.

When I became President, the Clerk was the redoubtable Barry Lyndon. He was very much in charge of the day-to-day running of the College, but he had given notice that he would soon be retiring. So, the newly installed President found himself looking for a new Clerk as well as new accommodation.

A number of alternatives were considered, including several London churches, but it soon became clear that we would not be able to find anything comparable to the spacious building in Kensington Gore. In due course agreement was reached with St Andrew's Holborn for the RCO to move there on a short lease. But there were some serious disadvantages – not least the limitations of the two-manual Mander organ in the church, which it was generally felt was unsuitable for the Fellowship organ playing diplomas.

Some honorary positions

After my two-year stint as President, I remained on the Council and was surprised to find myself being elected for a second term (1996–98) in succession to Dame Gillian Weir. In this term as President, I was much involved in helping to make things run smoothly at St Andrew's, but it became clear that the College would have to operate differently. Now the RCO does not own a building. In recent years, holding Council meetings and Conferment ceremonies at Southwark Cathedral has worked very well, alongside splendid new initiatives across the UK.

The Organists' Benevolent League / Organists Charitable Trust

The Organists' Benevolent League of which I was President from 1988–2018, was founded in 1909 by Sir Frederick Bridge "to relieve by pecuniary assistance or otherwise organists and their dependents who are in distress through poverty". The League was soon a real success, with the Royal College of Organists lending their offices and clerical assistance, and by 1918 over £1,000 had been invested, putting the organisation on a sound footing. Over the years the League has benefited from the generosity of many cathedrals, churches and individuals, and often organists have donated the proceeds from one or more of their recitals.

As a result of this generosity, the Organists Charitable Trust, as it became in 2009, has awarded grants to hundreds of organists. Beneficiaries' needs have changed since the establishment of the welfare state, but the Trust is still providing help, albeit in some different ways. To meet more relevantly the requirements of the 21st century, the Trustees in 2009 extended the aims of the charity to include, once the primary objects had been met, support for organ tuition in cases of hardship. It is vital, as Archbishop Rowan Williams encouraged us in his Centenary Message, that the Organists Charitable Trust seeks ways to support organists and organ music in our churches.

With this in mind, the Trustees decided to mark the Centenary with a concert at the church of St Giles' Cripplegate in September 2009, and by the publication by Novello of *The Little Organ Book*, which I edited. It consists of eleven relatively simple pieces of contrasting moods, with seven drawn from the period covering the first 100 years of the Trust's existence and four representing the start of the second century. Among many musical delights at the Centenary concert, John Eady FRCO, an OCT beneficiary, gave the premiere of *Paean*, the first work in the collection, composed by one of the Trustees, Philip Moore.

As well as Philip Moore's *Paean*, there are new commissions by three of the younger generation of composers, *Fanfare-Processional* by David Bednall, *Bluesday* by Iain Farrington and *Carnival* by Thomas Hewitt Jones, the last two with support from the Vaughan Williams Charitable Trust. Also being published for the first time were Herbert Howells's *Cradle Song* and John Rutter's *Prelude on Te lucis ante terminum*. The second half of the twentieth century is further represented by contributions from James MacMillan, Peter Hurford and Paul Spicer. Finally, acknowledging our inheritance, there are two works from the late 19th century, by Frederick Bridge and John Stainer, the Organist of St Paul's Cathedral, who, like Bridge, made such an impact on the quality and performance of church music.

As Sir Ernest Bullock, President of the Organists' Benevolent League from 1927 to 1944, wrote: "We are unsectarian, non-denominational ... our organisation extends to Anglican, Free Church, Roman Catholic and Cinema".

The Herbert Howells Society

From 1992 until 2024 I was Chairman of the Herbert Howells Society, which was set up in 1987 at the instigation of the composer's daughter, Ursula, and is based at Westminster Abbey where his ashes are buried. The aims of the Society over more than three decades have been to promote a wider appreciation of Howells's music and to support and publicise the performance, publication and recording of his works. Huge gratitude is due in particular to the indefatigable Secretary, Andrew Millinger.

It has only been since Howells's death in 1983 that a number of compositions he had put to one side have been discovered. The Society has been active, along with his biographers, Christopher Palmer and Paul Spicer, in trying to ensure that all his compositions will finally be published, and has collaborated with the composer's principal publisher, Novello, in bringing into print for the first time a number of choral and orchestral works. For eight years, I was also a Trustee of the Herbert Howells Trust which was set up in 2007 and is based at St John's College, Cambridge. The Society works closely with the Trust, to assist the publication, recordings and performances of the less well-known works.

Winchester Diocesan Choral Association

During my time as Organist of Winchester Cathedral, I was also Music Director of the Winchester Diocesan Choral Association. Each year in June, choirs from parishes across the diocese would join together in the Cathedral for a festal Evensong with the Cathedral Choir, involving as many as 400 voices. As well as selecting regular favourites, I tried to choose music a little beyond the standard repertoire, one of the most interesting works being the final section of Stravinsky's *Symphony of Psalms*, arranged for choir and organ by James Lancelot. By way of preparation, my colleagues and I led separate joint rehearsals in different parts of the Diocese.

On the day, the parish church choirs sang in the nave and stretched so far back that we needed a sub-conductor, perched precariously on a high stepladder to relay the beat from the pulpit – Winchester Cathedral has an extremely long nave and this was before the days of closed circuit television.

CHAPTER 20

Suspension and dismissal

"We decided to go through all the anguish of a court case rather than 'going quietly'."

For more than ten years from 1988, my wife Penny and I had enjoyed a varied and fascinating period at the Abbey involving many nationally important services, concerts and foreign tours. But on 20 March 1998 the situation changed dramatically when we were summoned to a meeting with the Dean and Receiver-General in the Jerusalem Chamber at the Abbey, and told we were being suspended. This left us shocked and bewildered. We had no idea what we had done wrong.

At the meeting I was ordered not to take the full choir practice for the weekend's music, due to start in a few minutes time at 4.00pm, even though I explained that my colleague was going to be late. Nor was I to have anything to do with the Abbey Choir, until the enquiries were concluded. The suspension soon became public knowledge, and the news went round the world – such is the iconic status of the Abbey.

The Abbey's concerns centred on the financial arrangements we had made over the choir's concerts and foreign tours over the previous few years. In summary, Penny (who was the Music Department Secretary) and I had operated a separate account to cover payments made to the altos, tenors and basses in the choir for events unconnected with the Abbey, including outside concerts and foreign tours. This enabled them to take responsibility for paying their own tax on this income, rather than paying it as part of their Abbey PAYE earnings. Penny was also receiving 'fixing' fees for recruiting the musicians and organising the events; this type of payment is standard practice in the musical world.

On returning to our house in Little Cloister, I called our then solicitor, Maitland Kalton; he was equally stunned, and immediately instructed me to write and deliver a letter to the Dean absolutely refuting any question of "financial irregularities" and asking that the suspensions be revoked. He could not believe the tone of the suspension letters and thought the only thing to do was to get counsel's opinion.

Around 6.00pm, Maitland telephoned to say that he had obtained the services of Cherie Booth QC, should this be necessary. Penny and I did not know what to do next, and (it seems incredible now) we continued with our plans for the rest of the evening, going to the 70th Birthday party of Sir David Lumsden, former Principal of the Royal Academy of Music (and my immediate predecessor before my first spell as President of the Royal College of Organists), as if nothing had happened.

During the weekend, I stayed away from the Abbey as ordered, and Penny went to Salisbury to sing in a performance of the *St Matthew Passion* conducted by David Stancliffe, Bishop of Salisbury. Later we learned from friends just how anguished she had looked. Then on the Sunday evening, still at a loss, I telephoned our friend, Frank Field, the Minister of State for Welfare Reform, who not infrequently would come to supper on Sunday evenings. Frank came round immediately, and after seeing the suspension letters, decided that he would seek a meeting with the Dean, the late Wesley Carr, whom ironically, he had backed over his appointment as Dean of Westminster 18 months earlier.

I do not intend to go over all the literally thousands of words written and spoken about our case. Until Dean Carr's arrival, I had been encouraged to run the Abbey Choir's outside engagements, including recordings and concerts, none of which were undertaken without the approval of the Dean and Chapter. But I should have realised that procedures which had worked well in the past might not necessarily be acceptable to the new Dean.

In the days immediately following the suspensions, I tried to establish some dialogue over, for example, what would happen to the Abbey's Holy Week Concert which I was due to conduct in less than two weeks' time, for which musicians had already been booked and tickets sold, but to no avail, and the language in every communication became progressively harsher. When we first met Cherie Booth, so that she could apply for an injunction to stop a 'disciplinary' hearing going ahead, her first words were: "Heavens, this looks as if you have committed murder!". Subsequently our case was taken over by another distinguished QC, Patrick Elias (now a retired Lord Justice of Appeal).

The Abbey post was my livelihood, and for over ten years I had worked to enhance the services through the music, to attract good young choristers to the choir and, perhaps above all, to give the choristers a sense of enjoyment and fulfilment. It might well be asked why, if the Dean did not want us there any more, we decided to go through all the anguish of a court case rather than "going quietly". We were insistent on one point, that any "settlement" must uphold unequivocally our integrity and honesty. However, despite the efforts of Lord Weatherill, the former Speaker (who, as High Bailiff of the Abbey, was an Honorary Lay Officer among the Collegiate Body) to persuade the Dean of this, he refused to budge, and so we had no option but to let him dismiss us and then to appeal. Until the morning of our dismissal, 22 April (which happened to be our 31st wedding anniversary), we thought that our integrity and honesty had been accepted. However, undertakings (such as appointing me Organist Emeritus) which had been given to Lord Wetherill were withdrawn, and at noon, at his Kings' Bench Walk Chambers in the Temple, Patrick Elias told us, in the presence of our solicitor, Stephen Levinson: "I cannot advise you to accept this offer".

So, we appealed to the Queen, as we were entitled to do because the Abbey is a Royal Peculiar, under the direct jurisdiction of the Sovereign as 'Visitor'. Following an initial hearing before the Lord Chancellor, Lord Irvine, directions were given for our appeal to be heard later in the year by a retired Scottish Law Lord, Lord Jauncey of Tullichettle.

In April came a wonderful offer from Professor Sir Bryan Thwaites (whose four sons had been in the Winchester Cathedral Choir) to write a letter to *The Times*, appealing for funds to help with our legal fees. Amazingly, this letter, signed also by Bishop John Taylor, Alex Wedderspoon, Dean of Guildford, His Honour Christopher Compston, John Gummer MP (now Lord Deben) and Dame Ruth Railton, raised over £120,000.

More funds were raised when a group of eminent musicians, the pianists Paul Daniel and Julius Drake, Joan Rodgers (soprano), Michael Chance (counter-tenor) and Ian Bostridge (tenor), gave a concert in May 1999 at the Barbican, devised and sponsored by Penny's sister, Amanda, and their three brothers.

The hearing began in September and was held over ten days at the House of Lords and at the Cabinet Office. The question of our honesty and integrity was addressed on the first day of the hearing. Counsel for the Dean and Chapter acknowledged that this was not a question of honesty. In my view if that crucial point had been conceded in April, the waste of time and the vast sums of money – the combined legal fees have been estimated at over

£600,000 – would have been averted. I will always regret that I was a part of the reason for such an appalling waste of the Abbey's resources, and the fact that the unfolding drama had brought such unhappiness not only to us, our families and friends, but also to so many other people.

The crucial point, over which we came unstuck in Lord Jauncey's view, and why he, in due course, found that our actions amounted to gross misconduct, was our alleged lack of openness about the account which we had used since 1994. I accept that I may have been misguided to have started this arrangement, and that I should have ensured that the Abbey authorities saw annual accounts. However, the account was set up so that it would be independent of the Abbey, and for this to be legal, it had to be separate.

On the question of whether the Abbey was aware of our separate account, there was conflicting evidence. The then Senior Accountant at the Abbey, the late Tim Fakes, was apparently persuaded to make a second witness statement, denying his awareness of the account, though this was at variance with his first statement. I felt this was extraordinary. Furthermore, his colleague, the late and very courageous Rodney Gould, came to the hearing in the Cabinet Office to confirm that he was certainly aware of the account. It would have been impossible for him not to have been, as he and others in the Chapter Office received cheques from the 'Neary Music account' in respect of Abbey charges or personal honoraria, as did the then Dean, Michael Mayne and the Choir School Headmaster, among others.

Our biggest difficulty was that Colin Semper, the Canon Treasurer, who was responsible for overseeing the Abbey's finances, had suffered a heart attack in December 1997, and had not only taken early retirement but was, at the time of the hearing, too frail to be rigorously cross-examined in front of everyone. Colin had provided a witness statement in our support, and later (unfortunately a year after the hearing) confirmed categorically in writing that he knew that the Nearys had received fixing fees, as happens in every aspect of the music business. Somebody had to spend time administering the account, and this was Penny, who had only undertaken the work to try to help the musicians. Moreover, she was completely open about the account and did not try to hide it from anyone. I have always felt aggrieved that she should have suffered when she was trying to help. Together with our solicitor I believed that, had it come earlier, Colin's evidence could have been decisive and turned the case in our favour.

Nonetheless, on the afternoon of 8 December, Stephen Levinson went to collect the Judgement from the Lord Chancellor's Office, prior to its public release the following day. Penny and I will never forget the sinking feeling when Stephen telephoned to tell us our fate, nor the look of absolute incredulity on Patrick Elias's face. We had to obey the confidentiality agreement made whereby nothing would be disclosed until the official announcement. Nevertheless, it was clear we were going to have to face the press and the television cameras, and so over the next few hours we prepared a press statement in which we said how disappointed we were by the ruling. It went on "But we are pleased and relieved that the decision makes clear, once and for all, that neither of us had been guilty of any dishonesty or deliberate concealment. Indeed, establishing this point was at the heart of our appeal and was our main objective. While we have been found to have made errors of judgement, which we accept and deeply regret, we consider that the penalty is out of proportion".

For the complete Press Statement we issued, see Appendix 8.

When I made that statement, at my side was the late Frank Field, MP, who throughout this nine-month purgatory, had never wavered in his support, often dropping into our house by the back gate (opposite the House of Commons). Even at 8.30am on 27 March 1998, the morning of his presenting his Welfare Report to Parliament (arguably one of the most important days of his Parliamentary career), Frank had gone to see the Dean to protest at the way we were being treated, warning him that if he continued in this way it would not only ruin the Nearys, but Wesley and his family as well. And apparently the Dean said: "I know".

The day after Lord Jauncey's verdict was released, *The Times* and *Daily Telegraph* both published leaders (sympathetic to us) about our treatment, the latter with the headline "Gamma minus", a direct quotation from Lord Jauncey's judgement about the way the Dean had handled our case.

The outpourings of public sympathy were quite extraordinary, not to mention the personal letters, including a most sympathetic one from the Archbishop of Canterbury, George Carey thanking Penny and me for our work for the church over the years, and hoping that it would not be long before we would be continuing that work.

Within a year the lawyer, James Behrens, in his book *Practical Church Management*, not only disagreed with the Judgement but was critical of the handling of the case. Indeed, virtually everyone thought that our case should never have gone to appeal. Lord Runcie, the former Archbishop, was to tell me when we met at Harvard in April 1999, that he thought it was the worst thing that had happened in the Church of England in his lifetime.

It is impossible for us to overstate just how much all the support we received meant to us, psychologically as well as financially, but in December 1998 we had to face moving out with few immediate prospects of any work. However, quite soon, some rays of light would come shining through the darkness.

CHAPTER 21

Cricket to the rescue

"I wondered when you would next turn up"

After the shock of our dismissal, out of the blue came some unexpected invitations. The first was from Peter McKenna, Artistic Director of the Australian Youth Choirs. Peter and I had been trying to find a time when I could spend a few weeks conducting his choirs, and after hearing Lord Jauncey's verdict, Peter immediately invited Penny and me to spend Christmas and the New Year as his guests in Melbourne, Sydney and Brisbane.

We flew out on Christmas morning and arrived in time to watch the second and third day's play, including a century by England's captain, Alec Stewart, of the post-Christmas Test Match at the Melbourne Cricket Ground. On day four, I thought it was only fair on Penny to have a break from cricket, so we visited the Twelve Apostles, a collection of limestone stacks (of which only seven remain) by the Great Ocean Road in Victoria, On the way back I asked our driver if he knew the score, only for him to answer: "It's all over". I replied, "So what was Australia's winning margin?" The answer was "We lost, and England won!". To think that I had missed the chance of seeing a rare England victory 'down under'!

We then flew to Sydney where we watched the first day's play of the next Test Match. To avoid the crowds, we decided to leave 20 minutes before close of play, but on the way out, we heard a roar, then a second and finally a third roar; would you believe it? The English fast bowler, Darren Gough, had taken a hat trick. I did however make contact with the England team at their hotel, when Peter McKenna somehow persuaded the tour manager, Graham Gooch, to have a drink with us after dinner; several players came to join us, including Michael Atherton, Nasser Hussain, Dean Headley and Dominic Cork, who entertained us with his graceful piano playing.

Our next encounter with the cricketers was at Sydney Airport, when it transpired that we were taking the same flight as the Australians to Brisbane (for some one-day internationals). We arrived rather late at the airport, and there were no places available for Penny and me to sit together. When the booking assistant was wondering what to do, Penny spotted that there was a vacant seat between Ian Healy, the Aussie wicketkeeper and Steve Waugh, the Aussie captain. I am not sure how pleased the cricketers were to discover that the seat between them was no longer vacant, not least when I tried to have a conversation. I did however produce a response from Steve, when I boldly declared that "these one-day games are a lottery". He disagreed, and we spent the rest of the flight debating the matter.

We returned to London, in time for Alice's highly praised début recital at the Wigmore Hall, following her winning the Pierre Fournier cello competition. My next London concert was at St John's Smith Square, conducting the BBC Singers and Century 21 in a performance of Jonathan Harvey's *Passion and Resurrection*, which was later transferred to CD.

Our next task was moving out of 2 Little Cloister. Fortunately, we had a house in Parsons Green, although it was too small to accommodate all our furniture and collections of music, quite a lot of which was kindly stored for us by our friend, Peter Dowling, and his wife, Sally, who had been a school friend of Penny's.

An invitation came from the Revd Peter Gomes, Professor of Moral Theology at Harvard, and Murray Somerville, director of the Harvard University Choir, to conduct the US premiere of *Innocence* by John Tavener in Harvard Memorial Church. This received a favourable Review in the *Boston Globe (see Appendix 3)*.

In January 1999 I was asked to help set up a new youth choir (age range 16–23) for the Royal School of Church Music. This was the brainchild of the new RSCM Director, John Harper, and the Archbishop of Canterbury, George Carey. It became very much a joint operation with Penny, who had recently been appointed to the administrative staff of the RSCM, and it was she who organised auditions in seven separate venues across the country. Thanks to the recommendation of the conductor, Paul Daniel, the choir's first engagement was to take part in the opening ceremony "One Amazing Night" at the Millennium Dome on 31 December 1999/1 January 2000. The 20 founder members of the new RSCM Millennium Youth Choir found themselves embracing popular classics such as *All you need is love*, along with new settings of Jonathan Dove's *To the Millennium*, and John Tavener's *A New Beginning*. And, of course, together with The Queen and the Prime Minister, we all sang *Auld Lang Syne* to welcome in the new Millennium.

For its first five-day course the choir was based at St Katherine's, a peaceful retreat house in Limehouse. On New Year's Day we took part in a midday Eucharist in the beautiful chapel, with the Tavener anthem, which had been sung in the Dome the previous night, as the Introit. The service also included Francis Grier's *Missa Trinitatis Sanctae*, composed for Westminster Abbey and a trial outing of a new anthem which I had written, *O worship the Lord*, concluding with the choir and congregation singing the opening verse together to the familiar tune *Was lebet* (O worship the Lord).

The original plan was for the choir to meet for two courses each year, and from the start we arranged for every member to receive individual coaching, mainly from the specialist voice teacher, Hilary Llystyn Jones, whose warm-up exercises were also most helpful. I aimed to choose a wide-ranging repertoire of sacred music, which was lapped up by the singers. The choir soon acquired a good reputation and was invited to take part in several broadcasts, including BBC *Choral Evensongs* from Exeter and Magdalen Colleges, Oxford. As well as preparing for the services, the choir also gave concerts, two of the most demanding being a summer concert in Merton College Chapel, which included Domenico Scarlatti's *Stabat Mater*, and a concert called *New York, New York*. The programme began with Aaron Copland's *In the Beginning* and ended with Leonard Bernstein's *Chichester Psalms* with the renowned counter-tenor, James Bowman, as soloist. Between these were settings by three York Minster organists, Edward Bairstow, Francis Jackson and Philip Moore. Our organist was Timothy Byram-Wigfield, who was the inspiring accompanist for all the early Millennium Youth Choir courses. I am very glad to say that the MYC, now known as the RSCM Youth Choir, is still going strong and is the RSCM's leading national choir. Among the singers on the first course were three former Abbey Choristers, Paul and Barnaby Smith and Dingle Yandell, who later became founder members of Voces8.

In July 1999 I was invited to take part in a sequence of music and readings at Fairford Parish Church in aid of the church's wonderful medieval stained-glass windows. This turned out to be quite an occasion, attended by the Prince of Wales, who when greeting me before the concert said: "I wondered when you would next turn up". It was the first appearance of my newly formed occasional choir, the English Chamber Singers, who were joined by Joanna Trollope and Donald Pickering as readers and Alice as solo cellist. She very nearly did not make it because on the same day she was playing a lunchtime recital at the Buxton Festival. Alice writes: "As I remember it, the organisers of the Fairford concert had arranged for a car to pick me and Mum up at the end of the Buxton concert, but it didn't arrive. I had my fairly old Ford Fiesta there, so was considering driving myself. But my future parents-in-law (John and Elizabeth Adams) kindly insisted that we take their faster and much more comfortable Saab. David drove Penny and me – I sat in the back and David remembers Penny encouraging his speeding to make sure we got there on time – which we did."

Another unexpected invitation came in a fax from Dana Marsh, the young director of the Los Angeles-based Paulist Boy Choristers of California, who wondered if I would be interested in taking his place while he had a year's sabbatical. Dana explained that the Paulist Choristers who had been founded in 1977, rehearsed four times a week after school, and in recent years had given complete performances of Handel's *Messiah*, with period instruments. I had first come across Dana when his father, a fine violinist who was about to take a sabbatical in the UK, wrote to me asking if his son, a chorister in the highly regarded choir at St Thomas on 5th Avenue in New York, might be allowed to sing with the Winchester Cathedral Choir for the coming academic year. Unfortunately, the choir school in Winchester did not have a space, so I recommended Dana to Richard Seal, who warmly welcomed him to Salisbury.

Dana's invitation could hardly have come at a better time, apart from for the fact that I had a number of commitments in England, for which I would have to make seven trips back, causing me to miss several rehearsals in Los Angeles. Dana however was able to arrange cover for me while I was back in the UK, and so he duly went ahead and at incredibly short notice secured the necessary visa and work permit. The Paulist choristers were good, and working with them gave me a welcome *modus vivendi*.

In due course I was able to explore new repertoire such as Britten's *Rejoice in the Lamb* and Bernstein's *Chichester Psalms*, as well as prepare the Paulist choristers to sing the ripieno choruses of the *St Matthew Passion*, conducted by Helmut Rilling. I was concerned however that the boys' sound might not be strong enough in the Los Angeles Music Center and brought in some girl choristers. Although not universally approved, the girls were soon accepted, not only for practical reasons, but also in the belief that they should not be denied the chance to make high quality music like the boys from the same school.

Incidentally, while acknowledging that the last year of a boy's treble voice often has a quality not frequently matched in girls of a similar age, I believe that the sound of the singers is much more determined by the teaching and vocal training they receive – as is reflected in the contrasting sounds of different boys choirs – than by their gender. Dare I say also that the girls' concentration is at least as good as the boys'?

Additional engagements in California came my way; conducting *Messiah* with the LA Master Chorale, and playing with the LA Philharmonic. There was more travelling to give organ recitals, as well as guest conducting and speaking engagements, including at the Annual Conference in Miami of the Association of Anglican Musicians, many of whose members had made generous donations towards our legal costs.

In July and August 2000, the English Chamber Singers made a tour of Australia, promoted by the Australian Youth Choirs, with concerts in Perth, Adelaide, Melbourne, Sydney (Opera House Concert Hall) and Brisbane. The varied programmes opened with John Tavener's Millennium piece, *A New Beginning* and included *Choral Suite* from *Becket, The Kiss of Peace*, by the Australian composer David Reeves, which the choir had recorded in London previously and given the premiere in Canterbury Cathedral.

There was a potential clash when I was invited by Nicholas Kenyon to play Bach's *Prelude and Fugue in C minor* at the BBC Proms on the day we were due to arrive back from Australia. I was keen to accept but with likely jetlag it was obviously risky, and I was very grateful to be allowed to miss the last concert of the ECS tour (in Brisbane), giving me an extra day in England before the Prom. The Brisbane concert was conducted by one of the singers, Aidan Oliver, who in due course became the renowned Director of the Glyndebourne Festival Chorus. Back in London the extra day made a huge difference, and the *Prelude and Fugue* seemed to go down well. Four years later came the challenge of playing on the newly restored organ at the First Night of the Proms the *Toccata in D minor BWV 565*, which was followed by Henry Wood's arrangement of the *Fugue* played by the BBC Symphony Orchestra conducted by Leonard Slatkin.

While directing the Paulist Boy Choristers, I also did a year as Director of Music at First Congregational Church of Los Angeles. The Great Organ of First Church is comprised of several organs joined together and is among the largest church pipe organs in the world, with 18,094 speaking pipes, 328 ranks, 15 divisions, and a total of 278 speaking stops. One of my first duties at "First Congo" was directing the music at a hastily arranged ecumenical service, five days after the terrible '9/11' bombings. One of the hymns selected was very appropriate: *Let there be peace on earth*, for which I made a new arrangement. At the church there was an annual Bach Festival, and I conducted the *St John Passion* with a fine team of soloists, choir and orchestra, who were joined in the chorales by a group of local singers. There were special events in the Hollywood Bowl, such as the First World Festival of Sacred Music in 1999 (about which I wrote an article for *The Times*), and in 2002 being on stage with the Paulist Choristers for the concert premiere of Howard Shore's *Lord of the Rings*.

I was also encouraged by the Los Angeles Da Camera Society to start a chamber choir specialising in Renaissance and Contemporary choral music. This repertoire was reflected in the first programme (Taverner and Tavener) of the Millennium Consort Singers in April 2007, in the presence of a full house at the Basilica in Los Angeles. Most of the excellent singers lived in the LA area, although one deep bass, about whom I had received the strongest recommendations, managed to travel to and from San Francisco. I auditioned all the singers, but the only time Hugh Davies and I could find to meet was one morning at Los Angeles Airport. I heard a resonant bottom D, and that was good enough. Our next concert for the Da Camera Society was another programme of English music in Pasadena.

For a short article about the Millennium Consort Singers see Appendix 4

By this time, I was paying numerous visits to San Diego, where I acted as Associate Director of the Pacific Academy of Ecclesiastical Music (PACEM), based at St Paul's Cathedral. This was mainly to conduct standard choral repertoire, such as Haydn's *Creation*, Mozart *Vespers* and plenty of Handel. I also went back for a further period as Artist in Residence at the University of California at Davis; and then in 2009, became Associate Director of the Grand Rapids Choir of Men and Boys. This was another exceptional choir, which had the benefit of being directed by an outstanding choir trainer, Scott Bosscher, who had spent five years singing in the choir at Wells Cathedral.

Back in England in 2000, I gave six Bach recitals with Alice at St John's Smith Square, featuring the Suites for solo cello, the Gamba Sonatas and a variety of organ works. The Independent's critic wrote: "Alice Neary's skill with sustained lines was apparent in Britten's first *Cello Suite Op 2*. There was an unforced quality in her playing that allowed the composer's voice to speak for itself, and displayed a wealth of character, from jauntiness to spellbinding melancholy".

MN with daughter, Alice.

CHAPTER 22

More Performances

"I am so pleased ... for church music at large"

In anticipation of John Tavener's 70th birthday on 28 January 2014, I was delighted to be involved in the planning of a weekend of celebratory concerts at St John's Smith Square. But John's shockingly sudden death on 12 November 2013 turned the proposed weekend into a memorial. John Lubbock and I shared the conducting – John directing *The Protecting Veil* with Alice as soloist, while I conducted the British premiere of *Miroires*, written in memory of the wife of John's heart surgeon, Sir Magdi Yacoub.

There were more Tavener performances, including several programmes with the Netherlands Chamber Choir, by far the longest of which was Sir John's monumental *Veil of the Temple* at the Oudekerk, Amsterdam in June 2005. Starting at 10.30 pm, it lasted until dawn, when I walked out of the church into the rising sun feeling euphoric and also relieved. I was much indebted to Stephen Layton for sharing his schedule and rehearsal notes for the first performance of this remarkable and demanding work at the Temple Church in 2003 (at which we were present). The piece, in eight cycles, is scored for soloists, three choirs and a children's choir with organ and duduk (a double reed woodwind instrument made of apricot wood, originating from Armenia).

Another unexpected opportunity came in 2005, when my friend Steven Abbott recommended me to Universal Music Classics and Jazz to direct an album called *The Choirboys*. Universal organised a nation-wide talent search to find a young chorister "to bring choral music into the current music scene". However, the judges could not agree which of the three finalists should be given the recording contract and decided to assemble them as a trio. Two (Patrick Aspbury and C J Porter Thaw) were choristers at Ely Cathedral, and Ben Inman was at Southwell Minster. They were all very receptive, quick to learn new repertoire (aimed unashamedly at the popular end of the market), which included Eric Clapton's *Tears in heaven* and Howard Goodall's *Ecce*

Homo and *The Lord is my shepherd*; another popular song was *He ain't heavy, he's my brother*.

Apparently, it was one of the fastest-selling classical debut albums in the UK, earning *The Choirboys* a gold disc which was presented to them on the BBC children's television programme, *Blue Peter*. This was sufficiently successful for Universal Music, Japan to organise a promotional visit to Tokyo in 2006, where I joined them, having flown in from Los Angeles. All the boys were in demand as soloists. But their time singing together as trebles was limited by their voices maturing and changing. Two years later I helped choose a new trio for a *Choirboys' Christmas Carols Album* – Andrew Swait was a member of Tewkesbury Abbey Choir, William Dutton at St Mark's Church, Harrogate and Bill Goss a pupil at St Peter's School, York. This album, more traditional than the first, attracted quite a lot of attention, with several new arrangements. Worldwide, however, it had less impact than its predecessor.

Between 2007 and 2012 I paid several visits to Washington DC, where James (Nicola's husband) was working at the British Embassy. The family lived in Bethesda, Maryland, and introduced me to Thomas Smith, the organist at Church of the Redeemer, who invited me to direct his choir whenever I was in the area and also commissioned a Mass setting for the choir and congregation – *Mass of the Redeemer*. Of my different compositions and arrangements, probably the most successful has been my setting of *We three Kings*, which was broadcast from King's College, Cambridge at the Service of Nine Lessons and Carols, and was several times included by Stephen Cleobury in televised Christmas programmes.

As well as making choral arrangements for services at Winchester and Westminster, for several years at Christmas I made settings for our six grandchildren, Isobel (viola), Harriet (voice), Emily (oboe), Jacob (French horn), Jessica (violin) and Leo (keyboard and later clarinet). Generally these were arrangements of Christmas carols, such as *Jingle Bells* and *See amid the winter snow*, and as well as playing their instruments each of them had a solo verse to sing. To begin with the arrangements were deliberately simple, but they became more challenging, reaching a climax with a setting of *Lord of the dance*, which they also played at our Golden Wedding celebration in April 2017 at St James' Clerkenwell. The party began in the church where, to call everyone to attention, I played on the full organ the opening chords of Messiaen's *Dieu Parmi Nous* after which David and Alice with Louise Williams (viola) regaled us with a gorgeous performance of the Schubert

String Trio in Bb D471. This was followed by the grandchildren playing and singing *Lord of the Dance*, with the unexpected bonus of the guests joining in the refrain!

In 2012, I was honoured to receive a Lambeth Doctorate from the Archbishop of Canterbury, Rowan Williams – "… in recognition of his outstanding contribution at national and international level as an organist and conductor and of his sensitive and dynamic interpretation of sacred and secular music in the choral tradition". It was a very happy occasion, not least because my fellow DMus recipient was Dr Francis Jackson, the distinguished former organist of York Minster. The choir from All Saints Fulham (where I had often deputised as organist or conductor) was directed by the much-admired editor, composer and arranger, Jonathan Wikeley. A number of our friends were there, led by the extremely supportive Celia Scott, a member of the St Margaret's congregation, who had done so much behind the scenes to further our cause. Among the messages was one from Anthony Caesar (former Precentor at Winchester and Sub Dean of the Chapel Royal) which particularly touched my heart: "Many congratulations on your Lambeth award. I am so pleased for you personally and for church music at large"

With Francis Jackson, former Organist of York Minster, when they both received Lambeth Doctorates.

I also enjoyed deputising at St Mary's Wimbledon, where the lively and dynamic Max Barley, then in his early twenties, was making his mark as Director of Music. It has been a great pleasure working with him on various works he has conducted, and it came as no surprise when he was appointed Director of Music at Holy Trinity Sloane Square, where he has already made a huge impact with his enterprising initiatives.

Thanks initially to the former Abbey chorister Philip Stopford (the boy who didn't like 'bad music'!), who by then had become an established composer and was Director of Music at St Ann's Cathedral, Belfast, I paid several visits to Northern Ireland. There I played recitals, directed courses and conducted, in particular at St Columbo's Cathedral, Londonderry, including a special service of thanksgiving and dedication honouring the hymn writer, Cecil Frances Alexander, and marking the centenary of the death of her husband, Archbishop William Alexander. As well as singing most of her famous hymns, such as *All things bright and beautiful*, we recorded some other musical settings of her texts, including Charles Gounod's moving *There is a green hill far away* for voice and piano.

In December 2014, I was organ accompanist and soloist at a Christmas concert at the Langholtskirkja (National Church) in Reykjavik, Iceland. I had heard the choir in London previously, and was very impressed – the conductor, Hilimar Örn Agnarsson was a Tavener fan. I took advantage of some time off to do some sightseeing and, very enjoyably, to bathe in the hot springs at Reykjavik's Blue Lagoon.

In 2018, Frank Field (MP for Birkenhead) asked me to direct the music at the Wilfred Owen Commemoration in Birkenhead, where Owen grew up, marking the centenary of his death. The principal event was in Christ Church, where Owen and his family worshipped, and his father taught at the Sunday School. This gave an opportunity to hear some of Owen's finest poetry, as well as a remarkable variety of music inspired by it. The programme began with my playing on the piano Chopin's *Funeral March*, which Owen had frequently played when he was in France during World War 1 and which, according to his biographer Dominic Hibberd, sometimes seems to have been the inspiration for his poetry.

Most of the performers had links with Birkenhead and they included Dame Patricia Routledge, who read Owen's *Futility*. Graham Ellis, whose *Trilogy of War Poems* with words by Wilfred Owen was sung by Nick Hardy and Paul Broadhurst, the Christ Church organist, whose fascinating choice for his organ solo was an extract from Philip Glass's *Koyaanisqatsi*. World War 1 composers and Merseyside poets were also represented, and the concert ended with a rousing performance of Parry's *Jerusalem*, composed in 1916. I also conducted a *BBC Songs of Praise* programme to mark the centenary, presented by Aled Jones.

CHAPTER 23

70th Birthday Concert, St John's, Smith Square, London, 28 March 2010

"I was glad"

It was Penny who not only had the idea of a concert to mark my 70th birthday, but who also overcame my initial reluctance and insisted that we went through with it. Fate seemed to have the casting vote when we discovered, to our surprise, that St John's, Smith Square was free on the day itself. We decided to invite some of my former choristers from St Margaret's Westminster (1965–71), Winchester Cathedral (1972–87) and Westminster Abbey (1988–98) to join the English Chamber Singers, and with a top line of excellent sopranos the choir proved more than equal to the considerable challenges I threw in their direction. The concert would be in aid of the Music Therapy Charity, from which our autistic son Tom had benefited so much.

Choosing what to perform turned out to be a pleasure and a challenge. Eventually I decided that, in the course of a choral and orchestral programme, each of my main musical resting places would be represented; and so we began with music by Henry Purcell, in whose footsteps I was extraordinarily privileged to follow, both as one of the Children of the Chapel Royal and as Organist of Westminster Abbey. After the rousing Rondeau from Purcell's *Suite to Abdelazer*, the choir launched forth into *I was glad*, set by Purcell for the Coronation of James II in 1685. We followed this with his remarkable verse anthem *My beloved spake*, composed for the Chapel Royal when he was barely 18. The programme then moved forward almost three centuries to works composed by Jonathan Harvey, who had found an unaccompanied setting of Wilfrid Owen's *Song of June*, written when we were at Cambridge together, but never performed; and so we proudly gave the world premiere. (*For an interview with Jonathan Harvey, see Appendix 1.*) This was followed by one of the commissions dating from my time as Organist at Winchester, *Come Holy Ghost*, in which Jonathan employed all manner of contemporary idioms including aleatoric techniques, when each singer, within prescribed limits, can choose to sing more or less when he or she chooses – brilliantly capturing the effect of 'speaking in tongues'.

As I wrote in the programme note, I only regretted that there was not space in the concert for anything by J S Bach. But to provide a leavening from all the weird and wonderful choral music, I could not resist including Haydn's *Cello Concerto in C* with the Goldberg Ensemble and Alice as soloist. Without a hint of nepotism, I can faithfully report that everyone thought that she played beautifully. What I had not expected however was the moment when, in the first movement cadenza, she inserted two unmistakable Bach snippets: the openings of the *Toccata in D minor*, and the *Fugue in G minor*. As the ever-buoyant nonagenarian, Sir David Willcocks, emailed the following morning: "Alice would pull her father's leg ...". This put everyone in very good heart and the second half of the programme seemed to go by in a flash. We began with a poignant rarity by Herbert Howells, his setting of Psalm 137, *By the waters of Babylon*, for baritone, violin, cello and organ. Then came the UK concert premiere of *Take him, Earth, for cherishing* by John Tavener, the other contemporary composer whose music I had specially championed, and who, like Jonathan Harvey, was present at the concert.

Finally, all the forces came together to perform Handel's *Dixit Dominus*, which I still consider to be the most demanding undertaking I ever gave my choristers, but this time with several of them as adult soloists. Then, just when I thought it was time to have a celebratory drink, a swarm of ex-choristers, now in their twenties and thirties, ascended the stage to be directed by Stephen Layton in a surprise encore – a specially composed version of *Happy Birthday* by John Rutter.

At the post-concert reception in the Footstool Restaurant there was a marvellous opportunity for past choristers and their families and friends to reconnect, while our other daughter, Nicola, who had been singing soprano, made a lovely speech. In response I noted with great pleasure how many members of my family had been taking part, but that I had been less pleased during the dress rehearsal when they (save for my tenor brother-in-law) kept interrupting me!

An unforgettable evening which, thanks to friends and family on and off the stage, truly did gladden our hearts. And the icing on the cake was to be found in *The Times* the following morning, not in a review, but in the crossword, most ingeniously set by the chief crossword editor (Richard Browne, one of the Waynflete Singers), with solutions including my name and age and various other relevant connections – extraordinary! (*For* The Times *crossword and its solution see Appendix 9.*)

With many of the performers giving their services, and thanks to the generosity of the audience and of many who could not be present, the concert raised over £6,000 for The Music Therapy Charity. The full house had also been egged on by Simon Callow's splendid introduction: "We like the tinkle of metal going into the buckets, but we like even more the gentle sound of the ... fifty-pound notes!".

CHAPTER 24

St Michael and All Angels, Barnes

"Would it help if I played for the next three weeks?"

In December 2012 I received an unexpected call from John West (my successor but one as Organ Scholar at Caius), asking if I would help audition a new Organist at St Michael and All Angels, Barnes, where he was the assistant. A high Anglican church (where, I was told, "if in doubt, genuflect"), I gathered there had been some tensions within the choir which would require firm handling by the next organist. Despite the musical competence of the candidates invited to audition, because of the difficult situation there was a reluctance to appoint either of them. So, in an unguarded moment and to allow more time, I said to John, that if they were desperate I could help out for three weeks before my next trip to America. John passed this on to the Vicar, Fr Paul Holland, and so it was that I became the temporary organist. Thanks to John's constant support, either accompanying or singing tenor, and the willingness of the singers to accept the temporary regime, things went quite well, and within a month or so I became Director of Music – and stayed for nearly nine years!

The musical menu was relatively simple, but what impressed me particularly was the willingness of the singers to do their homework before the weekly Wednesday practices; and within two years we performed Bach's *St John Passion* with the English Chamber Singers for the Barnes Music Festival – the St Michael's Choir (representing the congregation) singing the chorales and the first and last choruses. The performance was enhanced by an outstanding team of period instrumentalists, led by Alison Bury. Principally for economic reasons, we had just one instrument to a part, but this worked surprisingly well and encouraged some really expressive playing. Everyone was inspired by the superb Evangelist, Robert Murray, nephew of Bruce Houlder, one of the St Michael's tenors. Speaking of family connections, I should also mention that our own family was strongly represented, with Penny, Nicola, our granddaughter Harriet (sopranos), Amanda, Penny's sister, and Catherine, their sister-in-law (altos), and brothers, Antony (tenor) and Ben (bass) and were joined at later concerts by Alice (cello continuo) and David (violin).

Over the years, the St Michael's Choir, together with the English Chamber Singers, gave several concerts for the Barnes Music Festival, including the Fauré *Requiem* in a fine chamber arrangement by David Hill, my distinguished successor at Winchester, more masterpieces by Bach, the *St Matthew Passion* (again with Robert Murray as the Evangelist), the *Magnificat* and in 2020 the *Mass in B minor*. That was a mere three days before the first Covid lockdown, and I hate to think of the disappointment to musicians and audience if our performance had had to be cancelled.

The way the singers coped with the restrictions imposed during the lockdowns was truly inspiring – indeed I felt their singing improved. So that there would be at least some music even without the choir, I recorded some anthem accompaniments which the singers used when recording their parts at home. Jane Bennett-Powell, as well as contributing in countless other ways, collated the recordings, which she then sent to Fiona in Miami (daughter of congregation members, Nick and the late Rosemary Hurry), who did some editing (including subtle adjustments to hide occasional variations in tempo and pitch). Jane took over the later editing, and gratitude also goes to Hannah Childs for the live streaming of the services, which I know was greatly appreciated. We were also greatly helped by Lizzie Hackett-Brown churchwarden and parish secretary.

An important development, very much due to the initiative of Fr Stephen Stavrou, who had succeeded Fr Paul as vicar, was setting up choral and organ scholarship schemes for those still at school. This has really taken off, the 2023–24 organ scholar, Sophia Membury, having been awarded an organ scholarship at Pembroke College, Cambridge.

Speaking of the organ, we were greatly indebted to our organ builders, B C Shepherd and Sons, for refurbishing the St Michael's organ in 2016. In my view, the organ sound, enhanced by the splendid acoustics, was transformed, and was much enjoyed by all the organists who came to play – which brings me to John West. From the moment I arrived at St Michael's, until his sad and untimely death in 2018, I was immensely assisted by John, who served St Michael's as assistant organist for over 14 years. "Served" is indeed the word, for John unstintingly gave a huge amount of time to St Michael's. He was such a special colleague – not only a fine organist, but also an exceptional friend

– and his death left a horrible void. However, thereafter we were blessed to have Philip Berg and Emma McAllister as our organ accompanists on special occasions. Other special friends from St Michael's who have sadly passed on include the bass, Anthony Gardiner, who would send me thought-provoking poems after some of our performances, and the composer, Basil Moss, whose fine *St Michael's Mass* fits in so well with the liturgy.

My time at Barnes was very rewarding, and I was honoured in 2017 to be awarded a Lancelot Andrews medal "for Godly Service and Zeal for the Gospel" by the Bishop of Southwark. On my retirement Bishop Christopher also wrote very generously about my work at Winchester and Westminster.

I was very sad to leave St Michael's in January 2022, but because of my health problems it was the right decision, and the choir gave me a marvellous send-off. My successor, Laurence Williams, had been one of my Abbey choristers. As well as being a fine organist and choir-trainer, he has an outstanding voice, and at my final evensong he was the baritone soloist in the *Stanford in G Nunc dimittis* before I literally handed over the baton and he directed Edgar Bainton's appropriately named anthem, *And I saw a new heaven*.

With the Choir at St Michael and All Angels, Barnes, at MN's retirement.

Epilogue

Some years ago, when I first began these memoirs, I wrote:

> "For me, music is a life-long joy; it is not just 'for a while', it will always be a vital part of my life".

Now reluctantly I have to admit that much of the music I enjoy has to be in my head. In recent years it has not been easy to live with some serious medical issues. In 2017, Penny had noticed that I was speaking more quietly, which she discovered might be an early sign of Parkinson's Disease, and sure enough it was. Thanks to expert medical advice, not least from our daughter, Nicola, and Penny's brother, Antony, I was able to keep playing and conducting until reaching 82, but by then there was really no option but to stop, especially as I was also having episodes of tinnitus. Most disconcerting of all, however, has been deteriorating hearing, and quite frequently distorted pitch in the higher registers when listening to music. Given these problems, I feel fortunate to have been able to carry on so long for what I will immodestly call my "Indian summer". This would never have happened without the exceptional support of my wife and family, and indeed the patience and understanding of so many musicians with whom I have had the privilege and pleasure of working. I cannot thank them enough.

If music be the food of love, play on.

With daughter Nicola in 2024.

APPENDIX 1

Interview with Jonathan Harvey

Recorded in 2009 at his house in Lewes,
for the magazine *Cathedral Music*.

MN As I was driving down to your home in Lewes this morning, I began thinking of one or two constants in the way you have composed, right back to 1974/75 and the first Winchester Cathedral commission, *The Dove Descending*. I detected something which I have seen in many other of your pieces since – a fascination with one chord coming in and out of another, [JH Yes] and it seems to me that this technique is tailor-made for some of your work with live music and electronic music.

JH Very astute ... because I love the idea of structure, but structure which becomes fluid. It's almost as if (this has) become a kind of Buddhist aesthetic that all solid objects should dissolve. In the idea of emptiness; and in one form or another, this idea has been going on since then. With electronics, it's very easy.

MN But how would you describe the way in which these chords/ideas dissolve, and how they get resolved? When you start out, do you know?

JH No. It's quite different now. I used to have a grand plan, usually, an idea of the piece as a whole, but I don't really like that any more. I prefer to keep/give myself (more options) ...

MN Like going on a journey?

JH Yes, exactly; being open to the material and seeing where it might take you. That is even more interesting.

MN Yet from the first time we collaborated, you have been incredibly open and understanding over what we might call the limitations, the parameters within which we have asked you to work. I am sure you remember the first occasion (with *The Dove Descending*). The Bishop-elect of Winchester, John Taylor had invited me to set a text from Eliot's *Little Gidding* for his enthronement, but I had the sense to suggest that we approach a proper composer, and, with you living in the Diocese at Southampton, it was a perfect opportunity to ask you. However, given

	your reputation in 1975, when you were already established as a world authority on Stockhausen and delving into tonal or rather atonal areas that were not the norm in the cathedral world, I felt that the Dean and Chapter might need some reassuring …. do you remember coming to a Chapter meeting to face the clergy and hear what they and I envisaged for that service?
JH	Oh yes, that meeting.
MN	I remember encouraging you to take advantage of the antiphonal possibilities, but there were other elements which you picked up on, the harmonics developing from the chords coming in and out, in and among the cathedral acoustics, which really add another dimension.
JH	Well, as you know, Winchester Cathedral is a sacred place to me, and that time with you was absolutely one of the most, one could almost call it, a 'holy time'
MN	Yes, it was a creative time, thanks to John Taylor, and the Dean, Michael Stancliffe, in particular, all trusting, even though we did not (always) know where we were going.
MN	*The Dove Descending* did take some learning, but it was not long before we started work on another of your pieces. With Dominic, your son, by now a chorister, you had been attending Evensong on Sunday afternoons, and I will never forget the moment when you modestly came into the South Transept one afternoon and said: "I've brought you a little piece; would you like to see it?" And that was *I love the Lord*. Do tell me how that piece gestated.
JH	I had spent so much time in the cathedral listening to the choir, absorbing the whole atmosphere of devotion, the sacred sound and the resonant sound, hearing the beautiful, controlled in tune singing and so on … this had inspired me. It came all from the choir.
MN	By then you had already composed one or two bigger works, for the Three Choirs Festival, but, as far as I could tell, you hadn't written pieces which could be slotted into the daily liturgy.
JH	No, no liturgical pieces.
MN	And it is interesting, comparing you with someone like Messiaen, who had his great Catholic faith, but who felt unable to add anything to the liturgy.
JH	Yes, that's strange, isn't it? But I like the idea of the liturgy very much – so different from the concert world – you are part of a communal act

together; it's not a piece of music just for itself, and somehow that is what the old composers must have experienced. You feel you belong to the ancient tradition of service for the church; they were quite humble servants. The main idea was to fit into the devotion which was all around them, and that I liked very much, being part of it, belonging. It was very exciting.

MN And that comes through in the way you wrote. But how did you find an idiom, while keeping your own integrity, which would be right for the building and manageable by the fallible musicians, when you started work on *The Dove Descending*?

JH Well, you warned me, but at any rate I could hear quite clearly, that anything fast – semiquavers – for instance – doesn't work very well. And the best thing is this wonderful, rather slow and complex procession of sound, which is so powerful. So I always wanted to take advantage of that, and I think that's why my second Winchester anthem *I love the Lord* was the first tonal piece I had written for years, based on and in G major. And how could I write that without feeling that I had compromised? That was quite a question. I think the answer is that I gave up an 'ego' (Laughter).

MN Dying to yourself?

JH Yes, that's right. I did not feel that I was writing something old-fashioned, or stale or whatever. I did not want to join an *avant-garde* movement once more. I just wanted to do justice to the words, the beautiful words – which were very close to my mother, when she was dying, which was one of the impetuses to write the piece ....

And to be faithful to that was everything.

MN There was kind of follow up in *Resurrection* for the Three Choirs Festival at Worcester, but you also had a bigger denser group with low basses being asked to produce a bottom A, by an extraordinary technique, like a quint on an organ producing an overtone a fifth below. (Laughter.) But that was the only time since then that you have really limited yourself in quite that tonal way.

JH Yes, it was also tonal; it was also 'inversional', in a Schönbergian sense, as the inversion was fairly strict. But when you invert a major triad, of course you get a minor triad and its reflecting tonalities. And reflecting the title of *Resurrection* – (life and death) were the two twin themes, one going down and one going up, obviously, so they reflect each other –

	quite a philosophical concept being portrayed exactly in the music.
MN	Now, one of the most important aspects of your compositions for the liturgy has been to provide something <u>of our time</u>, but it's fair to say that often their difficulty has militated against their having as many performances as the compositions deserve.
JH	mmm Yes.
MN	I think the situation is getting better, and there are an increasing number of professional choirs in France, Germany and Holland who are doing these pieces, and a lot are appearing in concert programmes.
JH	Of course, I would love them to be done in the liturgy. I can't really tell, because I don't see the music lists.
MN	Well, I can assure you that there are one or two winners, which appear regularly, *I love the Lord*, and in particular *Come, Holy Ghost* (commissioned for the 1984 Southern Cathedrals Festival), with its brilliant use of aleatoric techniques, but at the same time making it possible not only for people to sense the plainchant but enabling the singers to grasp where they are in relation to it. It actually acts as a useful adjunct in keeping everyone within a sense of their own pitch
JH	Yes.
MN	… because singers are quite often alarmed, if they don't have accurate pitch themselves, by the sheer difficulty of pitching notes. The singers need some sense of where they are going to be.
JH	I have been aware of that, having been a singer myself, and I do know how difficult it is to pitch unless you have sense of where you are, or a tonality or a pentatonic mode.
MN	That's true of *Come Holy Ghost* …
JH	… which is basically pentatonic, so they do know pretty well where they are. But I sympathise with voices, and I try to give them that orientation.
MN	I have to say however that *Angels*, written for King's College, Cambridge Christmas Eve Carol Service, is very beautiful but very demanding. The two choirs are very separate, almost going off at a tangent from one another.
JH	It is difficult to pitch, more than I thought, perhaps.
MN	It worked beautifully with the Netherlands Radio Choir in the Concertgebouw in 2006; and I was delighted at the response of the packed audience, as well as that of the choir.

MN But perhaps of all the pieces commissioned for Winchester, the most original was the *Magnificat and Nunc dimittis* (Laughter). Michael Tippett's *St John's Service* in 1961 certainly felt as if it was breaking new ground, but 27 years later, you came up with something even more provocative – your *Magnificat and Nunc dimittis*, which no less an authority than Nicholas Kenyon, writing in the *Financial Times* about the première at the combined Evensong during the 1978 Southern Cathedrals Festival, recognized as a landmark for Anglican church music.

In the *Magnificat*, the 'Cantus firmus' moves from part to part in a Webern-like way, and there are also some spoken sections, aleatoric passages, while in the *Nunc dimittis*, we find an astounding fluctuation of sound to represent the light. How did you conceive that?

JH I liked the 't's in light, and I asked the singers to emphasize these 't's, which were aleatoric so they spattered about in chance formations – the more singers, the more 't's. The whole aleatoric idea of these passages was to build up to a climax until the organ, which has been little used until that point, crashes in with a huge chord, using all twelve notes. The organ gradually winds down, and that's the end. Light is represented by a very dramatic change of timbre and sound.

MN You mention 'twelve notes'. How often have you written using serial techniques?

JH Up to about 1982 I used it a lot, not very strict, often tinged with tonality. I was taught by two Viennese Schönbergians, Erwin Stein and Hans Keller.

MN Were they very strict with you?

JH Yes, they were strict, but neither of them said you <u>should</u> write serially, and they did not think that was the right way to go about it. Both of them thought that it should be very spontaneous, if I felt the need for it, to use it to give a kind of unity.

MN But when you say spontaneous, what do you mean? Where does the ear come into this?

JH That's exactly what they were saying. If you don't hear in the passage what you want, you shouldn't do it. ... I wanted to go into it quite a lot, and went to study with Milton Babbitt, the arch-serialist, at Princeton, but I came away from that period feeling that if it could not really be heard, – what was the point?

MN   It's an interesting point, because an audience, particularly the first time they hear a piece, is only going to pick up a certain amount. [JH Yes.] Has this ever made you think that you should write more simply?

JH   … Oh, yes, I have thought that from time to time, and that was in my decision to abandon serialism. I think the first example was probably the flute piece *Nataraja*. I also received a letter from Hans Keller, about being too intellectual and that if I would only forget my academic theories, I would be a good composer – pretty forthright, as usual!

MN   You were probably already trying to break away from academia. But let's move on to some of your electronic works, two of which were performed in Winchester. The *Toccata for Organ and Tape*, which is rather like a concerto for organ and tape, and which I premiered in New York, works very well but requires good speakers. And talking of speakers, one of the most remarkable sound experiences of my life (until last year's Proms 'performance') was hearing *Mortuos plango* (which features the tenor bell of the Cathedral and the electronically adjusted treble voice of Dominic, your son) in Winchester Cathedral – with the speakers right up in the clerestory.

JH   That was a dream, to have it come home. It took some trouble to get the speakers there (MN that's an understatement!) but it was worth it. Of course, it's a piece which owes everything to Winchester … (MN … and Dominic's voice)… JH … and the bell.

MN   It is the stage-managing of these things, isn't it, which is often time-consuming and expensive?

JH   That's been my battle throughout my life … you had to try and persuade people that it's worth doing, but people sometimes have been a bit lazy. It's not just money – they can find money for this, that and the other, if they want to – but they are suspicious and wonder if it's worth it.

MN   And concert promoters are often scared if you put something modern on the programme, thinking that it will deter the audience. But Louis Halsey, for example, in the sixties and early seventies was doing 'ancient and modern', with a mix of programmes, including your *Cantata I*, just as later we did at Winchester – drawing the audience in, and then giving them something which was completely outside their experience. But I am delighted to hear that St John's College, Cambridge is doing your *Canticles* soon after your 70th birthday.

JH   Yes and you had some say in that, I believe.

MN Well I just put a bit of pressure on, saying it was about time they did them!

JH They are hoping to do three things, an organ recital including the *Toccata, Fantasia and Laus Deo*, and some chamber music in the Master's Lodge. But I have a question for <u>you</u> about the *Canticles*; because without you, I would never have dared to 'challenge' and you said, yes, come on, write something challenging.

MN Well, it certainly ended up as a personal challenge, not least, dare I say, with my fellow organists at Chichester and Salisbury, as I knew that when they first saw the score there would be a reaction, and probably not a particularly favourable reaction. The only thing to do was to put it on the programme so that we had to do it. In the course of the early rehearsals with the Winchester Choir, we recorded sections on an old cassette machine, so that I could send John Birch and Richard Seal copies of how we thought it should go, for them to play to their choirs. One can't pretend that it's going to be easy for most cathedral choirs, unless they can make time for sectional rehearsals (as it happens, two of my most important innovations at Winchester, which were agreed before I arrived there, were to have a short full choir rehearsal before each service, and a man only rehearsal each Monday evening). But another help, and this is something which is such a blessing of the Cathedral system here in England, is that you see the boys or girls every morning and you can fit in ten minutes at the end of each practice; and so if you can just get the music into their systems, they barely have time to forget it, because there is a kind of not only mental memory but also a kind of muscular memory. But there is no substitute for the conductor who is taking it on to be absolutely clear in his/her own mind that they believe in the work.

I never did the *Canticles* at the Abbey, but that was primarily because of lack of rehearsal time with the men. But we were thrilled of course to get the *Missa brevis* which has recently been recorded very well by the current Abbey Choir under James O'Donnell. And that offers another technique of yours, namely using speech. What appeals to you about that (some might say 'extra musical') ingredient?

JH It's the idea of blurring, again, which you mentioned before – the combination of pitches and speech is a very definite blurring of musical pitches, so that the pitches and the speaking are somewhat random and cluster-like in effect. And if they are juxtaposed, they call each other into question, and the whole thing becomes more complex, becomes more ambiguous – I love that.

MN Do you feel that the spoken element is representing the congregation, as if part of the whole body corpus?

JH No. That's nice idea, but I had not thought of it. But maybe it does bring in the congregation.

MN In the *Sanctus* you chose very deep low beautiful sounds, which are sometimes quite difficult to hear, particularly in our cathedrals where the bass sounds tend to get lost. I was slightly surprised by that, but I knew that this must be what you wanted.

JH I love the deep low notes, very soft; I suppose I had thought that it would be fairly blurred, but anyway there are also the silences in the *Sanctus*, which are very much connected with Winchester and, I think, the Abbey. There is enough resonance to make the silences an integral part of the structure.

MN And silences also work beautifully in *Thou mastering me God*. My own test with that piece was keeping the choristers' interest while they repeated the same note (G above Middle C) for 44 bars, although at times the G almost seems to change in relation to the harmonies revolving around it.

JH That's very interesting.

MN ... and then eventually those words, 'Over again I feel thy finger and find thee' it's as if you were using those words of Gerard Manley Hopkins in music to find 'home'.

JH Your suggestion for the words is a very beautiful one, and in the notion of being touched by God, the touching is very musically explicit, isn't it?

MN There is at least one setting however which is basically very simple – the *Winchester Litany*.

JH I have only heard it once, with you, but not since then.

MN There the words are intoned and heard very audibly, with just the minimum of harmonic change, until finally having that lovely flowering, when we reach the words: 'Holy God, holy and strong'. (It's published by OUP.) Could you write something like that today?

JH Well, you see, that was really <u>functional</u>. At St Michael's (Tenbury) I had sung the Litany every Friday morning. That came back to me, and I remember how we functioned, and how we sang these little phrases in procession, right round to the West End and back; they had to be simple and had to work when we were walking ... all this was in my mind.

MN And it worked. This brings us to Bishop John Taylor (who had invited you to set the Litany), and without whom quite a few of the things at Winchester would never have happened, in particular *Passion and Resurrection*.

JH Yes.

MN when we were feeling our way.

JH So well done ....

MN not least thanks to the participation of so many local people. It became a kind of Winchester 'Oberammergau', when, even though some of the parts were quite difficult, they were managed valiantly by the excellent local voluntary chorus, the Waynflete Singers ...

JH Yes, that was very inspiring ...

MN and it gave the whole thing a feeling that it was their work too.

JH Local people gathered round in one way or another. some made costumes, and it all began with the cast and backroom team attending a Holy Communion service in the Epiphany Chapel (in the Cathedral), celebrated by John Taylor.

MN There is a video of the BBC documentary

JH ... which has been seen by a lot of people,

MN ... and it's crying out for a performance in America. Is there anything looking back now which you would change? Would you leave it exactly as it is, after nearly 30 years?

JH I always said that the procession to Calvary was written at some length because of the very long Winchester nave, but it does not have to be that long, and I think one or two cuts for a concert version are in order.

MN It has an inevitability, which made me think of the *Passacaglia* in Britten's *Peter Grimes*.

JH Interesting, or *Death in Venice*. That sense of inevitability was very much with me when I wrote it. I thought of it, as a ritualistic drama, as it must have been in medieval times; everybody knows the story ... over many centuries, and one is just waiting for the inevitable to happen.

MN It's always said it is easier to write music that produces an anguished mood; but yet you managed in *the Resurrection* to create a radiant orchestration, even though we were limited to the twenty players. You had the idea of the *Three Marys* from the libretto, but there is a sea-change in musical idiom, isn't there?

JH Yes, this was a turning point for me.

MN You could not have written it while you were writing serially, could you?

JH Well, it is influenced by serialism, because it's inversional. The whole piece is kind of 'skewed serial'; the plainsong is one element, largely the pentatonic scale, and the series adds the remaining seven pitches as one unified Gestalt. The work is a kind of dialogue between the two: the anguished part is very serial – all the interludes in the first part. Then in the second part, the mirror inversion used in the resurrection, I wanted to make very harmonious and triadic sonorities, but reflecting around the central axis, just as the axis of the world has changed at that moment – everything is different, a floating spiritual quality has occurred in some evolutionary jump ….

MN Since you came back from Stanford (California) nine years ago, you have devoted yourself entirely to composition, without having to do any other work. And it's clearly been a fulfilment of what you have always wanted to do. Have you found it a godsend to have this freedom, or would you like to be able sometimes to have a little break from composition? (Laughter)

JH I am forced to have a break, because my body demands it now, and I have to rest quite often.

MN Have you still time to write for the church?

JH St John's wants me to write something for their 500th in 2012, and Wells Cathedral have made me President of their New Music Wells Festival, and I have said that I will write them a little piece. I'm going over there to do a Round Table shortly.

MN When we look back at church music composed in the last quarter of the 20th century, it is absolutely clear that there are several of your works which are going to stand out: *I love the Lord, Come Holy Ghost, the Canticles* and *Missa brevis*, commissioned by the Dean and Chapter of Westminster. (I am constantly thrilled by the opening of the *Gloria* and the beautiful, augmented use of C major.)

JH Pentatonic again. I thought of God as pentatonic, and Jesus as tonal. In the *Gloria* there are two voices; the voice of and about God, and the

	voice of and about Jesus, and so I tried to juxtapose these contrasting elements.
MN	You have also spoken about the 'eternal feminine'; how do you think of the eternal feminine in music?
JH	Well, that was something I became more and more interested in in various ways, but it's usually linked to the divine. Often Indian words are very explicit and Indian poetry. It's such a mixture of the erotic and the divine. I have always thought that the ecstasies of the domain of love are very appropriate, just as some of the great mystics did – I have always found that connection very revealing.
MN	Have you ever been tempted to set anything from the *Song of Solomon*?
JH	I have used it, yes, but very early on, never I think since I was student.
MN	Well, it's fascinating to think from those early days at Tenbury, when you were already beginning to explore sounds, that for the next 60 years you have literally continued to do that, incorporating all these extra techniques; and coupled with your imaginative use of texts, you have actually given to the church such a precious and sacred legacy, which I believe is being more and more appreciated.
JH	That's very kind of you.
MN	My colleagues and I look forward to many more things to come, but on behalf of us all, I should like to end by saying: "Congratulations, Happy Birthday and Thank you".
JH	Thank *you*, Martin. Without you, it would not have happened. I say that quite categorically.

APPENDIX 2

Cathedral Opera: Passion and Resurrection

Stephen Walsh, *The Observer* 29 March 1981

Church opera has had a mixed history since Britten put it on the map with his three church parables in the mid-sixties. But Jonathan Harvey's *Passion and Resurrection*, which had its first performance in Winchester Cathedral last weekend, should do a lot to restore faith in what has often seemed a hybrid and equivocating genre.

Harvey is perhaps unusual in that he approaches opera specifically as a committed Christian who happens also to be a sophisticated modern composer. So, the new work is very far from being a straight transplant from the theatre to the cathedral nave. Harvey calls it a 'liturgical drama', and he makes it evolve, in an extraordinarily impressive way, out of the actual liturgy of the Eucharist.

Christians are used to being assured from the pulpit that the communion service is a re-enactment. 'Do this in remembrance of me' is the key passage. But it's all too easy to forget the full extent of the drama which is subsumed by those routine and familiar words. Harvey however takes them literally. The opera cuts into the liturgy at precisely the point where the priest intones the consecration; it then follows the passion story to the Crucifixion and Resurrection (using medieval mystery rather than biblical texts) and ends by cutting back into the service for what amounts to a brief 'post-communion' sequence.

This is a simple enough idea, and perhaps it has been done before (Britten himself used the framework plan, but never in a liturgical context). But I doubt if anyone has ever handled it with such a cunning blend of simple dramatic imagery and apparently effortless musical subtlety and elegance. The basis of Harvey's score, as of Britten's parables, is plainsong. The music emerges from plainchant and response, and it finally flows back into it; there are also plainsong congregational hymns at strategic points in the opera, and in between much, perhaps all, of the more dramatically specific music is in one way or another derived from lineaments of chant.

This material proves marvellously versatile. Harvey is able to find in it both very straightforward treatments, where the voice is simply doubled in a kind of pseudo-organum style, and far more complicated textures which suit the more extended episodes in the story and where the style and technique are chromatic/ serial. There is no hiatus. The plainsong episodes, whether very lightly accompanied by an isolated string or brass instrument or richly embroidered with organ clusters and orchestral quarter-tone trills, always seem fresh and vital; and the serial passages, like the long scene at the tomb, never lose touch with the mellifluous raw material. In the end the free-flowing, dance-like celebrations of the Three Marys merge imperceptibly with the *Alleluia* responses from the Easter Service.

Harvey has written for Winchester before, and in *Passion and Resurrection* he shows the depth of his respect for that shaft of light in the prevailing gloom of Anglican music by testing the cathedral's resources to the full. In the Bishop of Winchester's production only a few key roles (Pilate and the Three Marys) were taken by London pros, while other crucial parts, including that of Christ (Donald Sweeney), were movingly taken by locals, both professional and amateur. Admittedly it was fairly easy to tell from the acting which was which; yet certain crudities of gesture were not out of keeping with the mystery-play atmosphere of parts of the opera. And the music, helped no doubt by the superb natural theatre of Wykeham's great church, was consistently well done under Martin Neary's inspired and invigorating direction.

APPENDIX 3

Boston Globe, 10 April 1999

Neary conducts a noble 'Innocence'

By Richard Dyer
GLOBE STAFF

Music Review

CAMBRIDGE – The British composer John Tavener has been a media darling more than once in the course of a long and personally turbulent career. Now he is more popular than ever: Yo-Yo Ma has recorded his mystical cello rhapsody "The Protecting Veil"; the composer's austere face appears on the covers of two current magazines, looking like a figure in a Byzantine mosaic.

The man most responsible for the current worldwide interest in Tavener is Martin Neary, who selected Tavener's "Song for Athene" as the recessional at the funeral of Princess Diana, which was seen and heard by a billion people. At that time Neary was organist and choirmaster of Westminster Abbey, a position from which he was subsequently dismissed by the Dean because of a financial arrangement that had been approved by by the previous administration. To little avail, the British musical establishment lined up behind Neary, a much-respected figure. His career has since flourished because he is now at liberty to accept prestigious engagements outside the Abbey.

Neary has been associated with Tavener since 1972, and last night he conducted three works by Tavener at a concert by the Havard University Choir – "The Lamb," the "Song for Athene," and "Innocence," a 20-minute piece commissioned by Westminster Abbey for the unveiling of a statue to war victims. This was an

> 'Innocence' was an American premiere, and a poignant one to experience in a church dedicated to fallen sons and daughters of Harvard.

THE HARVARD UNIVERSITY CHOIR
Murray Forbes Somerville, conductor, and Martin Neary, guest conductor
At: *The Memorial Church, Cambridge, last night*

American premiere, and a poignant one to experience in a church dedicated to fallen sons and daughters of Harvard and in a week of indelible images of new innocent victims of war.

It's a piece constructed like a mosaic of different colored stones, arranged in a recurrent pattern – choirs and organ; low voiced singers; high soprano; and cello alternately perform the various strophes to construct the pattern which moves from a cry of "Lost" to the promise of redemption. The piece is striking, compelling, and not in every detail convincing. Chimes contribute a touch of tinsel, and the soprano must intone the words "Adam and Eve" while sustaining a high D, an effect that is phonetically impossible and, in the attempt, sounded more freakishly attention-grabbing than musical. Neary is clearly a superb musician, and the Harvard Univesity Choir, the 'Cliffe Notes, and the Din and Tonics served him and the piece nobly, as did the sweet-toned, young, British soprano Cecilia Osmond, the centered cellist Sam Ou, the clear-voiced bass Aidan Oliver, and the valiant tenor Thomas Gregg, who trilled in thirds.

The "Song for Athene" is serenely but not obliviously beautiful, the promise of paradise greeted by a chant of "Alleluia." "The Lamb," a setting of Blake's poem, has become one of the most popular recent choral works; the music, poised between sweetness and dissonance, has a sophisticated simplicity fully conveyed by the well-tuned performance.

The choir's regular director Murray Forbes Somerville came on in the second half of the concert for two fluently civilized pieces by Harvard's own Randall Thompson and two movements of a new Mass by Daniel Roihl, his senior honors thesis. This is less a personal statement than a survey of what the young composer enjoys hearing – if you had told this listener that the turbulent "Kyrie" was by John Knowles Paine (b. 1839) rather than Roihl (b. 1975), he would have believed you. The "Gloria" was more enterprising, mediating among a "Carmen" entr'acte with tambourine, a touch of Tavener, and Sondheim. The composer is an experienced choral singer, a fact manifest in his skillful handling of the medium; partisan cheers broke out when he emerged from the choir at the end.

APPENDIX 4

The Millennium Consort Singers, Los Angeles

The West-coast based Millennium Consort Singers came together in 2007 to perform choral masterpieces from the Renaissance and the twentieth and twenty-first centuries. Our opening concert, for the Da Camera Society, drew a full audience at St Sophia's Orthodox Cathedral in Los Angeles with works by the contemporary British composer John Tavener and his earlier namesake, John Taverner. Subsequent programmes included numerous American premieres of works by British composers, music by contemporary Americans such as Tom Flaherty and Kurt Rohde as well as a rich range of English music from the Golden Age and demanding repertoire from the twentieth and twenty-first centuries. Among the highlights were a notable appearance at Walt Disney Concert Hall in 2010 and several concerts at Bridges Hall of Music, Claremont. We also recorded *Water Ruminations* by Tom Flaherty with the Pomona College Choir, as well as his *Shakespeare Sonnets*.

In 2012, The Millennium Consort Singers gave a number of concerts for Pomona College, including a fascinating programme with the Pomona College Choir, conceived by the composer Tom Flaherty, with the theme of 'Music and Water'. Here is the programme:

A Choral Celebration – Music and Water

Millennium Consort Singers
Pomona College Choir – Donna M Di Grazia *director*
Edward Murray *organ*
Martin Neary *director*

Hard by a crystal fountain	*Thomas Morley (1558–1603)*
Napili Bay 2 pm	*JAC Redford (b.1953)*
Like as the hart	*Herbert Howells (1892–1983)*

Organ solo: Christ unser Herr zum Jordan kamm, BWV 684	*J S Bach (1685–1750)*
To be sung of a summer night on the water	*Frederick Delius (1862–1934)*
The Blue Bird	*Charles Villiers Stanford (1852–1924)*
Full fathom five	*Ralph Vaughan Wiliams (1872–1958)*
Water Ruminations, world premiere	*Tom Flaherty (b.1950)*
Organ solo: Naîades	*Louis Vierne (1870–1937)*
At twilight	*Percy Grainger (1882–1961)*
Shenandoah	*Percy Grainger*
Deep river (from A Child of our Time)	*Michael Tippett (1905-98)*

The Choir also took part in several programmes for Brit Week in Los Angeles, including in 2016 "*Shakespeare, Music & Love*", marking the 400th anniversary of his death.

APPENDIX 5

Commissions*, Premieres§ and other Significant Performances of Contemporary Music

1972	*§A Little Requiem	John Tavener	Winchester Cathedral
1972	§Grace	Herbert Howells	10 Downing Street
1972	§Ode for Sir William Walton	Arthur Bliss	10 Downing Street
1973	§Mar Português	Arthur Bliss	The Painted Hall, Greenwich
1974	*§The Dove Descending	Jonathan Harvey	Winchester Cathedral
1975	Ultimos Ritos (*British premiere*)	John Tavener	Winchester Cathedral
1975	Laus Deo (*BBC broadcast*)	Jonathan Harvey	North American premiere
1976	*I love the Lord	Jonathan Harvey	Winchester Cathedral
1977	Canticle of the Mother of God (*First broadcast performance*)	John Tavener	Winchester Cathedral
1978	*§Magnificat and Nunc dimittis (*BBC broadcast*)	Jonathan Harvey	Winchester Cathedral
1979	O praise ye the Lord (*BBC broadcast*)	Jonathan Harvey	Winchester Cathedral & Cheltenham Festival
1980	*§Toccata (*for Organ and Tape*)	Jonathan Harvey	Church of the Ascension, New York
1981	*§The Tree	Jonathan Harvey	Winchester Cathedral
1981	*§Prayer of Saint Andrew of Crete	John Tavener	Winchester Cathedral

1981	§Passion and Resurrection (BBC TV)	Jonathan Harvey	Winchester Cathedral
1983	The Lamb	John Tavener	Winchester Cathedral
	*§A Winchester Litany	Jonathan Harvey	Winchester Cathedral
1984	*§Come, Holy Ghost	Jonathan Harvey	Winchester Cathedral
	O Jesu nomen dulce	Jonathan Harvey	Winchester Cathedral
1984	§Requiem (first version)	Andrew Lloyd Webber	Sydmonton Festival
1985	*§Love bade me welcome	John Tavener	Winchester Cathedral
1986	§Hymns to the Mother of God	John Tavener	Winchester Cathedral
1987	§Lauds	Jonathan Harvey	International Congress of Organists, Cambridge
1987	§A Christmas Proclamation	John Tavener	Winchester Cathedral (commissioned to mark MN's time at Winchester)
1988	Akathist of Thanksgiving	John Tavener	Westminster Abbey
1988	§Today the Virgin	John Tavener	Westminster Abbey
1989	*§Mass	Jeffrey Lewis	Westminster Abbey
1989	§Thou mastering me God	Jonathan Harvey	Saint Cecilia Festival
1990	*§Missa Trinitatis sanctae	Francis Grier	Westminster Abbey
1991	*§Westminster Mass	Bryan Kelly	Westminster Abbey
1992	*§The Annunciation	John Tavener	Saint Cecilia Festival
1994	Christus vincit (first broadcast)	James MacMillan	Westminster Abbey
1995	*§Innocence	John Tavener	Westminster Abbey
1997	§Prayer for a child	James MacMillan	Westminster Abbey
1997	May the grace of Christ	Martin Neary	Westminster Abbey

Commissions, Premieres and other Significant Performances of Contemporary Music

1997	National Anthem arrangement	Martin Neary	Westminster Abbey
2000	Becket	David Reeves	Canterbury Cathedral
2000	§O worship the Lord	Martin Neary	Romford Parish Church
2010	§Song of June	Jonathan Harvey	St John's Smith Square
2010	§Miroires	John Tavener	St John's Smith Square
2011	§Mass of the Redeemer	Martin Neary	Church of the Redeemer, Bethesda, USA
2012	§Water Ruminations	Tom Flaherty	Bridges Hall, Claremont, USA

APPENDIX 6

Recordings – a selection

Winchester Cathedral Choir (1974–1987)

HEAR MY PRAYER (DOUBLE ALBUM)
Winchester Cathedral Choir, Clement McWilliam and James Lancelot *organ*

BRITTEN The Golden Vanity; Missa Brevis; A Ceremony of Carols
Daniel Cairns, Guy Meredith, David Hurley *treble solos*,
Clement McWilliam *organ*,
Robert Bottone *piano*, Marisa Robles *harp*
Pye Virtuoso TPLS 13065

HANDEL Messiah Highlights
Winchester Cathedral Choir, London Handel Orchestra
ASV

HANDEL Dixit Dominus and Nisi Dominus
Winchester Cathedral Choir and Winchester Baroque Ensemble (Roy Goodman),
Elisabeth Priday *soprano*, Charles Brett *alto*, William Kendall *tenor*,
Stephen Varcoe *bass*
HMV EL270945

THE GOLDEN AGE OF ENGLISH CATHEDRAL MUSIC
Winchester Cathedral Choir, The Viols of the Consort of Musicke
Byrd, Gibbons, Morley, Tallis, Taverner, Weelkes
ASV ALH 943

WINCHESTER CATHEDRAL ORGAN
Bach, Messiaen, Franck, Dupré
Martin Neary
TPLS 13066

Recordings – a selection

CAROLS FROM WINCHESTER CATHEDRAL
Winchester Cathedral Choir, James Lancelot *organ*
ACM 2036

EVENSONG FOR ASH WEDNESDAY
Barnaby Lane & St John Dyson *trebles*, Keith Ross *alto*,
William Kendall *tenor*, Allan Mottram *bass*
Winchester Cathedral Choir, James Lancelot *organ*
ALH 915

WINCHESTER CATHEDRAL CHOIR ON TOUR
Winchester Cathedral Choir, James Lancelot *organ*
ALH 922

ANDREW LLOYD WEBBER – REQUIEM
Paul Miles-Kingston, Sarah Brightman, Placido Domingo,
Winchester Cathedral Choir, English Chamber Orchestra, Lorin Maazel
COC 7471462

MUSIC FROM WINCHESTER CATHEDRAL
Paul Miles-Kingston, Martin Neary *EL2703721*

POULENC Mass in G; Quatre motets pour le temps de Noël;
HONEGGER: Une Cantate de Noël
Mark Harris *treble*, Donald Sweeney *baritone*,
Timothy Byram-Wigfield *organ*
Winchester Cathedral Choir, Waynflete Singers, English Chamber Orchestra
EMI EL 7 49559

IN DULCI JUBILO
Christmas polychoral music with the London Cornett and
Sackbut Ensemble,
Timothy Byram-Wigfield *organ*
Winchester Cathedral Choir
EL 270 5511

AT A SOLEMN MUSIC
Purcell, Croft, Pelham Humfrey, Blow, Battishill
Hilary Brooks *baroque cello*, Tim Byram Wigfield *organ*
Winchester Cathedral Choir, Baroque Brass of London
EMI

WESTMINSTER ABBEY CHOIR (1989–1998)

PURCELL – MUSIC FOR QUEEN MARY including the Funeral Music
"The best Purcell yet" *Classic CD*
Emma Kirkby, Evelyn Tubb, Michael Chance, Ian Bostridge,
Stephen Richardson, Simon Birchall
Westminster Abbey Choir, New London Consort
Sony/ Arc of Light SK66243

A MILLENNIUM OF MUSIC FROM WESTMINSTER ABBEY
including 11th century plainchant, Gibbons, Purcell, Blow, Handel,
Howells and Francis Grier's Missa Trinitas sanctae
Sony/ Arc of Light SK66614

JOHN TAVENER – AKATHIST OF THANKSGIVING
"The performances of the soloists and Choir are immaculate and
beautifully balanced" *Gramophone*
James Bowman, Timothy Wilson,
Westminster Abbey Choir, BBC Singers, BBC Symphony Orchestra
Sony/ Arc of Light SK64446 (CD), ST64446 (cassette)

JOHN TAVENER – INNOCENCE
"There is no finer disc than this to represent John Tavener as choral
composer – with Martin Neary drawing incandescent singing from
Westminster Abbey Choir". *Guardian*
Patricia Rozario *soprano*, Leigh Nixon *tenor*
Graham Titus *tenor*, Alice Neary *cello*
Charles Fullbrook *bells*, Martin Baker *organ*
Sony/ Arc of Light SK66613

Recordings – a selection

MUSIC FROM THE CORONATION OF HER MAJESTY QUEEN ELIZABETH II
"The organ is heard in all its magnificence" *Gramophone*
Martin Baker *organ*, Westminster Abbey Choir, English Chamber Orchestra, London Brass
Cantoris CRCD 3050 (CD), CRMC 3050 (cassette)

PSALMS VOLUMES 1 & 2
Westminster Abbey Choir, Andrew Lumsden *organ*
"... a release to make glad the heart" *The American Organist*
1) *Cantoris CRCD2361(CD), CR2361 (cassette)*
2) *Virgin VC 5 45032 2 (CD)*

CHRISTMAS CAROLS FROM WESTMINSTER ABBEY
Westminster Abbey Choir, Martin Baker *organ*
Cantoris CRCD 4000

MISERERE
A sequence for Holy Week, including two settings of the Miserere by Gregorio Allegri and Tommaso Bai (première recording)
Sony/Arc of Light SK66615

BENJAMIN BRITTEN
including Rejoice in the Lamb, A Ceremony of Carols, Abraham and Isaac.
Westminster Abbey Choir, Michael Chance, Ian Bostridge, Simon Birchall, Martin Baker *organ*, Aline Brewer *harp*
Sony/Arc of Light

CHRISTMAS CAROLS COLLECTION WITH EMMA KIRKBY
Sony/Arc of Light

PERFECT PEACE
Sony Classical

APPENDIX 7

A Year of Good Grace

From *The Times*, 24 March 1999, Martin Neary tells
Richard Morrison about life after Westminster.

It isn't exactly central to his repertoire, but Martin Neary has surely drawn inspiration during these past traumatic few months from the old Jerome Kern song: "Pick yourself up, dust yourself down, start all over again." Exactly a year ago he was suspended from his job, the grandest in all musical Christendom. He was organist of Westminster Abbey, a post once held by Henry Purcell. He had maintained an immaculate choral tradition. He had masterminded brilliant aural backcloths to majestic ceremonies, most famously the funeral of Diana, Princess of Wales. And, as a notable champion of modern British composers such as Jonathan Harvey and John Tavener, he had done much to ensure that the Anglican Church continued to have a living musical tradition.

All this counted for nothing when a new Dean, Wesley Carr, decided to make an issue of alleged financial irregularities in the relationship between the Nearys (Martin's wife, Penny, handled the paperwork) and the Abbey. The dispute was bitter, protracted and horribly public: a dire advertisement for the Church's professed belief in forgiveness and humility. Its conclusion, following a convoluted ruling by a high court judge, was crushing. Neary, a cathedral organist for more than 30 years, was ignominiously ejected from the world he loved.

Many in the church felt that, whatever the murky facts, this was a disgraceful way to treat one of Anglican music's most diligent and loyal servants. How on earth did this mild man survive, let alone bounce back with the vigour of a boxer stung by a blow below the belt?

"I don't see how anyone could have gone through that process without feeling hurt." Neary says. "But we have been sustained, first because we have faith – faith in our faith, and faith in ourselves – and secondly because we have had amazing, unrelenting support, day in and day out. We feel incredibly humbled by it. Only the other day I had a card from a cricket-loving friend who said: 'Whenever I see the third umpire making a nonsense of a decision, I think of your experience.' Joan Rodgers, Ian Bostridge, Paul Daniel and Julius Drake are even putting on a benefit concert for us, on May 9 at the Barbican. I'm very touched that such stars feel so strongly."

Perhaps the most distressing moment came when the Nearys had to quit the Abbey organist's traditional house in the Cloisters. "We'd done 16 years at Winchester Cathedral and more than a decade at the abbey, so we'd been members of closed communities for a long time. Luckily we had bought a place in Fulham, knowing the time would eventually come when we would need it. We didn't anticipate it would be quite so soon."

Remarkably, Neary believes that good may yet come out of this sorry mess. "As a result of the most unwelcome publicity the whole matter of security of tenure for cathedral musicians may well be improved," he thinks. He also says that he harbors no bitterness towards the Abbey. "I was blessed with the privilege of working there for 11 years, and obviously if things had gone differently, I'd have stayed there for another six or seven. We will never say anything to put down the Abbey."

Even so, it is with some relish that Neary lists the work he has been offered since leaving Westminster. The inference is clear. If he was untrustworthy, as the Abbey charged, he would be shunned by the rest of the church and the music profession. But the reverse appears to be true. "I have been asked by the Royal School of Church Music to be a consultant for its Millennium Youth Choir, which is very much the initiative of the Archbishop of Canterbury," Neary says. "I'm flattered and honoured that he should want me involved. I'm also doing lots of organ recitals this summer, then I'm off to Australia to work with the Australian Youth Choir."

And Neary is also in demand to conduct the modern English music with which he is so much associated. Tomorrow, for instance, he steers Sinfonia 21 and the BBC Singers through one of the most striking pieces of sacred music written since 1945: Jonathan Harvey's "church opera" *Passion and Resurrection*, which Neary commissioned and premiered when he was at Winchester in 1981.

The piece, says Neary, had originally been intended for Canterbury, "but the more they heard about it the more alarmed they got. It's certainly not your average choral society passion. There are an awful lot of difficult things for the performers. But the work also has wonderful lyricism and power. Indeed, for all its avant-garde moments, the Resurrection part has a Verdi-like flamboyance. I think it's Jonathan's most approachable piece."

Neary maintains that he is now having a "fantastic time" conducting such events: concerts that might never have come his way if he had stayed at Westminster. But ask him whether he will ever go back into cathedral life – even after the demeaning events of last year – and his eyes light up. "I think it's highly probable, yes. Some things about cathedral life I miss enormously: the very special rapport with the choristers, for instance. So I'm keeping all options open."

Meanwhile, if it isn't too blasphemous a thought, conducting a piece called *Passion and Resurrection* seems an appropriate way to close the book on the worst year of his life.

APPENDIX 8

Press Statement by Dr Martin Neary, 9 December 1998

Penny and I are very disappointed by Lord Jauncey's ruling, but we are pleased and relieved that the decision makes clear, once and for all, that neither of us has been guilty of any dishonesty or deliberate concealment. Indeed, establishing this point was at the heart of our appeal and was our main objective. We find it hard to understand how, if we have been found to have acted without dishonesty or concealment and in good faith, our actions can still be considered sufficiently ill-judged as to constitute gross misconduct. While we have been found to have made errors of judgement, which we accept and regret, we consider that the penalty is out of proportion. Back in April we had to lodge an appeal to clear our names against the Dean's allegations of dishonesty. We are deeply saddened that it should have taken over eight months, a 12-day hearing, and an inordinate amount of money to do this. The Dean and Chapter could have resolved this matter honourably, as the previous canon treasurer recommended and as many tried to achieve, but they declined. The judgement states: "It was surprising that nether the Precentor nor the Dean had asked Dr Neary directly about the fund and its operation as soon as they were aware of its existence. Had they done so and had the parties been prepared to discuss openly, and frankly, the Abbey's concerns, to acknowledge that serious mistakes had been made, and to consider the reasons therefore, it might have been possible to avoid the present unhappy situation with all its attendant publicity and to have reached a rather less dramatic resolution of their difficulties".

Lord Jauncey also condemns the Abbey's attempts to force us to attend a disciplinary hearing without allowing us any time to prepare our case, thereby justifying our decision to apply for a court injunction with the aim of achieving a postponement of the hearing. As the judge points out: "The Abbey's attempt to convene a disciplinary hearing at such short notice and without a detailed statement of the case being made against the Nearys must score gamma minus on the scale of natural justice".

Lord Jauncey has accepted that our primary concern when instituting the 1994 arrangement was to help the Lay Vicars to avoid tax deductions at source. For the arrangements to be genuine and not a sham, it was of course essential that the account be independent of the Abbey We are bewildered that there should be criticism of Mrs Neary receiving payments for extra work outside her Abbey responsibilities, which came in the form of fixing fees as customarily paid by concert organisers for arranging musical performances.

As well as acknowledging that the fundamental reason for setting up the 1994 arrangements was tax, Lord Jauncey also found that we neither concealed information from the Lay Vicars, nor in any way deprived them of income, and he applauded our hard work in obtaining extra remuneration for the singers through the increase in the number of engagements. Furthermore it should be noted that every one of the extra events, which we arranged, was formally approved by the Dean and Chapter. The basic criticism seems to be that we were not sufficiently open about the arrangements and that we did not disclose the fixing fees to the Dean and Chapter or the Lay Vicars. We are surprised that this lack of openness is sufficient to constitute gross misconduct, particularly as Lord Jauncey acknowledges that we acted in good faith.

We have had ten fulfilling and demanding years at Westminster Abbey, during which we believe we have contributed to the worship and to its musical reputation. We express our sincere thanks to our families and the hundreds of people who have so generously supported us. I particularly wish to thank my wife, Penny, for her work over ten years at the Abbey and to pay tribute to her strength, courage and unfailing support through these last months. We would like to pay a special tribute to the Westminster Abbey choir parents, whose sons it has been a privilege to train, and to the convenor of our Support Group, Professor Sir Bryan Thwaites, without whose initiative and relentless work our appeal would not have been possible.

We warmly thank our counsel Mr Patrick Elias QC and Mr Peter Irvin, and our solicitor, Mr Stephen Levinson of Paisner & Co, for their advice and support during the course of this case. We were also most grateful to Miss Cherie Booth QC and Mr Martin Richards of Kaltons for their advice before the disciplinary hearing in April,

This is a sad day for us and for Westminster Abbey. We are now considering our future, and very much hope we can continue our work with choirs. We wish the Abbey well.

APPENDIX 9

Times Crossword 24,497 Monday 29 March 2010

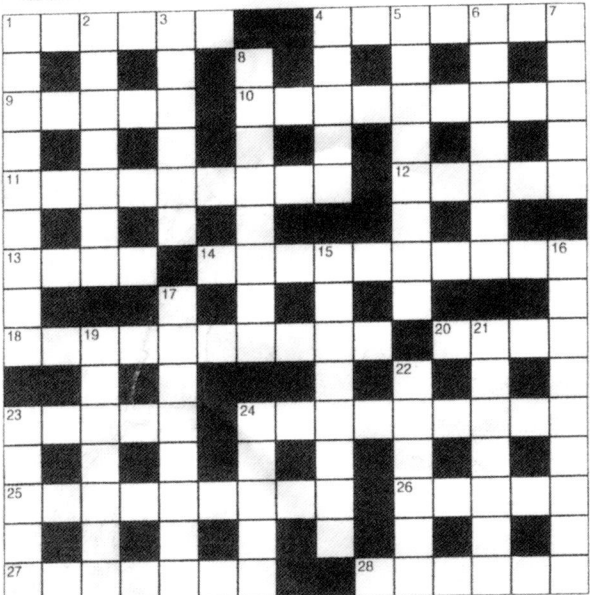

Across

1 I left alcoholic drink — I am a saint! (6)
4 Bird pulling back end of wing flying from here (7)
9 Good to avoid mountain tops in travels (5)
10 Slow change as popular uprising is headed off (9)
11 I am almost home, seriously! (2,7)
12 One speaking forgets lines — nicker results (5)
13 Take down spoken form of service (4)
14 For information, men grab computer industry founder (10)
18 Women's society does this, or fails (10)
20 Disadvantage of bomb development centre having mission taken away (4)
23 Cheap ticket, but initially restricted (5)
24 Operation determining the appearance of Macduff? (9)
25 Pay attention and note Hamlet stabbing king, in Shakespeare (4,2,3)
26 I agree to maintain a temperature that baker needs (5)
27 After many hours sailor sees the sun (7)
28 Member of religious society runs into the Devil (6)

Down

1 Male hanging around to enjoy festival (5,4)
2 Revolutionary assembly, we hear, is for no chicken (3,4)
3 Protect home? Of course (6)
4 Farm bird with missing foot (5)
5 Going out with reluctance at first in cold journey (8)
6 Deer fence thrown round river (7)
7 Singer's note has no vibrato in the middle (5)
8 What may make you a doctor? Look again! (8)
15 My attempt to secure honour in school subject (8)
16 Read notes carelessly, and struck a chord (9)
17 Zones included in domain name for region of world (4,4)
19 A number in disgusting housing, including flat (7)
21 We must support old woman (cow!) (7)
22 Advocate wife should be in bed (6)
23 Disposed of holding one had in firm (5)
24 Lift the mood of one in three, perhaps (5)

Solution to this crossword

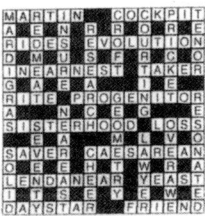

Happy Birthday, Martin!

Index of Names

Abbott, Steve 178, 197
Alain, Marie-Claire 44
Alcock, Walter 15, 131
Amis, John 48
Aprahamian, Felix 48, 62, 114, 116
Armstrong, Richard 40, 53, 57, 60
Armstrong, Robert 68, 70, 71
Ashcroft, Peggy 138, 141

Bach, J S vii, 34, 37, 42, 43, 50, 51, 52, 54, 55, 56, 57, 58, 60, 62, 63, 64, 66, 73, 84, 86, 91, 92, 96, 114, 115, 117, 120, 135, 137, 144, 153, 156, 170, 171, 173, 194, 195, 203, 205, 206, 226, 230
Baker, Martin 154, 160, 162, 163, 173, 177, 232, 233
Beeson, Trevor 122
Bennett Powell, Jane 206
Bertalot, John 166
Betjeman, John 61, 76, 153
Birch, John 83, 84, 97, 113, 217
Birchall, Simon 149, 150, 232, 233
Blair, Cherie 185, 238
Blair, Tony 158
Blech, Harry 50
Bliss, Arthur 72, 76, 90, 142, 227
Booker, Christopher 79
Bosscher, Scott 195
Boult, Adrian 16, 35
Bovet, Guy 44
Bowman, James 192, 232
Braithwaite, Nicholas 50
Brearley, Mike viii, 29, 114

Bridge, Frederick 1, 146, 181, 182
Brightman, Sarah 124, 125, 127, 231
Brink, Charles 39
Britten, Benjamin 39, 50, 71, 95, 154, 171, 174, 222, 230, 233
Broers, Alec 41
Bruce-Wilson, Richard 40
Byram-Wigfield, Timothy 82, 117, 122, 192, 231

Caesar, Anthony 82, 94, 199
Cairns, Dan 92, 230
Cairns, David 82, 88, 93, 105
Carey, George 188, 191
Carr, Wesley 185, 234
Chance, Michael 121, 149, 186, 232, 233
Charlton, Bobby 144
Clark, Geoffrey 29
Cleobury, Stephen 153, 198
Clinton, Bill 176
Compston, Christopher 186
Compton, Denis 26, 29, 145, 154
Copland, Aaron 45
Croft-Jackson, Harry 44

Dankworth, John 103, 124
Darke, Harold 4, 6, 53, 136
Dart, Thurston 40, 45
Davis, Andrew 44, 150, 154
Davis, Colin 105, 140, 143
Dawson, Les 145
Dawson, Lynne 160, 161
Dawson, Herbert 41, 48

Dearnley, Christopher 83
Del Tredici, David 46
Deller, Alfred 17
Domingo, Placido 126, 127, 231
Douglas-Home, Alec 73
Downes, Ralph 45, 62, 66
Dupré, Marcel 49, 230
Dykes-Bower, John 21, 22

Elias, Patrick 185, 186, 238
Emery, Walter 54
Evans, Geraint 143

Fenton, Barry 159
Field, Frank 185, 188
Fisher, Geoffrey 11
Fonteyn, Margot 140
Forbes, Sebastian 40, 54
Fox, Douglas 38
Frewer, Richard 41
Frost, David 67

Gabb, Harry 17, 27, 28, 48
Gaine, David 37
Gardiner, John Eliot 40
Gomes, Peter 191
Goodall, Jonathan 164
Grier, Francis 228
Guest, Douglas 66, 79, 80, 153
Guest, George 40
Guinness, Sir Alec 138

Hadley, Patrick 32, 34, 35, 36, 37
Halsey, Louis 57, 216
Handel, G F 14, 16, 26, 51, 70, 92, 108, 117, 121, 149, 154, 171, 172, 173, 195, 230, 232
Harper, John 256
Harries, Richard 34
Harris, William 21, 27
Hart, Henry St John 34
Harvey, Jonathan 2, 40, 90, 94, 97, 103, 109, 110, 111, 114, 125, 151, 152, 191, 202, 203, 211, 222, 227, 228, 229, 234, 235
Heath, Edward 51, 67, 68, 73, 75, 129
Heffer, Simon 36
Herrick, Christopher 58
Hickox, Richard 64
Hill, David 206
Howells, Herbert 25, 58, 71, 131, 141, 142, 182, 203, 225, 227, 232
Huddleston, Trevor 146
Hurford, Peter 47, 51, 153, 182

Irvin, Peter 238

Jackson, Francis 51, 192, 199
Jauncey, of Tullichettle 186, 237, 238
Jennings, Michael 129
John, Elton 159, 160, 161, 162, 164, 165, 167
Johnston, Brian 145
Jones, Geraint 42, 43, 48

Keener, Andrew 121
Kenyon, Nicholas 150, 194, 215
Keyte, Hugh 93
Kirkby, Emma 120, 149, 232, 233
Knapp, Merrill 108

Laine, Cleo 103, 124
Lancelot, James 82, 93, 94, 95, 97, 105, 108, 117, 126, 183, 230, 231
Landale, Susan 44, 49, 52, 55
Langlais, Jean 49
Layton, Stephen 95, 96, 197, 203
Ledger, Philip 40
Le Huray, Peter 40, 42
Leinsdorf, Eric 45, 47
Leppard, Raymond 32
Levinson, Stephen 186, 188, 238
Lister, Jane 119, 139
Litton, Jim 107

Lloyd Webber, Andrew 124, 127, 129, 155, 228, 231
Lough, Peter 13, 27, 33
Lumsden, Andrew 135, 138, 173, 233
Lumsden, David 93, 180, 185

Maazel, Lorin 126, 127, 231
MacMillan, James 182, 228
Major, John 72, 144, 152
Malcolm, George 47, 50, 61
Mandela, Nelson 176
Marchal, André 49, 52, 62
Marchant, Hugh 22
Marsh, Dana 193
Mayne, Michael 138, 140, 168, 177, 187
McFarlane, Ian 33, 39
McKie, William 21, 22, 23, 100, 131, 178
McWilliam, Clement 82, 85, 93
Messiaen, Olivier 52, 212, 230
Miles-Kingston, Paul 125, 127, 129
Millinger, Andrew 182
Montefiore, Hugh 34, 37, 39
Moore, Bobby 144
Morrison, Richard 120, 234

Neary, Leonard 3, 4, 6, 103
Neary, Jeanne 3, 4, 103
Neary, Alice 2, 48, 49, 53, 59, 86, 88, 109, 116, 121, 122, 143, 144, 173, 192, 195, 196, 197, 198, 203, 206, 232
Neary, Nicola 56, 58, 59, 88, 109, 116, 121, 203, 205, 208, 209
Neary, Penny 2, 50, 51, 52, 53, 54, 55, 56, 58, 59, 67, 77, 82, 86, 89, 101, 102, 184, 185, 186, 187, 188, 190, 191, 193, 202, 205, 208, 234, 237, 238 256, 256

O'Donnell, James 152
Olivier, Laurence 72, 138

Ormandy, Eugene 46
Overton, David 170
Owen, Eric 113
Owen, Wilfrid 202

Parry, C H H 16, 20, 168
Peasgood, Osborne 15, 178
Pears, Peter 14
Preston, Simon 41, 109, 134, 256
Pullan, Bruce 61
Purcell, Henry 1, 16, 17, 69, 77, 149, 150, 151, 171, 202, 232, 234

Radcliffe, Philip 40
Railton, Ruth 148, 186
Rattle, Simon 88, 126
Reynish, Tim 38
Robinson, Christopher 153
Roland-Adams, Gordon 131, 132
Roper, Stanley 7, 8, 9, 14, 15, 17, 18, 60
Ross, Alastair 63
Ross, Keith 81, 83, 231
Routledge, Patricia 200
Runnett, Brian 39
Russill, Patrick 142
Rutter, John 143, 203

Sargent, Malcolm 6, 16
Seal, Richard 79, 84, 97, 113, 154, 193, 217
Semper, Colin 177, 187
Seaman, Christopher 40
Simcock, Iain 134, 135
Smith, John 145, 146
Solti, George 143, 156
Somerville, Murray 191
Spicer, Paul 182
Stancliffe, David 92, 93, 97, 185
Stancliffe, Martin 92, 97
Stancliffe, Michael 41, 48, 53, 61, 65, 66, 79, 82, 121, 122
Stanford, C V 102, 153

Standage, Simon 40
Stopford, Philip 148, 200
Stravinsky, Igor 41, 256
Surplice, Alwyn 83, 131
Symeonides, Alexander 46

Tavener, John 2, 35, 85, 86, 92, 95, 122, 148, 158, 159, 160, 161, 162, 166, 171, 174, 191, 192, 194, 195, 197, 200, 203, 225, 227, 228, 229, 232, 234
Taylor, Leslie 13, 14, 18
Taylor, John and Peggy 78, 82, 90, 110, 121, 186, 211, 212, 219
Temple, Sebastian 165
Thatcher, Margaret 129
Thébault, Christian 3, 4, 11
Thurlow, Alan 113
Thwaites, Bryan 186, 256
Tobin, John 57
Tranchell, Peter 39, 49
Trollope, Anthony 144
Trollope, Joanna 192
Tutu, Desmond 146

Vaughan Williams, Ralph 6, 16, 25, 35, 37, 38, 84, 102, 182

Walsh, Stephen 41, 112
Walton, William 25, 26, 71, 72, 138, 139, 143, 156, 173, 227
Warren, Antony 206, 208
Wassertheurer, Gunter 57, 60
Watson, Angus 86, 105, 124
Weatherill, Bernard 186
Wedderspoon, Alex 82, 99, 115, 186
Wedderspoon, Judith 115
West, John 73, 205
Wheeler, Gerald 47
Whitbourn, James 152
White, David 18
Whitworth, John 17, 175
Wilkinson, Michael 14
Willcocks, David 40, 80, 90, 130, 151, 152, 154, 157, 203
Williams, Rowan 181, 199
Wilson, Harold 65, 78, 147
Wilson, Mary 67, 147, 148, 152
Wilson, Timothy 122, 232
Wlliams, Lawrence 207
Woodcock, John 2
Woolfenden, Guy 38, 141
Wray, John 13, 14, 30, 32

Xenakis, Giannis 46